PATHS TO THE CITY

NEW APPROACHES TO SOCIAL SCIENCE HISTORY

Series Editor: *Stanley L. Engerman*
Professor of Economics and History
University of Rochester

Published in cooperation with the Social Science History Association

New Approaches to Social Science History is a series of books designed to encourage publication and dissemination of scholarly works of social science history and historically oriented social science. The series is a key element in the publications program of the Social Science History Association, an interdisciplinary organization formed in 1974 for the purpose of improving the quality of historical explanation by encouraging the selective use and adaptation of relevant theory and method from the social sciences and related disciplines in historical teaching and research. By facilitating freer interchange between historian and social scientist, a more systematic reintroduction of the historical dimension into social science work and the application of historical data to test social scientific theories can be achieved. The series includes both single-authored volumes and edited collections of original essays devoted to substantive research, theoretical issues, methodological concerns, and curricular development.

Volume 1 *Class Conflict and Collective Action,*
Louise A. Tilly, Charles Tilly (eds.)

Volume 2 *Paths to the City; Regional Migration in Nineteenth-Century France,*
Leslie Page Moch

Leslie Page Moch

PATHS TO THE CITY

Regional Migration in Nineteenth-Century France

Published in cooperation with the
SOCIAL SCIENCE HISTORY ASSOCIATION

SAGE PUBLICATIONS
Beverly Hills / London / New Delhi

For information address:

SAGE Publications, Inc.
275 South Beverly Drive
Beverly Hills, California 90212

SAGE Publications India Pvt. Ltd.
C-236 Defence Colony
New Delhi 110 024, India

SAGE Publications Ltd
28 Banner Street
London EC1Y 8QE, England

Printed in the United States of America

Library of Congress Cataloging in Publication Data

Moch, Leslie Page.
Paths to the city.

(New approaches to social science history ; v. 2)
Bibliography: p.
Includes index.
1. Cities and towns—France—History—19th century. 2. Rural-urban migration—France—History—19th century. I. Title. II. Series.
HT135.m62. 1983 304.8'0944 83-2955
ISBN 0-8039-1985-9

FIRST PRINTING

CONTENTS

LIST OF ILLUSTRATIONS

MAPS

FIGURES

TABLES

PREFACE

Paths to the City: Regional Migration in Nineteenth-Century France is the second volume in a new series sponsored by the Social Science History Association with the goal of promoting a wider scholarly interchange between historians and social scientists. The series will include both single-authored works and edited collections of original essays devoted to applying social scientific methods to the study of historical issues, as well as to using the insights of historical research to broaden the perspectives of social scientific research.

In this volume, Leslie Page Moch provides an excellent example of the usefulness of social scientific approaches and methods in the study of a major historical problem — the role of migration in the process of urbanization. By utilizing a wide variety of sources, she has made a major contribution to understanding the social, economic, and demographic aspects of internal migration in southern France in the second half of the nineteenth century. Further, she has used this detailed case study to raise important questions for the study of the process of migration and its impact on individuals and families elsewhere.

— Stanley L. Engerman
Series Editor

ACKNOWLEDGMENTS

I am delighted to acknowledge the many debts incurred in the creation of this book. Charles Tilly's insight and intellectual vitality fired this study from the beginning. His genuine concern with historical questions and actors was inspiring to a beginning graduate student and remains so today. Louise Tilly graced this study with her interest, her broad knowledge of the nineteenth century, and her acute eye for the flawed argument. She offered aid and encouragement the likes of which few students experience. My most demanding mentor was Elizabeth Pleck, who, throughout my scholarly career, has been willing to train and to counsel. Time and time again she persuaded me to rethink and rewrite. By their character, intellectual sophistication, spirit, and their indefatigable research and writing, these teachers have become cherished friends and models. They enriched the scholarly experience which had its home in Ann Arbor in 1974, then migrated to France, to Champaign, Illinois, and then to Texas.

Scholars at the University of Michigan kindly read and commented on the manuscript in its initial phases. Fellow graduate students Donna Gabaccia and Bob Rudney saved my worst errors and most awkward prose from exposure. Professors Raymond Grew and John Knodel each improved the dissertation with advice and admonitions special to their respective expertise.

The Rackham School of Graduate Studies supported exploratory research for this project. Subsequently, a generous fellowship from the Social Science Research Council made it possible for me to devote 1976-1977 to research in France and to write the dissertation on which this book is based. The Department of Sociology at the University of Illinois gave me moral and material assistance at a crucial juncture. The Department of History at the University of Texas at Arlington provided excellent circumstances in which to create the manuscript.

In France, scholars Maurice Agulhon, Raymond Huard, Michelle Perrot, and the late René Lamorisse encouraged my research efforts. The directors of the Departmental Archives of the Gard in Nîmes, Monsieur Jean Sablou and Monsieur R. Debant and their staff, especially Monsieur J. Baccou, were unstinting in their cooperation and patience with endless requests for documents. Likewise, municipal librarians and the employees of the Protestant Consistory Archives tirelessly furnished materials. The hospitality and intellectual curiosity of the Nimois, Dr. and Madame Jean Paradis, Monsieur and Madame Pierre Martin, and many others, humanized both my research experience and the resultant study. Monsieur Pierre Gorlier and Mademoiselle O. Cavalier of Le Vigan, and Mademoiselle H. La Tour and Monsieur Benjamin Bardy of the Departmental Archives of the Lozère in Mende contributed hospitality, kindness, and their own insights into the evolution of Languedoc and its people. Pierre and Dora Atger, above all, offered friendship and community.

Eleanor Forfang provided expert and spirited mapmaking, and Michelle Bock typed the manuscript.

I owe a great deal to Sarah Page Moch, born two days after my Ph.D. dissertation was drafted, for infusing life with joy and fulfillment.

For his love and unstinting support, this book is dedicated to Michael Moch.

— Leslie Page Moch

Grapevine, Texas

INTRODUCTION

"I was born on May 13, 18___, in a city of Languedoc, where there were, as in all southern French cities, much sunlight, a good deal of dust, a Carmelite monastery, and two or three Roman monuments."[1] Thus began a semi-autobiographical novel by Alphonse Daudet. Daudet, *homme du Midi* and nineteenth-century realist, spent much of his career interpreting southern French culture to his curious compatriots of the North.

Daudet was born in Nîmes. His family had originated in the Lozère, one of the hilly departments in the Massif Central, north of the Mediterranean coastal plain on which the old Roman city stands. The Daudets' home town was Concoules, a few kilometers from Villefort, one of the towns on which Leslie Page Moch's graceful study concentrates. Peasant Jacques Daudet, the family patriarch, left Concoules for Nîmes during the French Revolution. His brother went with him. They joined a long-established migration from the rough mountains of the Cévennes to the plain. Jacques became a silk weaver in Nîmes and eventually built his own business. His son Vincent, Alphonse's father, contracted an advantageous marriage with the daughter of another silk manufacturer. The business failed at midcentury, when Alphonse was a boy. The family then moved to Lyon. There Alphonse received his education. His first job as a teacher's assistant was so miserable that he left the south to seek his fortune in Paris, where a brother had preceded him.[2]

Many more mountain people followed the Daudets' path to the city on the plain. Their migration, like that of the Daudets, was prompted by the search for better economic circumstances and was mediated by family connections. Like Alphonse Daudet, many migrants passed through Nîmes for a period of their lives. Some made it their permanent home. In Leslie Moch's warm, original, and sophisticated *Paths to the City*, we learn a great deal about this migration from hinterland to city, as well as about the regional economic change that promoted it. And we learn it while making close contact with the individuals and families who struggled to cope with migration and economic change.

Everyone who studies nineteenth-century industrialization and urbanization knows some of the lore of rural-urban migration: that most cities drew the great bulk of their migrants from their immediate surroundings, that average distance migrated tended to rise with skill, that cityward migrants from agriculture moved disproportionately into services and general labor, and so on. With a few historians of industrialization, such as Yves Lequin, we begin to get a sense of the connections between migration patterns within a region and alterations in the economy of that region. Occasionally — but no more than that — we find life histories of individual migrants, but it is very rare for anyone to look directly at the social structures of sending and receiving areas at the same time. The technical problems of doing so are formidable: City censuses may well identify birthplaces or previous residence, but they do not describe those sending areas or place the migrants within their structures. Migrants come from many places, many of which send only a handful of people; former migrants in the city at any particular point in time represent a residue of many arrivals and departures over a substantial previous period; identifying the "same" person in two different places using different records is no picnic. These and other technical problems explain why serious studies of whole migration streams are so few.

Yet if we are to understand the interaction among sending communities, receiving communities, and migrants, we need reliable observations on all three. The interaction matters because it bears on such questions as how much previous exposure to industrial production and/or capitalist property relations migrants to industrial cities had, to what extent migrants moved into ready-made networks of people from common origins, what sorts of information about urban opportunities and dangers migrants brought with them, and to what extent migration to a city was a last resort for impoverished villagers.

Leslie Moch helps us answer all these questions, and more. Her study of migration to Nîmes is the only European study we know that maps separate streams of migration to a city, describes the migrants within those streams, develops direct evidence concerning the sending communities as well as the destination city, analyzes the social processes bringing different types of migrants to the city, and provides accounts of the interpersonal networks they formed and joined in the city. Since Nîmes and its hinterland were divided sharply into Protestant and Catholic populations, she also contributes to our understanding of the rural and small-town bases of urban sectarianism. Once other scholars read this work, they will surely realize that the conventional, indirect reasoning from general information about migrants' places of origin is inadequate, and often downright wrong. They will want to emulate her methods and compare their findings with hers.

We hope that the specialists read and learn, but they are not the only ones who have something to gain from Leslie Moch's book. A lot of people who don't give a fig for Nîmes, for migration models, or for historical demography should nevertheless read her study of Nîmes and its hinterland for the light it sheds on the actual mechanisms of European urbanization and industrialization. Since we are all, like Alphonse Daudet, migrants and descendants of migrants, we may find ourselves in these pages, where real French people act out the processes that change the world.

— Louise A. Tilly and
Charles Tilly

NOTES

1. Alphonse Daudet, *Le Petit Chose: Histoire d'un enfant*. New York: Holt, 1922; first published 1868.
2. Ernest Daudet, *Mon frère et moi. Souvenirs d'enfance et de jeunesse*. Paris: Plon, 1882.

1

Migration and Urbanization

"My boy is going on with his studies," she said. "The master wants him to go to the city."

"Ours is going too," replied Elise. "He is going to get ready to work for the Company."

— André Chamson, *The Road*

In the "long nineteenth century" between the outbreak of the French Revolution and World War I, society, politics, and the economy of the West underwent major transformations. The hallmarks of change in this period — industrialization, expansion of the state, the growth of the middle classes and the proletariat — reflect the increasing importance of the city at the expense of the countryside. Cottage industry and rural artisans lost markets for their goods. As the agricultural sector declined, the prominence of the peasantry in the nation diminished. Departures from the countryside and small towns for the city were so massive at the end of the century that the phrase "rural exodus" was coined to describe them. On the other hand, a middle class and proletariat grew in urban areas; the majority of the white collar workers whose jobs were created by commercial and bureaucratic expansion worked in the city. In the forty years following 1851, the population of France grew by only 7 percent, with the rural population dropping by 8 percent while the population in towns of 10,000 and over nearly doubled.[1] Urban areas expanded, swelled by the arrival of thousands of newcomers — Henri Donzel and the Chevret sisters among them.

Henri Joseph Donzel was born in the small town of Le Vigan in the Cévennes mountains of southern France. He worked with his widowed father as a joiner-carpenter until he was in his twenties, when he landed the job of city hall secretary in Le Vigan and married schoolteacher Clemence Adèle Valat who was, like himself, a Protestant. Their son and daughter were born in the 1860s. When Donzel secured a promotion to work in the prefecture of the department, he moved his family to Nîmes. There he became an established member of the community: a bureau chief at the prefecture and an elector of the governing body of the Protestant church. The Donzel family settled in the northwest section of the city, between the Protestant cemetary and Nîmes' magnificent park, the Jardin de la Fontaine. Henri's son, like his father, became an employee in the prefecture. His spinster daughter cared for him after his retirement and his wife's death. At this time his young nephew, also an employee of the prefecture, joined the household. Henri Donzel died a respected citizen in 1906.[2]

Like her elder sister before her, Henriette Chevret came to Nîmes as a single woman from Langogne, a small town in the northeastern Lozère. While working as a cook in Nîmes, she met her husband-to-be — a café operator named Edouard Roche from the village of Villefort, south of Langogne. Henriette Chevret and Edouard Roche married in Langogne in February of 1901. They often moved after their marriage — back and forth with business between a mountain resort for the summers and Nîmes for the winters. Their daughters, Marie and Anna, were born during these travels in 1902 and 1904, respectively. In Nîmes, they always lived in the same neighborhood, usually on the same street as Henriette's elder sister Sophie.

Sophie Chevret had also worked in Nîmes before her marriage, after which her husband had come there and found work with the railroad. They had one daughter. Their working-class neighborhood was popular with railroad workers because of its location near the freight station and railcar repair depot. Sophie and Henriette's father was a saddle- and harnessmaker, and their older brother was a notary's clerk in Langogne. When their mother was widowed and in her sixties, she moved to Nîmes with an 18-year-old granddaughter and lived a few blocks from her daughters. The granddaughter, Rosine, worked as a clerk in the town.

The colorful and ancient city of Nîmes had had contact with the Cévennes mountains and the Lozère long before these migrants came to reside there. The people of the highlands had always refurbished this city on the Mediterranean plain, and for many years the silk industry had linked Nîmes with its mountainous hinterland. With the arrival of migrants like the Donzels and the Chevrets, the city expanded from 50 to 80 thousand between 1880 and 1900. It grew despite crises which virtually put an end to its silk, textile, and hosiery industries; its economy attracted clerks like Rosine Chevret, as well as workers to support its growing commerce in wine — produced in great quantities on the plain near Nîmes beginning in the 1880s. The implantation of the railroad and its subsequent extension north from Nîmes into central France enhanced the city's role as trade center and attracted men like Sophie Chevret's husband to work for "the Company." Others came to work in the shoe industry and the manufacture of ready-to-wear clothing. As the capital of the department of the Gard, Nîmes housed courts, secondary schools, normal schools, hospitals, and the prefecture that employed Henri Donzel and his son. One consequence of this growth was a thriving market for those mainstays of middle-class and urban life: domestic servants like the Chevret sisters, and café operators like Edouard Roche. Industry was not the mainstay of the economy attracting migrants to Nîmes, which renders it quite typical of French cities in 1900; great industrial centers were uncommon. Less typical of France was the important Protestant community of Nîmes, of which the Donzel family became a part.

If the Donzel family, the Chevret sisters, and Edouard Roche accurately represent the migrants to the city during the rapid urbanization in France during the closing decades of the nineteenth century, it would seem that migration to the city was a rather orderly process. Such a process would be based on strong professional, cultural, and personal ties between home towns and the cities, whether the migrants were servants, manual laborers, or white collar workers. The movement between home towns and cities capitalized on these ties and even may have enriched them in some ways. Yet contemporary French observers and many later scholars would disagree. Many believed both the "rural exodus" and cityward migrations to be dangerous and disruptive, damaging the countryside, confronting individuals with stress and society with problems of social control. Studies of the rural exodus emphasize the adverse demographic consequences of migration from the countryside. Decimated villages are likened to rotten grapes dropping from the vine of rural life, and the migration from villages to a cancer ravaging the countryside.[3] Relying on disease imagery of this kind, works on the rural exodus implicitly contrast healthy rural France with the dissolute city.

According to this starkly manichaean view, the individual risks ruin in the city. The migrant, in failing to cope with stress, encounters mental illness, crime, alcoholism, and prostitution. Contemporary concern is illustrated by the attitude of rural folk toward those who ventured into the city. An illustration in a *Semaine agricole* from 1882, for example, shows a worried mother giving her young daughter advice on how to survive the "urban adventure."[4] Zola's anti-alcoholic novel, *L'assomoir,* published in 1876, stresses the urban social institutions such as bars and wine shops which encouraged drinking.

Scholars, too, have emphasized the dangers of the city. A recent book on prostitution not only links migration with prostitution, but reveals that the recruitment of prostitutes was sometimes aimed specifically at newly arrived country girls in Paris' railroad stations and servants' employment agencies.[5] Others have emphasized the link between urban migration and crime. One might have thought that demographers guided by figures representing city growth and net migration flows would have avoided the anti-urban bias of other scholars. Yet they have provided a simplistic portrait of massive movements which, as one astute student of the rural exodus observed, puts the historian in the position of the physician who must make a diagnosis from changes in body weight alone.[6] The numbers describing such a large-scale phenomenon as urbanization create an impression of equally large-scale disruption, which enables them to characterize movements to the city as "destructive of ways of life" and to assert that "working conditions, customs of housing, of sustenance, familial relations, modes of thought were profoundly changed."[7]

Indeed, if aggregate trends alone are considered, the implications of massive human tides from countryside to city are sobering. The rural dweller is swept into urban areas, overwhelmed by an "irresistible current of population," bedazzled by the lights of the city and helpless in the face of its dangers.[8] The conclusion often drawn from studies of urban police records, the source for many studies of prostitution and urban crime, is that the burden of survival in the city falls on the newcomer, and that failure often results. In the words of an old woman who hastened to Paris from her village to attend the trial of her son: "It's Paris that's to blame; I'm taking my son out of it and I'll make sure he never sets eyes on it again."[9]

Such views of the departure from the countryside, the migrant, and urban life fit poorly with recent studies of migration and urbanization. Migration to the city is at once a more continuous, more collective, and more regionally defined process than it once was presumed to be. New evidence suggests that there is no simple connection between migration and breakdown. First, and fundamental to an alternative view of migration, is the fact that the rural countryside, often perceived as unchanging and therefore stable, was actually bustling with movement centuries before the rural exodus. This came to light with the first family reconstitution studies; close scrutiny of parish registers of baptisms, marriages, and burials found that only a very small proportion of villagers in traditional Europe remained in one parish for all three sacred events.[10]

The mobility patterns of preindustrial Europe included finely structured traditions of seasonal and temporary migration. Rural people came to the city in the winter to earn money to pay taxes or buy land — or simply to survive the season when their work was not needed at home. Young women worked in the city to earn their dowry as domestic servants. Groups of rurals traveled as peddlars, chimney sweeps, and agricultural laborers.[11] The significance of these temporary movements was that they "not only brought in complementary resources, they did more; they enriched experience and provided rural people connections with the exterior world."[12] Not only did rurals move about the traditional countryside, but those who remained in the country were not necessarily strangers to the outside world.

Other evidence indicates that not all migrants faced the city alone. Kin, friends, and prior contacts played a major role. Agricultural laborers, such as the teams of three or four grain harvest workers called *soques* in the south of France, made a collective journey from harvest to harvest. The masons from the central highlands of France who worked in Paris took to the road together every spring, and migrants who remained in the city encouraged others to join them. In this way, chains of migrants linked a city with a particular rural area or market town.[13] Anthropologists, sociologists, and oral historians attest to the use of personal ties in the decision to move, the choice of destination, and the search for work and housing upon arrival.[14]

These newcomers were not wandering across France; most of them were moving within the region of their birth. A late-nineteenth-century estimate was that half the migration in France occurred within the confines of the *départements,* and studies of the origins of city dwellers at the end of the nineteenth century — in cities such as Lyon and Bordeaux — attest to the regional nature of urbanization.[15] The image of the uprooted migrant rests on a notion of cultural dislocation, as well as economic and personal dislocation. Yet regional cultures were important to turn-of-the-century France. Regional dialect and attitudes may well have united the newcomer with the city as much as they alienated him or her.[16]

Small towns were the relay stations for the French en route to the city, and the inhabitants of small market towns and administrative centers were most susceptible to the attraction of urban areas. The words of a nineteenth-century interpreter of the peasantry evoke the experience of migration: "It is farther from the land to the market town than from the market town to the county seat."[17] "Mobility," concludes Yves Lequin, a twentieth-century historian, "is inscribed on the region's urban network."[18] Indeed, cities belong to their regions, and one must view the city, in its regional context, "as a resource for the understanding of the structures and processes of a more inclusive reality."[19] The regional economy should be seen as a single system rather than a rural-urban dichotomy. Yves Lequin's masterful study of the Lyonnais region shows that industrial development and migration were mediated by regional economic structures.[20]

Given the findings about preindustrialized migration, relationships among migrants, and the regional character of much migration, an interpretation of migration that emphasizes the destruction of rural life, or the lone migrant at the mercy of the city, is obviously inadequate. Although such models have justly come under fire in the last decade, historians have not yet replaced them with a more appropriate one.[21] For example, questions posed about internal migration ignore social organization in favor of other issues, despite the fact that evidence of the collective nature of migration has always existed. And the rich contextual information about migration streams, potentially fertile seed for an explicit alternative view of migration, has often been allowed to lie on the stony soil of the particularistically oriented study.[22] Consciously or unconsciously, it has proved difficult to move beyond ideas of uprooting and breakdown. This may be due to a bias toward a psychological view. Nevertheless, an orientation to individual success and failure is insensitive to the context of migration and to personal ties among migrants. For the historian, such problems are compounded by the difficulty of finding adequate sources for studying migration, of tracking people from origin to destination, and of evaluating relationships among people in the past. It is feasible, however, to reconstruct migration systems with care, and thus to sketch an alternative model of migration to the city.

How, then, should we view migration to the city? First, we must abandon the emphasis on *the* countryside and *the* city; these were places of population exchange within a region. Within this region, people had common origins, information, and traditions of migration. Consequently, the best alternative is to view migration in terms of migration *systems,* streams of migrants between a point of origin and destination, rather than in terms of gross flows from one region to another in terms of individuals. A model of migration systems emphasizes the historical and geographical context in which people moved — the traditions of migration in their region, the economic and cultural relationships between home town and destination, and changes in both these elements. It takes account of prior migrations, a flow of information among migrants, and a regional orientation. It varies from previous views insofar as it is collective, continuous, and more attuned to the region than to a dichotomy of city and countryside.

Within regions there were traditions of population exchange that had gone on for centuries. These traditions continued to operate in the nineteenth century. Gradually, though, the backward flow to the home town and rural area slowed and the urban population grew. As this happened, the class stratification and the labor force of the city changed. Some city-born had higher status than migrants, and migrants from some places did better than others. How and why did this stratification evolve? What were the origins of the labor force of the twentieth-century city, a labor force that worked in the large organization, the office, and in services as well as in the factory or workshop? With a focus on migration streams, such questions can be posed about the relationship between the growing city and its population. Moreover, with a model of migration systems it is possible to investigate how migrants affected the demographic substructure of urban society, for their patterns of family membership, marriage, and fertility clarify the process of demographic integration into the city. Also, a focus on migration streams and their origins in small towns and villages leads to questions about the changes in migration that resulted in urbanization. By looking at the evolution of small towns and villages, one can ask how and why migration patterns changed at the end of the nineteenth century. Thus, a focus on migration streams turns attention both to the evolution of migratory movement and to its connection with changes in urban society. It relates the evolution of rural and small-town society to that of the city.

Understanding migration as a system of migrants bound together by common origins, information, and personal ties does not deny the risks or costs of migration, nor does it presume that all migrants are alike. On the contrary, it predicts that certain groups will be concentrated in the city's dead-end jobs with no future employment security, higher income, or higher status. This outcome was a result of not only individual characteristics such as education and background, but of the nature of migrants' connections in the city and of urban society's attitude toward them as well. On the other hand, some groups may be funneled by their ideology, education, and connections into employment with potential for high status and possible higher income. This view posits that migration is a selective and responsive process, one which may find people in the hinterland of a city responding specifically to opportunities for young women to work as domestic servants, or for men to work repairing railcars or keeping business accounts. Information about selectivity and social context is only available when a migration stream is studied. Such a focus will be fruitful because it yields information about why newcomers fare as they do in the city rather than mere judgments of failure or success from the urban standpoint.

One way to investigate the implications of a model of migration oriented toward its collective and continuous characteristics is to compare several migration streams within one region; for example, streams leading to the same regional capital. In this way, both the similarities and differences among migrant streams in terms of their origins, the impetus to move, and their urban lives can be investigated. Moreover, this can be done within the context of a regional history of temporary and permanent movement. Such a strategy was adopted in this investigation of cityward migration in Eastern Languedoc in southern France, focusing specifically on the city of Nîmes. Nîmes was chosen because it was one of the few towns in France that fulfilled criteria for growth in the nineteenth century, size, economic function, and research facilities.[23] Nîmes was particularly attractive as a site for a study of migration and urbanization. First, like other towns on the Mediterranean littoral, for centuries it has been receiving temporary and permanent residents from the mountains and uplands of Languedoc. A study of the citizens of Nîmes is all the more fascinating because the population has been divided into two distinct, if not hostile, camps; an important minority of Protestants live in Nîmes, and both Protestants and Catholics migrated to the city in the nineteenth century.

I have chosen migration to and from three towns in Eastern Languedoc — as well as their native sons and daughters living in

Nîmes — for specific study. These are: the small town of Le Vigan, home of Henri Donzel; the trading center of Langogne, home of the Chevret sisters; and the village of Villefort, birthplace of Edouard Roche. These towns were chosen because each sent a visible stream of migrants to Nîmes, more than one would expect given the town's size and distance from the city.[24]

I used a combination of sources to study Nîmes, Le Vigan, Villefort, and Langogne, the history of movement around them, their economies, and their inhabitants. Some of these sources are familiar to students of migration, and others are more familiar to social historians and to those who study France exclusively. The census lists of Nîmes and birth records from Le Vigan, Villefort, and Langogne provide primary identification of the migrants. Each of these sources yields information that is marvelously rich by some criteria, though overly narrow by others. (The census lists and birth records are evaluated in Appendix I.) Individual military conscript records further identify and fill in life histories for many migrants. Marriage records from Nîmes, Le Vigan, Villefort, and Langogne provide a sketch of regional migration patterns, while government reports on the local economy and contemporary published materials on the region help to complete the history of migration in Eastern Languedoc. A key resource is the sensitive account of the aspirations and lives of migrants from the Cévennes mountains provided in *The Road* by André Chamson. Three autobiographical accounts of life in prewar Nîmes, one by a middle-class Protestant, one by a Protestant from a family of artisans, and one by the offspring of an impoverished Nimois family, in addition to newspaper accounts, all offer more personal insights.[25] In combination with archival documents, census and civil status records, these materials illuminate the role played by culture and community for newcomers to Nîmes.

By its methodology, its focus, and its sources, this study of migration in urbanizing France seeks fresh insights into the experience of migration to the city between the beginning of the rural exodus in the 1880s and World War I. The study was undertaken with an eye to a broader understanding of the change experienced by those who, like the Donzels and the Chevret sisters, began their lives in villages or small towns and moved to cities like Nîmes. It confirms that people like them were not jolted from a motionless traditional countryside into the industrial city. Historical reality is at once more complex and more interesting than such an account suggests. Departure from a changing rural and small-town world for an urban society in flux was a journey along paths that had familiar contours. This study illuminates the meaning of cityward migration through a close investigation of the context in which it occurred, rather than inferring that meaning from the deserted village or urban "social disorganization." It is part of a larger effort to understand the large-scale changes wrought by the nineteenth century — industrialization, urbanization, the demographic transition — through a focus on the men and women whose lives were at the heart of these historical dramas.

NOTES

1. Adna Weber, *The Growth of Cities in the Nineteenth Century* (Ithaca, NY: Cornell University Press, 1963), 68, 71. See also Georges Dupeux, "La croissance urbaine en France au XIXe siècle," *Revue d'histoire économique et sociale* 52 (1974), 180.

2. To protect the anonymity of individual migrants, who in some cases lived until quite recently, I have utilized fictional names. I have pieced together the biographies here and in Chapter 2 from: (1) the census lists of Nîmes, 1906 (Archives Départementales du Gard — hereafter ADG — series 10M, 260, 261, 262); (2) *Etat civil* records, particularly acts of birth and marriage from the Lozère and the Gard; (3) individual conscript records (ADG and Archives Départementales de la Lozère, series R); (4) a census of consistory electors from the Archives of the Reformed Church of Nîmes (Archives du Consistoire de Nîmes, series C53); (5) a list of donors to the Protestant poor, "Collecte annuelle pour les pauvres," *Bulletin de l'Eglise Reformée de Nîmes* 18 (January 1905), 1-11; and (6) reports from local newspapers such as *Le Petit Républican du Midi*, 1906; *Le Petit Midi*, 1906.

3. Raoul Blanchard, *Le Comté de Nice* (Paris: Arthème Fayard, 1960), 50.

4. A.J.B. Parent-Duchâtelet, *De la prostitution dans la ville de Paris* (Paris: Baillière, 1836); drawing reproduced in Maurice Agulhon, Gabriel Désert and Robert Specklin, *Historie de la France rurale, Vol. 3* (Paris: Editions Seuil, 1976), 399.

5. Alain Corbin, *Les filles de noce* (Paris: Aubier Montaigne, 1978), 75-76, 109-111, 166-168, 304-305.

6. Jean Pitié, *Exode rural et migrations intérieures en France* (Poitiers: Norois, 1971), 39. Frustration at the paucity of information about migration eminating from such sources has been expressed by Sune Åkerman, "Towards an understanding of emigrational processes," *Scandinavian Journal of History* 3 (1978); Michael Anderson, "Urban migration into nineteenth century Lancashire: some insights into two competing hypothoses," *Annales de démographie historique* (1971); André Armengaud, "Un siècle delaissé: le XIXe," *Annales de démographie historique* (1971); Karl Obermann, "De quelques problèmes et aspects socioéconomiques des migrations allemandes du XVIe au XIXe siècle," *Annales de démographie historique* (1971).

7. Pierre Guillaume, *Démographie historique* (Paris: Armand Colin, 1970), 276.

8. Journal d'Agriculture Pratique, "Une école de fermières à New York," *Bulletin de la Société d'Agriculture de la Lozère* 50 (1899), 133.

9. Quoted in the *Journal des debats,* 1828; from Louis Chevalier, *Laboring Classes and Dangerous Classes* (New York: Fertig, 1973), 309.

10. For example, see Etienne Gautier and Louis Henry, *La population de Crulai, paroisse normande* (Paris: I.N.E.D., 1958). See also R.S. Schofield, "Age-specific mobility in an eighteenth-century rural English parish," *Annales de démographie historique* (1970); Steve Hochstadt, "Migration and industrialization in Germany, 1815-1977," *Social Science History* 5 (Fall 1981), 445-468; Charles Tilly, "Migration in modern European history," pp. 48-74 in William McNeill and Ruth Adams, eds., *Human Migration: Patterns and Policies* (Bloomington: Indiana University Press, 1978).

11. A summary of these patterns in France is provided by Olwen Hufton, *The Poor of Eighteenth-Century France* (Oxford: Clarendon Press, 1974).

12. Abel Chatelain, *Les migrants temporaries en France de 1800 à 1914* (Lille: Publications de l'Université de Lille, 1976), 1106.

13. The primary observations of this phenomenon in French history are those of Louis Chevalier, *La formation de la population parisienne au XIXe siècle* (Paris: Presses Universitaires de France, 1950); Alain Corbin, *Archaisme et modernité en Limousin au XIXe siècle,* 1845-1880 (Paris: Marcel Rivière, 1975; David Pinkney, "Migrations to Paris during the Second Empire," *Journal of Modern History* 25 (1953). For other countries see, for example, Lynn Lees, *Exiles of Erin, Irish Migrants in Victorian London* (Ithaca, NY: Cornell University Press, 1979); Allen Neuman, "The influence of family and friends on German internal migration, 1880-1885," *Journal of Social History* 13 (1979); John MacDonald and Leatrice MacDonald, "Chain migration, ethnic neighborhood formation and social networks," *Milbank Memorial Fund Quarterly* 42 (1964).

14. For example, Grace Anderson, *Networks of Contact: The Portuguese and Toronto* (Waterloo, Canada: Wilfrid Laurier University, 1974); Isabelle Bertaux, "The life history approach to the study of internal migration," *Oral History* 7 (1979); Sidney Goldstein, "Circulation in the context of total mobility in Southeast Asia," Papers of the East-West Population Institute, No. 53 (1978); Janice Perlman, *The Myth of Marginality: Urban Poverty and Politics in Rio de Janeiro* (Berkeley: University of California Press, 1976); Charles Tilly and Harold Brown, "On uprooting, kinship and the auspices of migration," *International Journal of Comparative Sociology* 8 (1968). For an informative essay on migrants' "biased information field," see Allen Pred, "Behavior and location: foundations for a geographic and dynamic location theory," *Lund Studies in Geography* 27, series B (1967).

15. Louis Desgraves and Georges Depeux, *Bordeaux au XIXe siècle* (Bordeaux: Fédération Historique du Sud-Ouest, 1969), 418-419; Yves Lequin, *Les ouvriers de la région lyonnaise* (1848-1914), Vol. 1 (Lyon: Presses Universitaires de Lyon, 1977), 238-239; Jean-Pierre Poussou, "Les rélations villes-campagnes en Aquitaine dans la deuxième moitié du XVIIIe siècle: quelques reflexions méthodologiques sur les attractions urbaines et les échanges migratoires," in *Démographie urbaine* (Lyon: Centre d'histoire économique et sociale de la région lyonnaise, 1977), 185-196; Weber, *The Growth of Cities in the Nineteenth Century,* 254.

16. Eugen Weber, *Peasants into Frenchmen: The Modernization of Rural France* (Stanford, CA: Stanford University Press, 1976), 67-94 and passim. J.J. Lee concludes, upon surveying the regional character of internal migration in Germany: "Insofar as specific regional cultures existed, then migration may not have required as rapid or as traumatic a psychic journey as some models suggest" in "Aspects of

Urbanization and Economic Development in Germany, 1815-1914," in Philip Abrams, ed., *Towns in Societies* (Cambridge: Cambridge University Press, 1978), 285.

17. Agulhon, Désert, and Specklin, *La France rurale,* 472.

18. Lequin, *Les ouvriers de la région lyonnaise,* 270.

19. Philip Abrams, "Introduction," in P. Abrams, ed., *Towns in Societies.* For an intriguing investigation of the importance of region to population patterns, see John Knodel, "Town and country in 19th-century Germany: urban-rural differentials in demographic behavior," *Social Science History* 1 (1977).

20. Lequin, *Les ouvriers de la région lyonnaise.*

21. For some most explicit critiques, see Goldstein, "Circulation"; Lees, *Exiles of Erin;* and Perlman, *Myth of Marginality.*

22. Some particularly rich descriptions of migration systems are found in Roger Beteille, "L'originalité de l'emigration rouergate: filières, migrations et comportement socio-professional," *Actes* du XLIIe Congrès d'Etudes de la Fédération Historique du Languedoc Méditerranéen et du Roussillon (Rodez: Fédération Historique, 1974); Corbin; *Archaïsme et modernité en Limousin.*

23. I looked for a city that had grown by at least 50 percent during the nineteenth century to assure that it had attracted some migrants, and that had a population of not much more than 100,000 in 1901. As census lists are a primary source for this study, a larger city would have proved unwieldy. Use of the census lists also required a city with microfilming facilities in its archives. I also looked for a city with some industry, which I thought would render the labor force more visible to the researcher. Four cities filled the first two criteria (Avignon, Chalons-sur-Saone, Monpellier, and Nîmes), but only two (Chalons and Nîmes) met all four requirements.

24. These two towns and the village were chosen because each sent a visible stream of migrants to Nîmes — more than one would expect given the town's size and distance from the city.

A gravity calculation was used to estimate the number of migrants that one would expect, to be compared with the number observed in a 5 percent sample of migrants taken from the census lists. This calculation was figured for the 48 sending areas with the most migrants in Nîmes in 1906.

$$M_c = \frac{P_1 P_2 K}{D^2} \qquad K = \frac{P_1 P_2}{D^2} \Big/ \Sigma \frac{P_1 P_2}{D^2} \qquad I = \frac{M_o}{M_c} 100$$

M_c = expected number of migrants from a specific location
P_1 = population of Nîmes in 1906
P_2 = population of home town in 1906
D = distance between home town and Nîmes
K = proportion of migrants expected from any one town
M_o = number of migrants observed from a specific home town
P = total number of migrants from the 48 top birthplaces in the sample (N = 448)
I = index of observed to expected migrants

Five towns had a ratio of observed to expected migrants of over 1000. Three of these were chosen for further study. Two were eliminated because they had ambiguous place names; that is, names that could apply to several communes in the area.

After combing the census lists for a second time and gathering data on all migrants from the three areas, it was discovered that one area had only 83 people in Nîmes, too small a group for specific study.

Upon returning to France to begin research on the home towns, I discovered that none of these towns had a Protestant tradition, and I chose to add the Protestant town with the highest ratio of observed to expected migrants. Le Vigan, with a ratio of 550, was chosen.

25. André Chamson was born in Nîmes and raised in Le Vigan. He was named to the Academie Française and presided over the National Archives of France for many years. Autobiographical accounts of life in Nîmes are Marc Bernard, *Pareils à des enfants* (Paris: Gallimard, 1941); Lucie Mazauric Chamson, "*Belle Rose, Ô Tour Magne*," (Paris: Plon, 1969); Paul Marcelin, *Souvenirs d'un passé artisanal* (Nîmes: Chastanier, 1963).

2

Migration and Economic Change in Eastern Languedoc

> Certainly, rurals of the Massif Central or Brittany, for example, where urban networks have little structure, are more directly attracted by the great cities than those of Provence, Languedoc, the Alps or of Alsace where a local urban structure, a human tradition, and a physical and social climate retain them in neighboring locales.
>
> — Pierre Merlin, *L'exode rural*

Pierre Merlin observes that Languedoc is one of France's provinces in which migration patterns are distinctly regional. This raises questions about the nature of regional movement and its relationship to urbanization. In particular, what are the human traditions and structural elements that unite a region? More pointedly, which historical changes produced the shift in migration patterns that resulted in urbanization?

In order to investigate the context and causes of urbanization in a regional frame of reference, this chapter begins with a brief account of migration in Eastern Languedoc: its history, structure, and the shift from temporary migration to permanent settlement in a regional capital. Then, with an eye to evolving migration streams, the focus narrows from Eastern Languedoc to three home towns: Le Vigan, Villefort, and Langogne. The investigation discusses specific changes in migration for each town and the historical circumstances in which they occurred. Finally, in order to assess the selective nature of migration, the people in the migration streams which emerged between each home town and Nîmes are identified and compared with those who did not take the same path. Finally, biographies are reconstructed for a few people in each migration stream. Regional patterns are appropriate to a broad perspective; variations in home town conditions provide an account of changes in migration patterns and in the origins of migration streams.

THE EVOLUTION OF MIGRATION

Migration was significant centuries before the rural exodus of the 1880s; men and women have traveled between the mountains and plains of Eastern Languedoc since the Middle Ages. In the sixteenth century, Braudel's *"éternel immigrant montagnard"* resuscitated many plague-depleted cities. Le Roy Ladurie recounts the descent of begging men, women and, most pitifully, children into the Languedocian plain in search of bread and warmth. Records of montagnards from the Cévennes mountains and from the uplands of Gévaudan and the Rouergue living on the plain indicate that some prospered, or at least survived, and stayed on.[1] Others returned home, gradually transforming Languedoc into a single region. People in the south of France migrated for short-term employment more frequently than those in the north, as the Massif Central, "a reservoir of men and human suffering," forced its people out to earn their bread.[2] In the eighteenth century, long before the upland areas were accessible to wheeled vehicles, mule paths were used by men, women, and children who left their homes on foot. Unlike most migrants from the Alps and other regions of the central highlands, such as Auvergne and Limousin, who went to Northern and central France, those from the Lozère and the Cévennes mountains traveled toward the south coast.[3]

The origin of temporary migration was the centuries-old transhumance of sheep from the highlands to the plains for the winter and to the uplands for summer pasture (see Map 2.1).[4] Many uplanders earned cash through seasonal harvest work. At the beginning of the nineteenth century, when a variety of crops were cultivated on the coastal plain, the first movement would be the descent of male and female silk workers from the Cévennes and the plateaus *(causses)* of the Lozère to mountain valleys and the plain for a month of intense work. In June, laborers from outside the department of the Gard harvested the grain around Nîmes. Cevenols often moved to the tidal flats to gather salt during the month of August. By mid to late July, ripening began in the uplands, and day laborers found work harvesting rye around Langogne and Clermont-Ferrand in the Massif Central. The grape harvest took place in September on the coastal plain.

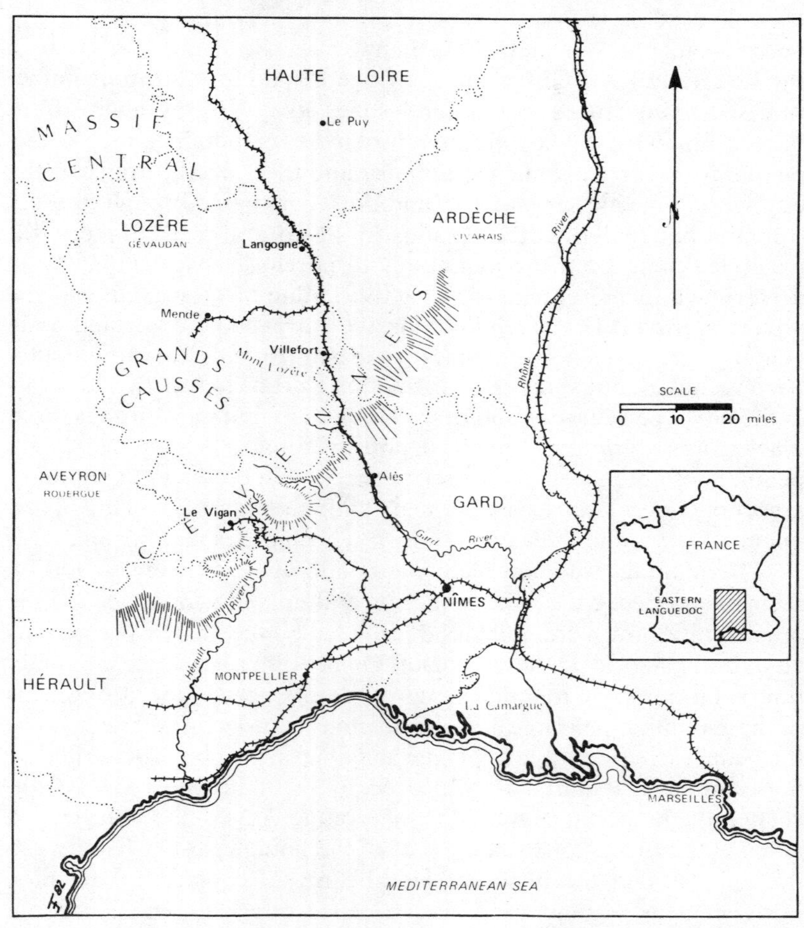

Map 2.1: Eastern Languedoc

After that, their own potatoes and chestnuts called the montagnards home.[5]

Temporary migration also touched the cities; agricultural workers passed through town to beg and buy. "As the wine harvest approached, or just after it was finished, Nîmes filled with bands of Cevenol peasants that we called *gavots* — men and women carved from the hardest of wood," a Nimois recalled of seasonal workers.[6]

Other montagnards found work in town, many in urban textile industries. For example, one enterprising Nimois manufacturer recruited young women to spin and young men to card cotton through a curé in the Lozère in 1781. Girls from the Lozère spun for cotton manufacturers, leaving traces in workers' songs like "The Spinner," from Nîmes, about a girl who longs to return to her mountain home. Young people from the Cévennes mountains and the Lozère furnished the city with domestic servants. In addition, commerce brought traders from market centers in the uplands to the coastal plain. Bakers, for example, came from the mountains to purchase wheat flour. Mule drivers, who were crucial to the provisioning of Gévaudan and the Vivarais, traveled between the Massif Central and the lowland trade centers. The existence of temporary urban workers has infrequently been recorded, but shreds of information alert us to the myriad rurals in the city's petty trades and services, such as chimney sweeps, boot blacks, knife grinders, pan and pottery repairmen, cobblers, and peddlers of both sexes with every conceivable product. In addition, abject outsiders such as abandoned children, beggars, and the ill and unemployed found their way to the city's charities and hospitals.[7]

The montagnards and plainsmen of Languedoc were united by their interdependence. The mountain and upland people needed the opportunities for work and bread provided by the nearby prosperous cities and plains in a milder climate. On the other hand, the manufacturers, farmers, and middle classes of the city needed the strong arms of the mountain peasant to perform arduous tasks. And the cities of the plains, so susceptible to plague and illness, particularly during the hot summers, required new people to maintain their size. Consequently, the permanent settling of montagnards in the villages and cities of the plain constituted a part of the human exchange between the uplands and the plains of Languedoc. Most of the exchange, however, was a temporary one, because upper Languedoc could support its population for most of the year. Temporary migrations took the form, for example, of a trader's days at a lowland fair, the summer of a shepherd from the plains spent in mountain pastures, a young woman's season as a cotton spinner in the city, or the years a domestic servant spent while earning a dowry. In Languedoc, at least, montagnards were not stay-at-homes; rather, they knew something of the lowland plains or the coastal cities.

Temporary migration in Languedoc fluctuated to meet the needs of the migrants for employment, cash, or food and the needs of the manufacturer or landowner for labor. For example, when there was an unusually difficult season in the mountains, more people would descend, and when workers were needed, more were recruited from the highlands. After the 1840s, the balance shifted between seasonal or temporary migration on the one hand, and permanent emigration on the other. Permanent emigration from the uplands increased, and this was a turning point in the population history of the region.[8]

A decline in opportunities for seasonal employment was partially responsible for this shift. A series of crises undermined the fragile systems of seasonal earning. After 1853, a long silk crisis strangled cash-earning opportunities for Lozerians and Cevenols. Twenty years later, the phylloxera epidemic virtually eliminated vine harvest work. As French vineyards were replanted, they expanded, and the plains were given over to the wine industry. This eliminated the cultivation of grains and other products, which had provided seasonal employment in the early summer, though some opportunities for harvest work appeared when the development of the railroad promoted fruit and vegetable production in the Rhone delta for the markets of Lyon and Paris. Rhone valley farms needed pickers for short periods, and girls came from the Cévennes to do the job. The development of the wine and fruit and vegetable production reflected an increased concentration of capital in the lowlands. The general result of these crises and developments was that the staggered series of harvests that provided work on the Languedocian plain in the spring and summer disappeared. The grape harvest remained, but little else. Moreover, women were less often hired for this task. In a region where the migration of women was of great importance, such a change devastated the system devised by rural people to maintain themselves.[9]

The acceleration of permanent migration to the lowlands is clearly reflected in the evolution of population by department. Before the 1840s, few departments in France lost population. By 1851, there was a dramatic change; the census that year showed that 40 departments had suffered a loss of people. The upland departments of Eastern Languedoc, the Lozère, and the Ardèche, lost badly while the Hérault and the Gard gained. The Lozère, a department with an extremely high birth rate and natural increase, exported people constantly (Table 2.1). After 1851, when it registered its peak population, the Lozère lost a greater proportion of its people through emigration than any other department in France.[10] The Gard received many Lozerians.

But department-level population figures are a crude indicator of how people migrate. They mask important phenomena of step migration and urbanization — departures from rural areas to valley towns,

TABLE 2.1 Population Trends by Department in Eastern Languedoc, 1836-1911

	Department			
	Gard	*Hérault*	*Lozère*	*Ardèche*
1836-1851				
Population at Time 1	366,259	357,846	141,733	353,752
Population at Time 2	408,163	389,286	144,705	386,559
Net Migration[a]	+12,700	+14,200	−9,600	−12,600
Migration Intensity[b]	+3.5%	+4.0%	−6.8%	−3.6%
1851-1866				
Population at Time 1	408,163	389,286	144,705	386,559
Population at Time 2	429,742	427,245	137,263	387,174
Net Migration[a]	+5,400	+30,500	−17,900	−27,200
Migration Intensity[b]	+1.3%	+7.8%	−12.3%	−7.0%
1872-1891[c]				
Population at Time 1	420,131	429,878	135,190	380,277
Population at Time 2	419,388	461,012	135,517	371,269
Net Migration[a]	−4,300	+45,000	−21,100	−29,200
Migration Intensity[b]	−1.0%	+10.5%	−15.6%	−7.7%
1892-1911				
Population at Time 1	419,388	461,012	135,517	371,269
Population at Time 2	413,458	480,484	149,917	374,469
Net Migration[a]	+10,000	+40,000	−27,100	−42,600
Migration Intensity[b]	+2.4%	+8.7%	−20.1%	−11.5%

a. Net migration is the difference between the population at time 2 estimated from birth and death records and the population censused at time 2; see Pitié, *Exode rural,* 108 and note 30, this chapter.

b. The intensity of migration measures net migration relative to the population at time 1; Pitié expresses this by an index rather than by a proportion; see Ibid., 108.

c. The 1866-72 period is omitted because the demographic impact of the Franco-Prussian war renders the required statistics of birth and death unsuitable; see Pitié, Ibid., 79.

SOURCE: Jean Pitié, *Exode rural et migrations intérieures en France. L'exemple de la Vienne et du Poitou-Charentes* (Poitiers: Norois, 1971), 109, 123, 143, 159.

and movement from these towns to regional or national centers. Not only did seasonal migration give way to permanent emigration, but movement to agricultural areas gave way to city-bound migration. Young people led the movement from rural areas; we find them in small towns and in railroad station towns. Townspeople, in turn, moved to larger centers. In the case of lower Languedoc, the regional centers were the benefactors.[11] A detailed focus on the countryside will show the connections among attenuating temporary migration, step migration, and urbanization. The link is changes in the rural economy, the human response to which was a massive shift in population. To see how economic changes affected the people from the uplands of Languedoc, and how their migration changed as a result, I will turn to the town of Le Vigan in the Cévennes mountains in the department of the Gard, home of Henri Donzel; the village of Villefort, in the mountains of the southern Lozère, and birthplace of Edouard Roche; and the small town of Langogne, north of Villefort, and home of the Chevret sisters.

LE VIGAN

Le Vigan is a small town on the edge of the Cévennes mountains, about 58 miles west of Nîmes. The steep forested mountains open to a wide basin on the Arre river at an elevation of 700 feet, where Le Vigan sits on the north side of the river. Terraced slopes rise steeply above it. In the nineteenth century, Le Vigan was a town of 5000, an industrial and administrative center for the western portion of the department of the Gard. Under the old regime, Le Vigan had been the seat of a subdelegate of the Generality of Languedoc. Its administrative function continued after the revolution, when it became a subprefecture in the department of the Gard, thus linking its courthouse, schools, and offices directly to the prefecture of Nîmes.[12] These administrative functions capitalized on long-lived commercial ties with Nîmes, based primarily on the silk industry.

Silk production involved both agriculture and industry in the canton of Le Vigan. When silkworms hatched in May, they voraciously devoured the leaves of the mulberry tree that had been gathered by women and children.[13] Then the silkworms mounted twigs in specially heated chambers to spin their cocoons and hibernate. Breeders tended fires to keep the cocoons warm. By the end of August, girls and women could dissolve the cocoon in boiling water and draw the first fine silk threat from it. The remainder of the silk production — evening, spinning, and milling the thread — continued throughout the year, but the manufacture of raw silk was an intense seasonal activity that provided cash for peasant worm-tenders, as well as for large-scale producers, since the spinning of silk and the manufacture of hosiery were year-round industries in Le Vigan. Families of the region depended on their daughters' annual cash earnings from drawing the silk thread, or on their earnings from the mills. Stocking knitters, on the other hand, were men.[14]

Le Vigan had a quasi-rural character that was reflected in the vital role agriculture played in the town's life. Crops that required mild weather, such as grains, vegetables, and some grapes, were cultivated on the broad valley floor, while the cultivation of more hardy crops, such as chestnut and mulberry trees, began at the outer edge of town and spread over the surrounding hills. About one-fifth of the people of the commune were sharecroppers and peasants living outside the town in isolated farms or hamlets, but many Viganais were landowners. In his study of the region, Dugrand calls Le Vigan "the little land-owning metropolis of the western edge of the causses and primary valleys of the Cévennes."[15]

Le Vigan had long been a crossroads of east-west mule paths from Nîmes to the Rouergue to the west, and ancient paths for transhumant flocks moving between the plain of Languedoc and the Cévennes mountains. For centuries it acted as a trade center at which goods from the plain were traded with those of the uplands. Wine and salt from lower Languedoc, wheat and rye from the plateaus, and fattened pigs and chestnuts from the mountains were bought and sold.[16] When Le Vigan tried to alter its annual schedule of fairs, comments and objections came from the north, from communes in the Lozère beyond high mountain passes, from the Aveyron and the Causse of Blandas to the west. These replies indicate that Le Vigan was more important as a trade center as the twentieth century approached, because it became more accessible to its hinterland. Mail service and roads opening to the north in midcentury solved transport and communications difficulties with the mountains. By the end of the century, the commune of Le Vigan held fourteen fairs annually.[17] Commerce with the plain, particularly the silk trade between Le Vigan and Nîmes, predated the revolution. This too was facilitated when the mule path toward Nîmes was made passable by wheeled vehicles in 1774. A century later, the railroad linked Le Vigan to the Mediterranean littoral.

The southern Cévennes had a venerable tradition of Protestantism predating the seventeenth-century Camisard revolt against the armies of Louis XIV, which followed the revocation of the Edict of Nantes. The Protestant population of Le Vigan was diluted during the nineteenth century as Catholic peasants from the mountains of the Lozère gradually became a more important part of the population. By the turn of the century, Le Vigan was about half Protestant and half Catholic. Each camp had its own politics, with Protestants traditionally being republicans and Catholics traditionally being royalists. Each group had its own social institutions, be they mutual aid societies or social clubs. For example, La Philharmonique Viganaise was the Protestant musical society, La Musique Saint-Pierre the Catholic society. A general synod of the reformed church of France was held in Le Vigan at the turn of the century, and at about the same time the Catholic church was renovated, largely with local funds; both Protestants and Catholics were active in Le Vigan.[18]

One reflection of the active religious life in Le Vigan, and of its multifaceted economy, is the level of schooling for the Viganais throughout the nineteenth century. A secondary school was established in 1836 that employed nine professors by the time of the Second Empire. Although the school was not open continuously, it attests to the town's interest in education. At midcentury, boys' and girls' schools — Catholic and Protestant — existed in the commune. As a consequence, literacy was relatively high in midcentury Le Vigan. Over 86 percent of the men marrying in Le Vigan in the early 1850s signed their name to their marriage records, as compared with 80 percent of the grooms in the Gard and 72 percent of all the grooms in France over ten years later in 1866. Women, too, were likely to be literate. Nearly 60 percent signed their name to marriage records in the years 1851-1855, compared to 55 percent for France and 60 percent for the Gard in the next decade.[19] By 1880, the Association des Amis de l'Instruction Populaire had instituted night classes for adults in the Catholic and Protestant schools.

Several factors promoted schools and a high rate of literacy in Le Vigan. The size of the commune alone (between 4650 and 5390 in the period from 1851 to 1881) made it a likely site for substantial educational institutions. Moreover, because Le Vigan was a subprefecture, it offered more employment for white collar workers than towns without an administrative function. Its commerce also helped in this regard. Both commerce and administration made the uses of literacy and some education visible to every school child, reduced the isolation imposed by the Cévennes mountains, and made the town relatively sophisticated. Finally, the religious composition of Le Vigan promoted literacy. Protestants in the region say that they have been reading the Bible for 500 years, while Catholics have only been reading a century. A Catholic reponse to Protestant literacy, as well as the Bible-reading Protestant population, promoted literacy in the Cévennes quite early in the nineteenth century.[20]

Le Vigan's role as a small regional capital for industry, commerce, education, and administration generated an exchange of persons between the Viganais and the Cévennes mountains, the high plateaus to the west, and the Mediterranean plain. Le Vigan had long played the role of relay station in systems of seasonal and temporary migration. In the late eighteenth century, the subdelegate in Le Vigan described the arrival of migrants from the Auvergne and Rouergue to the north and west for the winter.

> Regularly, every year, when the rigor of the climate forces the inhabitants of Auvergne and the Rouergue into inaction, they come in numbers to lend us help and to share our work; they spend the winter and part of the spring with us.[21]

Twenty-two years later, the subprefect reported on seasonal migrations to and from Le Vigan. Sawyers, coppersmiths, and chimney sweeps, he wrote, came from the uplands for the winter. An important contingent, which included women, left Le Vigan annually to work the silk harvest and the grain harvest in the Hérault to the south and to gather salt along the coast. Others departed to work as agricultural laborers for the winter, to pick chestnuts in the fall, and to harvest grain on the plateaus of the Lozère at the end of August.[22]

Some temporary migrants from the Auvergne and the Rouergue "even stay and establish their permanent residence here," reported the subdelegate in 1786. And the subprefect, writing in 1811, added Lozerians to the list of immigrants settling in the area.[23] Marriage records from Le Vigan in the 1830s show that the Languedocian plain was also within reach of the Viganais. Over one-tenth of the brides and grooms were from the uplands, and another 10 percent from other locales outside the canton of Le Vigan. Compared with a nearby town similar in size and industrial vocation, Le Vigan had broader contacts. In contrast with its twin, St-Jean-du-Gard,

> Le Vigan maintained closer relations with more distant areas (the Rouergue to the West and, East of Ganges, lower Languedoc). It is entirely possible that the administrative function of Le Vigan accentuated the intensity of human movement and thus contributed to opening a broader marriage market than St-Jean's.[24]

People attracted to Le Vigan came primarily from the rocky plateaus *(causses)* to the west and from the Cévennes mountains. Marriage records from the early 1850s show that about one-quarter of the brides and grooms had moved to Le Vigan from other areas, and most of these areas were within twenty kilometers in the uplands, the river valleys and the plateaus to the north and west. Birthplace and residence of marriage partners in Le Vigan are analyzed in Table 2.2. The census of 1876 reflects the same movement from the upper valleys of the Hérault and Arre rivers and the north side of the plateau of Blandas to the west.[25]

André Chamson has portrayed this movement from the highlands to Le Vigan in *The Road,* the story of two peasant families who were drawn off the land to Le Vigan by working on the road through the mountains into the Lozère in the 1850s. After the completion of their work on the road, the peasants returned to their land only on Sundays, where they often reflected on the choice they had made to move to town. One Sunday when the two men cultivated Combes's land together, Audibert asserted:

> "You feel lost in the city. I would never go back to live in these deserts. If my father died, our house would give its stones back to the mountain. It takes five whole hours to climb up there; it is even wilder than here and nothing is worth anything. . . . Rotten planks and stones without cement. My father lives up there like a wild boar; there won't be four sticks of furniture to take away."

Combes replied:

> "But just the same, life wasn't as bad as all that in our mountains."

But the men were divided on this.

> "We lived off animals and trees and expected nothing of anybody. Every house had enough sunlight to ripen its vegetables. A spring made the wealth of a family, or if not the wealth, at least the security."
>
> Sometimes Audibert seemed convinced. He agreed with Combes, but an hour later he would say appropos of something entirely different:
>
> "No, in spite of everything, you can't live in these solutides."
>
> But more often, instead of going off with Combes to the mountain, Audibert spent his day of rest at Saint-André. He dressed himself in his Sunday best.[26]

The wives of the two men preferred town life. Madame Combes, in fact, had been the one who urged the move. In his portrait of Anna Combes, Chamson sensitively evokes the peasant woman's search for security in town, which was enhanced by her employment in the silk mills.

> in the mountain farms and sheepfolds where she had passed her childhood, on the farm to which she had come as a young woman, mistress of a little world that had hardly permitted one to earn a living, one never escaped from a continuous poverty, a poverty that was without great destitution but without one hour of abundance,

> and she had long suffered from this frugal life in which economy resulted in nothing laid by, in which sobriety enabled one merely to exist from day to day, without the promise of any security for the morrow. She had wished therefore to live in town, not to become rich but to assure her future. Like her, since the beginning of the century, other mountain women, poor and anxious, had come down.[27]

Did Le Vigan's attraction for people of the mountains change during the nineteenth century? Did the Viganais themselves become more likely to leave home? Traces of the evolution of migration to and from Le Vigan are left in the marriage records. Indeed, marriage records are a particularly helpful source for the study of migration patterns because they list both the birthplace and the residence of the bride and groom at the time of their marriage. In addition, they list the groom's occupation. A detailed evaluation of marriage records as a source is included in Appendix I. A comparison of marriage records for two periods, 1851-55, and 1901-05, shows that migration patterns did change. (The first period was chosen because the largest cohort of Le Vigan's migrants residing in Nîmes in 1906 was born at this time; see the section on migrant streams below.) The attraction of a little town like Le Vigan grew, and its area of contact expanded. Grooms' residence reflects these changes most acutely because women generally married in their home town; consequently, brides' residence changes very little over time. The marriage records for Le Vigan for 1901-1905 reflect a very different residential pattern from those for 1851-1855.

At the turn of the century, women from Le Vigan were meeting and marrying men from a larger region than fifty years earlier. Nearly three-quarters of the women marrying in Le Vigan in the 1830s married men living in the commune. In all, 65 percent of the women marrying in the 1850s married men living in Le Vigan, yet fewer than half the brides in the 1901-1905 period married men living in the commune. The proportion of bridegrooms born and residing in Le Vigan and its canton dropped off sharply in the last half of the century, while the proportion residing outside Le Vigan nearly doubled (see Table 2.2).

In addition, bridegrooms came from farther away. This may be because local men went farther and took local women with them, or because unmarried women themselves had contacts farther from home because they left home to work, visited friends and relatives outside the canton, and/or received visitors from more distant places.

TABLE 2.2 Birthplace and Residence of Marriage Partners in Le Vigan, 1851-1905

	Grooms		*Brides*	
	1851-1855	*1901-1905*	*1851-1855*	*1901-1905*
Born and residing in the canton* of Le Vigan	57%	41%	76%	69%
Born outside Le Vigan, residing in the canton of Le Vigan	23	19	21	30
Residing outside the canton of Le Vigan	20	40	3	1
Missing data	1	0	0	1
Total	100%	100%	100%	100%
N	156	179	156	179

*The canton includes the commune of Le Vigan and nearby hamlets.
SOURCE: ADG E5 and ATN *Etat civil*, Le Vigan.

Most likely, both occurred. In a few cases, the bridegrooms residing outside Le Vigan had been born there and returned home for a bride. In most cases, though, it seems that the bride's employment and family contacts had produced the engagement with an outsider. Unfortunately, it is impossible to tell whether women met their husbands while working in Montpellier, for example, or while visiting relatives or friends there. This is because marriage records give legal domicile at the time of marriage, and brides were usually silent about their residences, as well as their employment, before marriage. Because women often married in their home town, marriage records underreport their premarital migration to an unknown degree. Consequently, we can only conclude that marriage records reflect connections between Le Vigan and grooms' residences, and we cannot know exactly how those connections were formed. In the 1850s, the marriage records show, Nîmes was the single most important point of contact outside the immediate area; five women married men from there in five years.

At the turn of the century, nearly one-third of the grooms, as opposed to 8 percent in the 1850s, lived over twenty kilometers from Le Vigan. More important, of the men who came to Le Vigan to marry, only one-third came from the Cévennes or nearby small towns like Valleraugue. They more often came from the south, from the Hérault, the Gard, and the Bouches-du-Rhone. Of the 72 grooms living outside Le Vigan, the largest group resided in the Hérault, particularly in Montpellier. Contact with the Hérault had taken precedence over the Gard since the 1850s. In all, over half this group resided in the three coastal departments, concentrating in and between Montpellier and Nîmes. This pattern reflects the connection between the Protestant Cévennes mountains and the Protestant wine-growing coastal plain called the Vaunage.[28] One-fifth of these grooms lived even farther from Le Vigan — five in Paris and a suburb, two in Lyon, others in towns of the Ain, Tarn, Hautes-Alpes, the Ardèche, and Vaucluse.

Grooms also tended to reside in cities and towns, although a minority were peasants from rural communes. The vast majority (80 percent) lived at least in *chef-lieux de canton,* akin to county seats. There is a clear network among the region's cities that is reflected in the destinations of most couples who left Le Vigan after the wedding: Montpellier, Marseille, Nîmes, Sète, Arles, and Alès, Valleraugue, Ganges, and St-Hyppolite du Fort in the Cévennes. Long-distance connections were almost exclusively urban. The women from this little town, then, would form urban families.

Among grooms' occupations, government, other white collar work, and professions now dominated, whereas the urban grooms of the 1850s had been mostly artisans. The largest group of grooms consisted of railroad workers and railroad white collar workers in Montpellier, Paris, on the Mediterranean littoral — everywhere. Next came government employees: the science teacher in the Alps, policemen in Provençal towns, tax clerks in Languedoc, career army officers stationed in Montpellier and Nîmes. Only six grooms born in Le Vigan figure among those residing elsewhere; all of them worked for the railroad or the government — four as railroad employees on the Mediterranean littoral, one as a tax officer in the Ardèche, and the last as a postal clerk in Lyon. The sons of Chamson's ex-peasants in Le Vigan, Audibert and Combes, would fit easily into this group, for Audibert's son went to Nîmes for his schooling, and Combes's son was stationed in the railroad drafting office in a suburb of Paris.

As the contacts of the Viganais reached south and to major cities by the turn of the century, the town continued to attract people from upland areas. This is apparent in the steady attraction of brides and grooms born outside the canton who lived and married in Le Vigan (Table 2.2). Indeed, Le Vigan's population would have declined without the in-migrants from its hinterland, because deaths consistently outnumbered births between 1850 and 1900.[29] During this period, the crude birth rate dropped from 28.6 to 20.2 births per thousand (see Table 2.3).

TABLE 2.3 Crude Birth Rate, Crude Death Rate, Population, and Net Migration, Le Vigan, 1849-1908

Period	*Crude Birth Rate*	*Crude Death Rate*	*Period*	*Population at Time 1*	*Net Migration*
1849-1853	28.6	28.6	1851-1856	4993	−288
1854-1858	25.2	30.0	1856-1861	4656	+812
1859-1863	24.8	28.9	1861-1866	5376	−145
1864-1868	25.3	30.7	1866-1872	5104	+247
1869-1873	27.0	33.7	1872-1876	5204	+232
1874-1878	28.3	29.2	1876-1881	5389	+ 47
1879-1883	24.4	29.3	1881-1886	5268	+198
1884-1888	22.4	29.0	1886-1891	5353	+237
1889-1893	21.7	30.4	1891-1896	5374	− 4
1894-1898	23.4	27.5	1896-1901	5199	+ 24
1899-1903	20.2	24.2	1901-1906	5126	−449
1903-1908	19.1	25.3	1906	4595	

SOURCE: ADG E5 and ATN *Etat Civil, Le Vigan;* ADG *Actes Administratifs,* 1852-1907.

Net migration figures sketch the balance between immigration to Le Vigan from the uplands and emigration to the lowlands and cities (Table 2.3). Although these figures measure population movements imperfectly, when used over a period, they do reveal migration trends.[30] Le Vigan continually attracted more people than it lost between 1860 and 1890. This period was surrounded by two important periods of loss: the silk crisis of the 1850s, and the years 1901-1906.

The silk industry, lynchpin of Le Vigan's economy, was subject to crises. The market for silk stockings, for example, dropped after the revolution when men began wearing long pants and women, boots. A more serious crisis occurred when the silkworms themselves were stricken by the illness *pébrine* in 1852. As a result, the population of Le Vigan dropped from nearly 5000 to 4650 before the census of 1856, increasing to 5370 in the early 1860s. This increase did not reflect a recovery from the crises, however, but the inundation of Le Vigan by refugees from the countryside, who were affected by the crisis even more severely than townspeople.[31] Over a dozen years were required to find a cure for *pébrine* and to put the silk industry back on its feet. By this time, less expensive oriental silks had been introduced in France, silks that became even less costly with the opening of the Suez Canal in 1869.

After this, only a heavily subsidized silk industry (which began with the Méline tariff in 1892) could survive. The rural Cévennes produced silk and silk stockings, once again in vogue by the 1870s. At the end of the century, a new silk industry was developed when scraps of silk called *schappe* were processed for use with other materials in novelty fabrics. It employed about 1000 people in Le Vigan, out of a population of some 5000. By the turn of the century, nonetheless, the silk industry in Le Vigan was living on borrowed time; it owed its survival to subsidies and to the fact that the *schappe* mills were owned by Lyonnais and Swiss, who closed and relocated factories at their discretion. Finally, the mills became a less attractive employer because the wages were shamefully low, hardly higher in 1900 than a century earlier. As a consequence, Italian women worked in the mills because only they would accept the low wages.[32]

By the end of the century, Le Vigan's economy was stagnant. Although it was hetereogeneous — commercial, industrial, agricultural, and administrative — its elements were interdependent, so that slumps in one area affected others. The agriculture which was a source of wealth for townspeople and peasants alike declined in value. Chestnuts, already decimated by disease in the 1870s, were spurned as a marketable source of human food, and the price they could bring at market declined. The market for the area's livestock, goats and pigs, did not expand as rapidly as the wages of the farmworker increased. For example, while the market price for potatoes, rye, and chestnuts dropped at the Le Vigan markets in the twenty years after 1880, the price for 33 days of farm labor increased from 46 to 60 francs.[33] The value of mulberry leaves, which were used to feed silkworms, depended solely on the level of silk subsidies. The decline in the proportion of workers in small industries such as wooden shoemaking, cabinetry, and masonry between the 1850s and 1900 suggests that the town was not expanding rapidly enough to support the building trades, and locally made articles were less marketable. Indeed, Pierre Gorlier observes that the annual September 9 fair declined with the opening of the railroad, which increased the variety of goods available at the end of the century.[34] Thus the decline of agricultural prices, competition of goods from the outside, and the atrophy of raw silk production, as well as the troubles of even the most prosperous sectors of the silk industry, contributed to the town's decline. As a result, the population decreased between 1890 and 1906 from over 5300 people to fewer than 4600.

Migrants continued to come to Le Vigan from its hinterland, but more Viganais now left home. Rural workers left the unprofitable land. Artisans, whose goods were now produced in the city and distributed by the railroad, may have been inclined to leave. Marriage records indicate that there were fewer male domestics of bourgeois in Le Vigan than before. The bourgeoisie was choosing to live in the city.

For example, the Baronesse de Clauzon, who donated 50,000 francs toward the restoration of the church of St. Pierre in Le Vigan, lived in Nîmes when the restoration was effected.[35] The children of the bourgeoisie and highly paid officials were also likely to leave, since the secondary school closed in 1890.

Le Vigan exemplifies the type of town most likely to send people to large cities: an administrative center, relatively urbane, and long connected by cultural and economic ties with Nîmes and the Mediterranean littoral. The stagnation and periodic decline of its population masks the key role that towns like Le Vigan played in the urbanization of French society. On the one hand, they provided a first urban destination for migrants from the mountains, such as Combes and Audibert in Chamson's novel. On the other, these towns prepared people like the sons of Combes and Audibert for large cities, where they would find new horizons in normal school or in work for the railroad. Nevertheless, the story of Le Vigan and its place in the changing migration patterns of Eastern Languedoc is only part of the story of the region. The histories of Villefort and Langogne demonstrate how varied the faces of change were.

VILLEFORT

Villefort and Langogne are northeast of Le Vigan, on the eastern edge of the department of the Lozère. Here, rugged and forested highlands at the border of the old provinces of Gévaudan and the Vivarais hid draft resisters from the Republican army in 1801.[36] When Robert Louis Stevenson traveled through the area in October of 1878, he found it quite cheerless: "One of the most beggarly countries of the world. It was like the worst of the Scotch Highlands, only worse; cold, naked and ignoble." As he journeyed down the road from Langogne to Villefort, he observed sourly:

> The hills of Gévaudan on the right were a little more naked, if anything, than those of the Vivarais on the left. . . . A low dotty underwood . . . grew thickly in the gorges and died out in solitary burrs on the shoulders and summits. Black bricks of firwood were plastered here and there upon both sides, and here and there were cultivated fields.[37]

Stevenson was following a long tradition in traveling this path. It had been a Celtic route and a Roman road, named the Regordane, which connected the province of Nîmes with the central highlands. Mule trains traveled this road throughout the eighteenth century to transport goods between the Massif Central and the Mediterranean plain. In an effort to persuade the government to build a royal road along the Regordane corridor, Gévaudan boasted in 1760 that 100 mule-drivers transported goods along the route, maintaining over 150 bridges and providing a prosperous business for the inns along the way.[38] Langogne is at the northern edge of the Regordane in the Lozère, Villefort at the south end.

Villefort is a small rural commune snuggled into a narrow mountain valley 1800 feet above sea level, 61 miles north of Nîmes. In 1851, about 1600 people lived in the village, its hamlets and scattered farms. Villefort's rocks and trees resemble those in the southern Cévennes; it has the same steep valleys, mountain streams, and rough granite as the hinterland of Le Vigan. There, too, local agriculture produced chestnuts rather than grain, and its livestock consisted of sheep and goats. Cultivation was only possible on the hand-fashioned terraces that striped the hillsides.

Villefort, north of the broad Mount Lozère which borders the Protestant area, is Catholic. Despite physical resemblances, the history and religion of Villefort profoundly separate it from the southern Cévennes, intimately linked with sustained Protestant resistance to royal authority and a continued Protestant tradition. In Villefort, the Reformation is remembered for acts of destruction and bloody deeds, not for heroism or resistance to royal forces; the village's Reformed church was destroyed in 1662, never to be rebuilt. In the nineteenth century, the faithful in the area would undertake a pilgrimage to the Chapelle Saint-Loup located on the crest of a mountain in the commune. Nearby lived a famous surgeon-priest who performed miraculous surgery and made fools of medical doctors by doing so in court.[39]

Villefort was a trading center, capitalizing on its location at the crossroads of two routes: the Regordane, which runs north and south, and an important east-west mule path linking the Rhone valley with Gévaudan. Both roads were probably impassable to wheeled vehicles until the mid-nineteenth century in the rough terrain around Villefort. Nevertheless, a lively commerce was carried on by muleback. The rich variety of goods marketed in the fairs of Villefort in the eighteenth century included:

> salt and vinegar from lower Languedoc, oil from Provence, wines from lower Vivarais, dried and salted fish and Mediterranean fruits (figs, almonds, oranges, raisins), wool, combed and raw hemp, druggists' items (soap, paper, copper acetate for grape vine illnesses, alum for tanning, soda, wax, pitch), and hardware.[40]

At the beginning of the nineteenth century there were eleven fairs annually in Villefort, and two markets a week.

Even before then, Villefort played the role of population center in a localized system of migration, attracting and exchanging people within a small radius. Between 1762 and 1789, four-fifths of those married in Villefort were born in the parish, and most others were born within twenty kilometers, along the trading route to the west or north. The only exception was the few miners who had come to work in canton's lead mines from eastern France and Germany.[41]

The people of Villefort did not intermarry with those of the Protestant Cévennes to the south. In his study of the Cevenol population, René Lamorisse describes the origins of marriage partners south of the crest of Mount Lozère; in no case, as late as 1855, did anyone choose a partner from the other side. He comments:

> Without doubt, the closed topography favors stay-at-home habits; but these articulate the social and economic stability in a population which retains its goods, its activities, its familiar sphere. In addition, the religious factor contributes to the maintenance of demographic isolation.[42]

Seasonal migration acquainted Villefortais with the plain of Languedoc. Men and women traveled south in the late spring to work for silkworm breeders and in summer for grain harvests. Before and after the phylloxera epidemic, the grape harvests brought migrants to the plain in late summer. The Villefortais were seasonal miners as well. Only about twenty kilometers to the south lay the coal basin of Alès-Grand'Combe, which expanded rapidly in the 1840s. Peasants from the area were recruited to the mines; the movement of peasant-miners from the Regordane corridor between Villefort and Longogne can be traced by still-extant miners' *carnets*. They spent winters working in the mines, then returned to their villages for the agricultural season.[43]

Nîmes, too, attracted Villefortais as early as the 1830s, when its stocking-knitters were a visible presence in the city. Girls who worked as spinners in the same era may have come from Villefort. By midcentury, young women may also have begun work in Nîmes as domestic servants. The village's bakers (who had to go south for wheat flour), cattle and sheep merchants, and other tradesmen had contact with Nîmes as well.[44]

The plain may have been particularly attractive for Villefortais early in the nineteenth century, because its own commerce and industry were beginning to decline. In 1839, Villefort was described as a market town in decline in the *Nouvelle topographie descriptive du département de la Lozère:* "The Gard and the Ardèche exchange products of the Haute-Loire, Loire and Puy-de-Dome in Villefort; its field of action no longer includes Languedoc or Provence."[45] Trade was blocked continually by washed out bridges and roads — inevitable in this rough terrain after spring and fall rains — so that money had to be sought to rebuild roads and bridges. In addition, trade decreased as Villefort found fewer markets for locally produced goods. Outlets declined for the rough woven products of the local wool industry because of finer wool imported from Australia and rising standards of production nationwide. The lead mines closed. Villefort's decline is painfully apparent from the records of the commune. According to the tax lists of 1789, 25 artisans produced wool in Villefort, but a century later only one family of spinners and carders were at work, and its children were a more-than-sufficient labor force.[46] Tanning and leather shoe production also suffered. Villefort had supported 25 artisans in the leather industry, including 17 shoemakers and four tanners in 1789. A century later, the centralization of the glove industry and shoe production had nearly eliminated this work. The bridlemaker of the village did some tanning with his son, but only occasionally.[47]

By the mid-nineteenth century, Villefort was a small rural commune that had lost much of its commercial and industrial vitality. It was becoming an exclusively agricultural village, one that lived primarily on potatoes and chestnuts. Rye and oats were produced north of the commune, and the narrow valley floor of the village and hamlets sheltered vegetable gardens, a few vines, and fruit trees. "The equilibrium of the local economy, which gave an appearance of relative prosperity," concludes a study of prerevolutionary Villefort, "was broken as soon as the artisanal and commercial activities ceased which had compensated for the poverty of the climate-threatened agriculture."[48]

In such a village, educational facilities were minimal. Villefort was without an administrative function, a strong commerce, or a Bible-reading Protestant population to promote the uses of literacy; its small size did not warrant schools of importance. Although literacy improved markedly in the first half of the century, fewer men were able to sign their marriage records in the late 1860s (75 percent) than in the rest of the Lozère (90 percent). The figure for women (65 percent), however, matched that of the department. In the 1860s and 1870s, the only schools for local children were a boys' school operated by the

Frères de Sacre-Coeur, and a girls' school under the Soeurs de Saint-Joseph-de-Vans. These must not have been well attended, because Villefort was an undereducated commune by the standards of the Lozère. In a department in which nearly one conscript in five was unable to read as late as 1880, those from Villefort rated among the least literate.[49] The students, mostly children of peasants, very likely were similar to those in the hamlet of St-Julien-des-Points, twenty kilometers to the south. Attendance at school there dropped off at the end of April when the children were needed to plow, shepherd, and care for geese and pigs. In November, when the potato and grain harvests were complete, attendance increased.[50]

This history of relative isolation and slow decline was interrupted abruptly when:

> The workers of progress set up their tent
> And the Railroad
> From Langeac to Villefort
> Became for these regions a stroke of good luck.
> Bridges were constructed, trenches opened
> Tunnels were pierced through high-perched peaks
> Everywhere one saw housetops spring up.[51]

Railroad construction through Villefort's rough terrain began in 1867, bringing several thousand outsiders into the canton and transforming Villefort into a boomtown. Abel Chatelain estimates that 6000 workers constructed the section of the rail line passing through Villefort. Members of the work crews came from the Auvergne to the north and from the Rouergue, west of the Lozère; a few came from Belgium, Spain, and northern Italy. Local people worked as station personnel rather than in construction.[52] For three years, the crews remained in the area of Villefort, because the rugged topography required time-consuming construction of tunnels and viaducts. Because the altitude rises sharply from 650 to 1800 feet between Alès and Villefort, 37 tunnels were required within the borders of the commune of Villefort alone. Completion of the line was a triumph of engineering and human effort. Just north of the village, for example, the track runs through a tunnel and out along a viaduct over 220 feet above a steep-pitched valley. Villefort's death records attest to the treacherous nature of the task; in 1869, 29 railroad workers from central France, Spain, Belgium, and northern France were buried.[53]

Although the construction crews lived in barracks outside the village, the population of Villefort rose to nearly 2,000 between 1861 and 1866. Workers' families and railroad personnel, such as station employees, engineers, and managers, moved into Villefort. The crews needed food and supplies; in one year, for example, they consumed 1,500 head of cattle, 3,500 sheep, 300 pigs, 500 horses, 400 mules, 52,000 kilos of butter, and 3,600 kilos of cheese. Prostitutes, innkeepers, and barkeepers who helped the workers spend their salaries in this backwoods area also flocked to Villefort. Although commerce flourished, an international work crew, drinking, and payday violence took their toll on municipal order. The Prefect, a judge, six brigades of police, and 200 soldiers stationed in Nîmes rushed to Villefort in the aftermath of one altercation![54]

The railroad boom also left its traces in Villefort's marriage records, which show that Villefort was a prosperous and attractive place in the period from 1866 to 1870. (During this period, the largest cohort of Villefortais migrants residing in Nîmes in 1906 were born; see the migrant streams section below.) The number of marriages nearly doubled over that of the early 1860s. Over half the grooms and nearly one-third of the brides in Villefort were born outside the commune and were drawn there before their marriage (see Table 2.4). The majority of grooms born outside Villefort came from over twenty kilometers away—from the Loire, Corrèze, and Puy-de-Dome in the Massif Central, the Isère to the east, and the Meurthe in Lorraine. Although half the grooms were employed by the railroad, the others attest to Villefort's lively commerce and services during this period; they include a notary, a medical doctor, blacksmiths, a harnessmaker, a butcher, and three bakers. Some brides married men living outside Villefort, as Table 2.4 shows. Most of these men resided within twenty kilometers, in the Lozère or the coal basin of the Gard; three lived in Nîmes.

Villefort's prosperity lasted as long as the railroad construction. With the departure of the work crews, its decline resumed more precipitously than before. By 1872, the population had returned to near its 1861 level of 1539; by 1876, it had dipped below that. Opportunities dried up and people moved on to brighter prospects. By 1875, commerce had so declined that the town asked authorities to approve an additional trade fair, because if Villefort did not increase its commercial activity, more people would be forced to leave. Market records show that its trading zone shrank as those of other communes impinged on it.[55] Upon the heels of the decline in trade and services came the agricultural depression of the 1880s and 1890s, which made it harder for the peasants of Villefort to earn a living from their pigs and chestnuts, much less to assure a future for their large families. As a consequence, the young people of Villefort at the turn of the century

TABLE 2.4 Birthplace and Residence of Marriage Partners in Villefort, 1866-1905

	Grooms		*Brides*	
	1866-1870	*1901-1905*	*1866-1870*	*1901-1905*
Born and residing in the canton* of Villefort	36%	35%	67%	73%
Born outside Villefort, residing in the canton of Villefort	51	12	32	15
Residing outside the canton of Villefort	13	53	1	12
Total	100%	100%	100%	100%
N	92	51	92	51

*The canton includes the commune of Villefort and nearby hamlets.

SOURCE: ADG 4E 198 and ATM, *Etat civil,* Villefort.

had fewer opportunities at home than they would have had 35 years before.

Their options were to turn to the few sources of support remaining in Villefort — government jobs, such as postmen — or to leave. Many joined the "army of steady workers, looking forward to steady positions" with the railroad, an army whose size grew between 1876 and 1907 from about 172,000 to 308,000. Some began railroad careers in the local station, for "the railway station offered steady jobs for steady people — in the long run an influence more subversive [than construction gangs]."[56]

A comparison of marriages from 1866-70 and 1901-05 shows how these choices affected migration and employment. The marriage rate dropped; the number of weddings in Villefort between 1901 and 1905 was about half that of 1866-70. The precipitous decline in population and marriages suggests that for many young people, there was no sense in returning to their home town to marry because even their parents were no longer there. The number of grooms living in Villefort dropped from 73 in the 1860s to a mere 16 at the turn of the century. With one exception, the grooms living in Villefort were born within ten kilometers of the village. This is an indicator of the weak attraction exerted by Villefort after the railroad boom.

By the turn of the century, women were likely to live and work away from Villefort before they married. About one bride in eight even declared her residence as elsewhere when she came home to marry (see Table 2.4). Among these were the daughter of a day laborer living in Alès, in the coal basin, and a peasant's daughter living in the ancient village of Saint-Gilles, near the Camargue. These young women — 22 and 24, respectively, at marriage — may well have worked as domestics, but their occupations were not listed in the marriage records. Another was employed as a clerk in a mining town.

Whatever the work experience of young women from Villefort, they chose to marry men who were living elsewhere than their hometown; by 1900, the geographic arena in which their husbands lived had broadened considerably, with few women marrying men who lived in the Lozère or nearby in the Ardèche. Only two of the (27) bridegrooms living outside the canton of Villefort were from these departments. Eleven worked in the coal basin, and eight on the Mediterranean littoral between Nîmes and Marseille; thus, Villefort's contacts concentrated in the coal basin and the south. Some bridegrooms lived outside Languedoc, in such scattered places as the Pyrenees, the Alps, and near Paris.

Moreover, the great majority of couples moved to cities and towns. The largest group went to the towns of the coal basin: La Grand'Combe, Alès, Genolhac. With one exception, the coastal destinations were towns and cities such as Arles, Beaucaire, Marseille, Nîmes, and Tarascon. Those who left the region altogether resided in suburbs of Paris, garrison towns, and a *bourg* in the Alps — all but one in urban locations.

Nearly half the grooms living outside Villefort were employed by the government (five), or by the railroad (eight). Two more were soldiers. Six of the bridegrooms were born in Villefort, and their work sheds light on the possibilities open to young men from an agricultural village at the turn of the century. The first, son of a widowed innkeeper, was serving as a foot soldier garrisoned in the Alps. A butcher's son taught school in a village near Paris. The son of a peasant worked for the railroad in Nîmes. Another worked as a gendarme in the Alps. There were two coal basin workers: a carter and a stonecutter. The government, railroads and mining companies presented the opportunities, and the coal basin and towns were the sites of these opportunities.

Villefort's history is a most dramatic one. The commune consistently attracted local people, and in the late 1860s it drew from a much wider area. The railroad boom interrupted a gradual decline, after which the steady income of railroad work elsewhere and employment in mining lured away young people. The Villefortais themselves became more mobile and formed contacts to the south in the coal fields of the Gard and nearly all of France by the year 1900. Competi-

TABLE 2.5 Crude Birth Rate, Crude Death Rate, Population, and Net Migration, Villefort, 1849-1908

Period	*Crude Birth Rate*	*Crude Death Rate*	*Period*	*Population at Time 1*	*Net Migration*
1849-1853	36.2	33.0	1851-1856	1614	−103
1854-1858	28.9	33.7	1856-1861	1530	+ 34
1859-1863	29.5	31.3	1861-1866	1539	+427
1864-1868	42.0	45.2	1866-1872	1943	−328
1869-1873	46.0	39.2	1872-1876	1638	−141
1874-1878	38.4	33.4	1876-1881	1535	−104
1879-1883	31.9	28.3	1881-1886	1455	− 37
1884-1888	30.5	33.1	1886-1891	1418	+ 30
1889-1893	25.9	26.1	1891-1896	1449	−219
1894-1898	26.0	21.3	1896-1901	1201	− 46
1899-1903	20.9	25.1	1901-1906	1139	− 4
1903-1908	18.7	25.9	1906	1111	

SOURCE: ADL E4 198 and ATM, *Etat civil, Villefort;* ADL *Receuil des Actes Administratifs*, 1852-1907.

tion with more powerful markets after the installation of the railroad further damaged the commune's commerce. As a result, the impetus to leave Villefort after the 1860s was quite strong.

The demographic trends of the village reflect its devitalization following the railroad boom. Fertility declined from a late 1860s high of 46 births per thousand to 20.9 at the turn of the century (Table 2.5); at the end of the century, fertility dropped dramatically and simultaneously, while the death rate rose. These shifts reflect the aging of Villefort's population, also apparent from the reduction in marriages at the turn of the century.

Net migration figures show only the railroad construction period as one of significant in-migration (Table 2.5). They suggest that the completion of rail construction triggered a great wave of emigration, and that the agricultural depression prompted a second wave in the 1890s. By 1906, a little over half as many people lived in Villefort as had lived there forty years earlier.

In many ways, Villefort's history is a story of rural exodus and urbanization, because the village became more rural with the decline of its commerce and industry. The peasantry fared well until the second half of the nineteenth century, and many villagers went to larger cities. Yet the Villefortais were influenced by particulars of geography and history; the coal basin of the Gard was within easy reach, migration traditions connected Villefort with the Mediterranean plain, and historical circumstances bound Villefort with the railroad. The story of Langogne, however, is quite different.

LANGOGNE

Langogne is a little town in the Massif Central, nestled in a gentle valley at an elevation of over 3000 feet. The topography and climate of France's central highlands separate it from both the Cévennes and the Mediterranean plain, for it is located on a high rolling plateau, much of it forested with pine rather than chestnuts or mulberry trees; the winters are long and the summers cool. This town is located near the top of the Regordane corridor in the Lozère, some 30 miles north of Villefort and 92 miles north of Nîmes. In the middle of the nineteenth century, Langogne had an extraordinarily homogeneous population; out of 3000 inhabitants, there were only two Protestants and one foreigner in residence. As in Villefort, the Reformation left memories of violence rather than heroism in Langogne, most visibly marked in the damage inflicted on the town's Romanesque church.

Like Le Vigan and Villefort, Langogne is located at a crossroads, namely the junction of the Regordane way and the road from Mende (the capital of the Lozère), to Puy-de-Dome and the Rhone. Langogne was the center of the high plain between the mountains of the Ardèche, the Cévennes, and the Haute-Loire.[57] More accessible than Villefort because its terrain was less rough and closer to Lyon, Langogne was a natural passageway between lower Languedoc, the Auvergne, and Lyon. This function was enhanced by the opening of new roads at the end of the eighteenth century toward Le Puy, Villefort, and the Rhone.

As a consequence, Langogne became an important market center. Its three-day fairs attracted merchants from Limousin to Provence, as well as convoys of mule-drivers who would market goods from the highlands and plains; grain, wine, vegetables, and oil from the south; livestock, cheese, and wood products from the north. Wooden buckets, shoes, wash tubs and railing, wool and copper products came from Langogne and its immediate hinterland. The town was "a sort of granary for the Cévennes and the Vivarais," an entrepôt for the region's food.[58] At the end of the eighteenth century, a new grain market was built just outside the medieval town walls, one that proved too small as soon as it was built.

The grain market was important partly because all wheat had to be imported. The 3000-foot elevation, cool climate, and rather infertile soil meant that the schoolmaster's laconic 1874 report that "the town of Langogne is very commercial, but its soil is hardly productive" would have been equally appropriate a century earlier.[59] Rye was the primary crop of the commune because it was hearty and resistant to late frosts. It provided animal feed and bread for the hamlets. The potato became a staple in the nineteenth century.

The municipal council petitioned the central government in 1789 to name Langogne the prefecture of the new department of the Lozère. The council cited Langogne's extensive commerce as proof of its importance, and touted its industry as well. "There are in this town over a thousand persons continuously occupied at working wool; over a hundred looms are in use." So much wool is worked, the council wrote, that some had to be imported. Wool was also processed and dyed in Langogne. In 1787, industry produced 5208 pieces of cloth — serge and rough *cadis* with a market value of over 200,000 *livres*.[60] A copper industry employed at least twenty men in two foundries. Moreover, the tanning industry was relatively important. The Langouyrou river was diverted to form a canal running through the municipal wash house, then under the tanners' quarter in the Rue de Calquières. In 1789, twenty tanneries lined the river. They used the waters of the Langouyrou to process the skins of sheep and goats of the region.

These vigorous industries did not endure; English competition hurt the wool trade in the eighteenth century, and French manufacturing and Australian wool delivered the final blows in the nineteenth. By the second half of the century, little remained of Langogne's wool industry. In 1861, less than one-tenth of the population was supported by the manufacture of various textiles. These were home industries, with one exception: the widow Boyer, who employed about eight workers and operated the one wool-spinning mill in town. In his report, the mayor noted that manufacturing in Langogne could hardly be described as industry. Of the town's workers, he wrote: "These are only simple lone laborers, working by the piece or by order, but not at all engaged either in continuous work or fixed prices, which would put them into the category of *industriels*."[61] The centralization of the glove industry, which organized tanning and processing in the same location as manufacturing, had robbed Langogne's tanning industry of its market. By 1861, only five tanners lived in Langogne, and only one remained in 1880. Thus tanning, like wool processing, declined as Langogne entered national and international markets.

Yet Langogne did not suffer as much as did Villefort. Rather, it "continued a slow but steady demographic increase for 260 years. . . . It owed that especially to its favorable geographic position, to an increase in routes of communication."[62] Commerce continued to be important throughout the first half of the nineteenth century. Moreover, a high birth rate kept the population up, for the Lozère was a high-fertility area. A rough indicator of fertility in Langogne is its crude birth rate, which stood at over 34 per thousand in midcentury (see Table 2.7).

Although Langogne was never an administrative center, it was large and commercial enough to offer a living to some government employees such as administrators, police, and clerks. In 1861, it supported several doctors, surgeons, and pharmacist-herbalists. Its commerce meant that there were merchants, clerks, notaries, and lawyers. Clergy staffed the hospitals and schools. Like Le Vigan, it had a relatively important landowning bourgeoisie. In 1861, more property owners were living off their rents than working their own land in the commune, following Langogne's history of large-scale property ownership and sharecropping rather than small owner-peasant farming.[63]

The Lozère was an overwhelmingly rural department dominated by its agricultural population; in midcentury there were only 500 government employees, 350 school teachers, and 70 doctors and pharmacists in the entire department. From this perspective, Langogne was relatively important as a center for the Lozère's nonpeasant population. One consequence was that the schools of Langogne improved literacy substantially in the first half of the nineteenth century. At the end of the old regime, less than half the grooms marrying in Langogne could sign their name to the marriage record, but this proportion had grown to 65 percent by the 1830s and to over 90 percent by 1860. During the Second Empire, a secondary school was opened.

Women, however, were not schooled in Langogne. Only one-third could sign their name to marriage records under the old regime, and fewer than one-half could do so in the 1830s. According to marriage records, literacy did not improve for women in Langogne in the next thirty years, for only 45 percent of the brides of 1857-61 could sign their name. For the late 1860s the figure is 50 percent. For the women of Langogne it was only the compulsory schooling of the 1880s which taught a clear majority to read and write. Langogne, for all its urbanity relative to the hamlets of the rural Lozère, was clearly part of the nonliterate, intensely Catholic culture of the Massif Central.[64]

This does not mean, however, that the Langognais had no acquaintance with the world. Patterns of growth and migration suggest that Langogne was affected by movement between uplands and plain, and by the movement of people within the highlands. As an eighteenth-century center for industry and trade, Langogne grew by attracting men and women from throughout the region. Seasonal laborers and beggars came for the winter in the beginning of the nineteenth century. Harvest teams from the causses, the Cévennes, and the Ardèche cut rye in Langogne. In turn, there was an exchange of harvesters. An Auvergnat observed in 1858:

> The Lozerian population does not emigrate: it pours out periodically, on fixed days, by entire families and without distinction as to sex. It is a tide composed of all the able-bodied members of each parish. They leave Sunday after mass, with the priest's blessing, carrying for baggage some linens, a sickle, a flail. The day and if necessary the night is sufficient to reach the villages where special fairs are held; whole families hire themselves out together.[65]

With the decline of local industries, seasonal movements probably increased. Indeed, in the first half of the century, observers noted that Lozerians increasingly could speak French because their seasonal migrations were taking them to cities. By midcentury, many Langognais went south to work in the mines and the vineyards of the Gard. The neighboring canton of Grandrieu sent teams of vine-trimmers and vine harvest workers to the south.[66]

Marriage records from the late 1860s show Langogne to have been the center of a small area oriented to the highlands of the Lozère and bordering departments. (The largest cohort of Langognais migrants residing in Nîmes in 1906 was born during this period; see the migrant streams section below.) Figures from the marriage records appear in Table 2.6. About one-third of the grooms who were living in Langogne came from outlying hamlets and nearby villages with names like Chauderyac and Cellier-du-Lac. A smaller group came from other locations in the region, many of whose residents were working on the railroad built through the canton in 1869. Because the terrain around Langogne was less rugged than around Villefort, the work crews were relatively small and their stay short.

About one-fifth of the grooms lived outside Langogne, but these were likely to be from within a radius of twenty kilometers. They were tanners, flour merchants, and government clerks who would have had business in Langogne. Only one groom was living in the department of the Gard to the south — an elderly widower working in the coal basin who had returned to his home town for a wife.

How was this pattern affected by the coming of the railroad to Langogne and the agricultural crises of the end of the century? Unlike Villefort and Le Vigan, Langogne prospered after the coming of the railroad. It advanced as a regional center partially because the prod-

TABLE 2.6 Birthplace and Residence of Marriage Partners in Langogne, 1866-1905

	Grooms		Brides	
	1866-1870	*1901-1905*	*1866-1870*	*1901-1905*
Born and residing in the canton* of Langogne	41%	35%	69%	66%
Born outside Langogne, residing in the canton of Langogne	38	18	27	26
Residing outside the canton of Langogne	22	46	4	9
Missing data	0	0	1	0
Total	100%	99%	100%	101%
N	111	141	110	141

*The canton includes the commune of Langogne and nearby hamlets.

SOURCE: ADL E4 80 and ATM, *Etat civil*, Langogne.

ucts of the area were more marketable by rail. The "black bricks of firwood" described by Robert Louis Stevenson became great assets once the pine could easily be delivered to the coal basin in the Gard to serve as mine timbers. Wooden items, such as the buckets and tubs sold in eighteenth-century fairs, and *sabots* manufactured into the twentieth century, were old Langognais products that developed a mass market thanks to the railroad. At the turn of the century, the commune of Langogne included over 300 acres of forest owned by peasants and wood merchants.

Butter, game, fish, eggs, fowl, mushrooms, and medicinal plants — all perishable items in plentiful supply — found outlets when they could be exported quickly to Paris or the Mediterranean littoral. In January of 1881, for example, one merchant sent 100 kilos of butter to Nîmes and 177 kilos to Paris. He also shipped game to the Gard. The same month, three other merchants between them shipped 47 kilos of butter to Montpellier, Alès, and Paris.[67]

Livestock had been sold at Langogne's fairs for a century, but with the coming of the railroad, livestock raising became the area's primary industry. Throughout France, one of the most important economic consequences of the late-nineteenth-century agricultural depression was the development of cattle raising. France's consumption of meat, butter, and milk was on the rise, while the market for rye fell. Given the decline of grain prices relative to the price of meat and dairy products, the reduction of grain production in favor of cattle raising was logical for communities like Langogne. Its grazing land and access to rail transport enhanced its competitive position. The use of land around Langogne shifted as the production of rye decreased and more of the commune was given over to meadow- and pastureland. By the end of the century, little other than oats and some fodder was cultivated. Teams of harvesters no longer came to Langogne at the end of the summer. Rather, butchered meat and livestock transformed Langogne into a meat entrepôt. By 1880, a number of slaughterhouses were established along the Langouyrou river, which runs through the town. The rail records of 1881 show that one merchant sent 369 kilos of meat to Toulon and Nice in the first month of the year, while another dispatched 87 kilos to Marseille and 173 kilos to Nîmes and Lunel. The station was expanded to house the animals awaiting departure. The production of meat continued to grow, and by 1913, 14,000 head of veal were slaughtered in Langogne. In all, 224 railcars of animals left the town that summer.[68]

Unlike Villefort, then, Langogne continued to grow after the railroad construction. It alone, among the towns along the rail line north of Alès, grew after the railroad installation, and by the beginning of the twentieth century, Langogne's population stood at nearly 4000. The mechanisms behind this growth are a complex of changing demographic patterns. The crude birth rate dropped significantly from over 34 per thousand in midcentury to around 24 by the turn of the century (Table 2.7). Nevertheless, the rate of 24 represents greater fertility than in Le Vigan or Villefort, and births usually outnumbered deaths after the 1860s. The balance of births and deaths shows that Langogne's population, unlike that of Villefort, did not age at the turn of the century. This is also suggested by an increase in the marriage rate from 6.0 in 1851 to 8.7 at the turn of the century. Net migration figures show sizable fluctuations in the attractiveness of Langogne (Table 2.7). After the railroad connection was made with the south, a wave of migrants came to Langogne and a sustained attraction appeared with the expansion of the cattle industry around the turn of the century.

As prosperous as Langogne was, its attraction was limited to a more local sphere at the turn of the century. At that time, of the men married in Langogne who resided there, the majority were born in the commune, a much larger proportion than in the 1860s (see Table 2.6.) Another quarter of them had been born within a twenty-kilometer radius. What distinguishes this pattern from the 1860s is that a much smaller proportion of grooms came from outside the twenty-kilometer radius. The railroad, improved roads, and opportunities elsewhere may have taken the regional population farther away, leaving Langogne's commercial success for its natives, especially males.

TABLE 2.7 Crude Birth Rate, Crude Death Rate, Population, and Net Migration, Langogne, 1849-1908

Period	Crude Birth Rate	Crude Death Rate	Period	Population at Time 1	Net Migration
1849-1853	34.7	33.8	1851-1856	2996	−155
1854-1858	31.4	31.5	1856-1861	2804	+232
1859-1863	32.1	34.1	1861-1866	3057	+ 8
1864-1868	34.3	32.2	1866-1872	3036	− 33
1869-1873	40.6	39.1	1872-1876	3040	+429
1874-1878	38.6	29.5	1876-1881	3611	+ 9
1879-1883	36.7	30.9	1881-1886	3696	− 13
1884-1888	32.0	28.7	1886-1891	3808	−288
1889-1893	27.3	29.4	1891-1896	3495	+133
1894-1898	24.7	23.5	1896-1901	3634	+ 95
1899-1903	26.7	24.4	1901-1906	3552	+301
1903-1908	23.8	21.7	1906	3917	

SOURCE: ADL E4 80 and ATM, *Etat civil*, Langogne; ADL *Receuil des Actes Administratifs*, 1852-1902.

The women of Langogne clearly were leaving this little town. Although Langogne continued to attract women from the region through the end of the nineteenth century, Langognaises frequently left home before marriage, and one bride in ten declared her residence as elsewhere when she returned home to marry at the turn of the century (see Table 2.6.) The women in Langogne also listed their occupation at marriage more than the brides in Le Vigan and Villefort. They worked as cooks in Langogne, Montpellier, and Marseille. One was employed as a presser in Bèziers.

Nearly half the brides in Langogne married men living away from their home town. This was a change from the 1860s, when only about one bride in five married a man living outside the canton. One-third of the brides married men living over twenty kilometers away, and most of them went to the south. Of the 65 bridegrooms who worked and lived outside Langogne, many (20 percent) resided in the coal basin of the Gard, and a larger contingent (38 percent) lived on the Mediterranean plain, particularly between Nîmes and Marseille. The single most important residence was Nîmes, to which nine brides moved. Finally, five bridegrooms lived outside the area altogether, in Paris and a suburb, in Grenoble, and at a rural post in the Loire.

The majority of destinations were regional and urban — such as Nîmes, Grand'Combe, Genolhac, Alès, Marseille, and Arles. Yet over 40 percent of the contacts represented by these marriages were rural; that is, they were contacts with small communes of the Massif Central and the wine-producing plain of Languedoc. Thus, while urban areas became important for Langogne, its location high in the Massif Central yielded fewer urban contacts than Le Vigan or Villefort.

Nevertheless, urban occupations had their place. Nearly one-third of the bridegrooms worked as *cheminots* (railroad workers), and most of them did so in cities like Nîmes, Paris, and Marseille and in towns like Alès, Arles, Mende, and Le Puy. Other workers, such as bakers, barrelmakers, masons, and miners, were employed in towns. White collar workers, however, were virtually absent. Perhaps the women from Langogne married men with less education than did women from Le Vigan and Villefort. The eleven bridegrooms born in Langogne had moved to the coast (four to Nîmes), to the coal basin (two), and to Paris (one). The majority worked for the railroad.

The pattern of movement to and from Langogne changed markedly during the second half of the nineteenth century. Although the town continued to attract men and women, thus serving as a relay station for the general movement of population from the uplands, it did so from a smaller area by the turn of the century. The number of young people did not decline drastically as it had in Villefort. When people left Langogne, they moved farther away than before. The zone of contact for this town, like Le Vigan and Villefort, expanded remarkably. In the case of Langogne, the town turned south to the Gard, and specifically to Nîmes.

When Robert Louis Stevenson traveled through the region by donkey in 1878, he was greeted at the gates of Langogne by a young girl. His response was to declare her broad accent unintelligible. In a similar vein, Eugen Weber has described towns in the Massif Central under the Third Republic in terms which undeniably apply to Langogne — people spoke the local *patois* rather than French, the streets were muddy, and cattle entrails fouled the air and polluted the waters of the River Langouyrou.[69] Yet a closer look shows that even a town with these characteristics was expanding in demographic, economic, and social terms. The history and evolution of opportunity in even this most provincial town reflect the complex factors that gave rise to cityward migration. The town's secondary school, which by the turn of the century had 100-150 pupils, over half of whom were boarders, is only one manifestation of this little town's role of central place. Although there were fewer opportunities for artisans — tanners, weavers, carpenters, woolens workers — others such as clerks, butchers, and tenant farmers, as well as the merchants and clerks working for them, could make a life in Langogne.

These were opportunities for men. In Langogne, clerks and slaughterhouse workers were male at the turn of the century. A decline in domestic service and the absence of landowners among the bridegrooms at the turn of the century suggests that the bourgeoisie of Langogne was living elsewhere. With the decline of the textile industry, women may have had difficulty earning their own way or contributing to their family's needs in Langogne. Hints come from other quarters as well that the women, particularly, were leaving. The departmental journal at the time found women's temporary emigration before marriage normal, but was alarmed by the rate of permanent departures.[70] It was painfully obvious to people in the Lozère at this time that its women were eager to migrate. The marriage records of the turn of the turn of the century from both Villefort and Langogne suggest that women readily left before marriage to work, and the proportion who came home to marry a city-dweller indicates that many stayed in the city.

Le Vigan, Villefort, and Langogne each experienced unique histories between 1850 and 1900. Le Vigan declined but succeeded in maintaining a mixed economy. Its silk industry and its agriculture each underwent crises that visibly shook the population. Local artisanal production declined. Government employment, however, remained relatively steady. At the end of the century, Le Vigan continued to attract immigrants from its hinterland, but it lost more people to the Mediterranean littoral and to large cities elsewhere in France.

The rural commune of Villefort suffered the most severe economic and demographic decline. Before midcentury, local industries (wool and tanning) and trade were in trouble. They faded to nothing with the installation of the railroad, which favored other market centers and imported better manufactured products. With the depression of agricultural prices at the century's end, rural people also began to leave Villefort. By 1906, they were emigrating in considerable numbers; most went south to the Gard and the cities of the Midi.

Langogne's traditional industries also declined, but it developed a new and prosperous economy. The railroad enabled Langogne to export timber, along with meat and other perishables, throughout France. Thus commerce and animal husbandry replaced agriculture. Although some Langognais left home for other areas, more people remained or were attracted to the prosperous little town.

Le Vigan and Langogne began the period as regional centers, Villefort as the center for a smaller arena. The allure of the Lozerian towns diminished by the turn of the century. By then, all three towns were integrated into a larger arena. Migration patterns changed in terms of both distance and permanence.[71] As local and regional seasonal and temporary movement faded, cheminots, government employees, miners, urban workers, and their brides replaced the temporary urban domestic servant, harvest worker, and seasonal miner. As migration patterns shifted, so did destinations: The three migration systems broadened and turned toward the Mediterranean. The Viganais concentrated in the city of Montpellier and the plain between Montpellier and Nîmes. The Lozerians, on the other hand, focused on the coal basin and the Mediterranean plain toward Provence between Nîmes and Marseille. More people from all three towns left the region than in the past. The importance of urban destinations — particularly for the Viganais and Villefortais — highlights the shift in migration patterns to permanent urban residence. Viganais, Villefortais, and Langognais were among the Europeans who at the turn of the century went from a rural village or bourg to regional urban centers like Alès, to large cities like Montpellier, Nîmes, or Marseille, and even to Paris.

A most striking change in employment patterns accompanied the evolution of migration. In the 1850s and 1860s, the bridegrooms in the three hometowns who had lived elsewhere had been employed primarily as artisans or laborers, such as locksmiths, bakers, tanners, carters, miners, and traders. Yet by the turn of the century, these bridegrooms were more likely to work for the railroad, the government, or the educational system. (The proportion of bridegrooms living outside hometowns who were employed by railroad or government was 35 percent for Le Vigan, 56 percent for Villefort, and 35 percent for Langogne.) This was relatively secure, year-round employment that sometimes promised a retirement income. These aspects of their work were perceived as very advantageous by government clerks, teachers, and railroad workers and their families. Mesdames Audibert and Combes, mothers of a railroad employee and a teacher, respectively, squared off comparing the advantages of their sons' chosen careers:

> "In the Company, you know, one has advantages."
>
> "Yes?"
>
> "You travel for nothing, second class, and then you get your clothes . . . and the pension."
>
> "Oh, but you get a pension in the schools too, and your lodging."
>
> "Yes, but what about your traveling expenses?"
>
> "Good heavens, one doesn't travel as much as all that in this life. You have never taken the railroad, have you? Well."

> "Oh, us! That's exactly it. If we could take it for nothing . . . and the clothes."
>
> "But the schoolhouses often have gardens. . . . You get your vegetables."[72]

The significance of this kind of employment for migration patterns is twofold. First, the employer often determined the destination, whether it was a tax office in the Ardèche, the railyards of Lyon or a rural schoolhouse in the Ile de France. Thus, career migration could break the connection between family or friendship and destination characteristic in chain migration. For example, Audibert's son worked in a large rail suburb of Paris only because "the Company" sent him there. Friendship and preference sometimes continued to play a role, however. After normal school training, Combes's son received the position he desired near his home town with the help of his former schoolmaster's influence. In local government jobs, also, one could be sure of employment within a given area. In general, however, employment with the government or the railroads moved people at the employer's discretion. This had long been true. "I see no man more constantly in motion," wrote Jules Michelet, of the civil servant in midcentury. "Without speaking of cutbacks and dismissals, which sometimes come and are always feared, his life is a series of changes, journeys, and sudden transfers from one end of France to the other for some electoral mystery or other."[73] What was new was the large scale of career migration.

Career migration usually meant permanent departure. Students (who had special train fares) and cheminots (who traveled free) returned home cheaply. Other migrants returned home for vacation also, for these visits were important to them, their families, and to other villagers.[74] Before retirement, however, one rarely moved back home, simply because most employment was located elsewhere. Career migration, then, reinforced the trend of permanent emigration from home.

The marriage records from Le Vigan, Villefort, and Langogne provide an extraordinary picture of the broadening of geographic horizons for women in the last half of the nineteenth century. Marriage records attest to women's legendary eagerness to leave the mountains and rural life succinctly expressed in the proverb from Western Languedoc: Goats ascend, girls descend.[75] The women of the *belle époque* simply went further than their mothers. They were less likely to marry a local man or a peasant and much more likely than their mother to set up their household in the city. They may also have been more likely than their mothers to live away from home before marriage, since employment prospects for young women at home shrank in the last half of the nineteenth century.

MIGRATION STREAMS

People from all three little towns had contacts with Nîmes. In the case of Le Vigan, connections were the most long-lived, predating the revolution. They were broadly based on ongoing administrative connections, as well as on contacts established by the capital and labor of Viganais. The connection between Villefort and Nîmes, on the other hand, was born primarily of the work experience of the Villefortais on the Mediterranean littoral and on traders' contacts with Nîmes' markets. It is likely that the contacts between Langogne and Nîmes have the same base, but these find the least expression in home town marriage records.

These connections and the towns' economic histories allow a fair prediction of the social background of emigrants to Nîmes. Children of artisans, of the bourgeoisie, and of silk workers in Le Vigan would be likely to emigrate as their economic base deteriorated. Workers' offspring simply found it increasingly difficult to find work at home. Children of the bourgeoisie, on the other hand, may have been more inclined to leave because local horizons were too restrictive for their aspirations to become high-level officials, lawyers, doctors, or urban rentiers. For some, it was economic need, and for others, a desire for wider possibilities. There was indeed a flight of capital as well as people from the Cévennes to the cities of the littoral.[76]

Emigrants from Le Vigan were relatively urbane, because their home town had long been in contact with Mediterranean cities and it had an active associational life. Because it was a subprefecture, the town's population included such professionals as lawyers and judges who had been educated in cities of the littoral, if not in Paris. For these reasons, emigrants could be expected to include a large proportion of people with white collar ambitions.

Emigrants from Villefort were less educated and less urbane than those from Le Vigan, for it was a rural village at the turn of the century. Because it had few government functions and little trade, Villefort housed few government personnel and few commercial or white collar workers. Moreover, Villefort's link with the cities of the Mediterranean coast was less strong than with the coal basin, where education and training was less salient.

Emigrants were likely to come from Villefort's large agricultural households, as well as its artisan, trade, or railroad workers' families.

Men who left Villefort were not likely to be already trained for white collar work, because the commune's schools were weak and male literacy relatively low. Because Villefort was a rural commune, single female emigrants tended to follow the rural tradition of working as servants in the city.

Migrants from Langogne would often come from its declining artisan sector. Although it is impossible to tell with the information available, emigrants could have been members of families that lost small-scale rural livelihoods due to competition from larger-scale cattle raising and livestock commerce. These were the groups least able to prosper in a small town whose commerce and animal husbandry offered employment on the land, in slaughterhouses, and in commercial clerical jobs. In short, the emigrants from Langogne to the Mediterranean littoral were among its least skilled and least educated people. On the other hand, the commerce of Langogne itself could employ men with petty bourgeois ambitions.

An examination of the social origins of the migrants who moved to Nîmes from each town reveals who left for the city and demonstrates what kinds of selective mechanisms were at work creating migration streams. It can suggest both why people left home and why they fared as they did in the city. Information about migrants' social origins comes from the father's occupation at the time of their birth, as listed on the birth record (see Appendix I).

Most of the parents of emigrants from Le Vigan to Nîmes worked in what the census called industries, including artisanal production, foodmaking, hostelry, and such services as barbering. Their occupations are analyzed in Table 2.8. The silk industry employed the largest single group (13 percent) as carders and stockingmakers. Other parents in the industry category worked as carpenters, shoemakers, innkeepers, and tailors. Agricultural laborers (15 percent) and members of the liberal professions (17 percent) — lawyers, teachers, government employees — were also important.

This occupational distribution confirms the predictions offered above. The declining sectors of the economy of Le Vigan were well represented in the migration streams, as the children of these groups pursued their fortunes in Nîmes. Children of the liberal professions and some of the bourgeoisie went to seek a secondary education and broader social and economic horizons than those in the home town. Commercial and bureaucratic structures had created connections between the liberal professions and the commercial sectors of Le Vigan and Nîmes.

The selection process in the Le Vigan-Nîmes migration is illustrated by comparing the migrants' parents with the resident marrying (and presumably childbearing) population of Le Vigan at the time when the largest cohort of migrants was born, 1851-55. Migrants appear disproportionately in the liberal professions and bourgeoisie categories (Table 2.8). Nîmes, then, was an especially important destination for those in a position to seek broader horizons for career, social, and educational mobility.

The parents of Villefort's migrants, on the other hand, were primarily rural agriculturalists (31 percent) and railroad and transport workers (18 percent). The second largest "industrial" group was the food and lodging trade — café owners, innkeepers, and shopkeepers (10 percent). The members of the liberal professions — government employees necessary to a village the size of Villefort — a policeman, a postal worker, and a notary — contributed 10 percent (see Table 2.8).

In Villefort as in Le Vigan, decline fostered emigration. Agriculture and transport, the two largest employers in Villefort in the 1860s, could not provide for future generations. The end of railroad construction decimated the town's service sector; cafés and inns that catered to railroad employees had gone under a decade later. The most important groups of parents of migrants, then, were those whose legacy was most affected by changes in the late-century economy.

Migrants from Villefort were disproportionately children of agricultural, rural parents, for migration to Nîmes was especially attractive to peasants. The fact that children of the hostelry sector, and of industry and government employees were also disproportionately represented is characteristic of the rural exodus, the exit of trade and commerce from Villefort.

The majority of Langogne migrants were the children of artisans and workers in the town (see Table 2.8). Unskilled laborers, workers in carpentry, building, shoes and leather, and hostelry made up an important proportion of the parents (44 percent). Relatively few were children of white collar or agricultural parents.

Again, economic history and previously established networks had an effect on the composition of Nîmes-directed migration. Although Langogne had its contingent of government employees, as well as medical, legal, and teaching professionals, these people did not have a particular link with Nîmes, but rather with Mende, the capital of the Lozère. The commercial community also had links with many places besides Nîmes, such as Paris and Marseille. Moreover, commerce in Langogne was booming at the turn of the century, so that the children

TABLE 2.8 Fathers of Migrants Compared with Resident Populations

	Fathers of Migrants			*Resident Grooms, 1866-1870*		
Occupation	*Le Vigan*	*Villefort*	*Langogne*	*Le Vigan*	*Villefort*	*Langogne*
Agriculture	15	31	12	14	14	15
Industry						
Silk	13	—	—	11	—	—
Railroad and transport	—	18	—	—	47	—
Railroad and building	—	—	15	—	—	37
Other	42	36	64	52	32	38
Building and carpentry	(8)	(6)	—	(na)	(na)	(na)
Food and lodging	(7)	(10)	(15)			
Clothing and toilette	(6)	(4)	(10)			
Shoe and leather	(10)	(6)	(10)			
Unskilled labor	—	(4)	(19)			
Textiles	—	—	(5)			
Other	(11)	(6)	(5)			
Commerce	5	4	2	6	1	1
Liberal Professions	17	10	2	8	4	4
Domestic Service	2	0	2	3	0	4
Bourgeoisie	5	0	0	9	1	1
Illegitimate	1	2	3	0	0	0
Total	100%	101	100	103	99	100
N	164	51	59	102	73	79

SOURCE: ADG E5 *Etat civil*, Le Vigan; ADL 4E 198 *Etat civil*, Villefort; ADL 4E 80 Etat civil, Langogne.

of commercial people may not have been tempted to leave. The prosperity of livestock husbandry should also have kept agricultural workers in Langogne.

In fact, a comparison of the parents of migrants from Langogne with the resident marrying population of the town reveals that commerce, the liberal professions, and agriculture were underrepresented and that industry was very important in the parent group (see Table 2.8). The largest group comprised building and railroad workers. The importance of unskilled laborers, carpenters and masons, woodenshoemakers, and tanners (and among the children, bastards) suggests that many migrants to Nîmes were among the poorest people in Langogne.

Emigrants from Le Vigan, Villefort, and Langogne in Nîmes, then, represented certain parts of their hometown society and were selected from particular groups in each community. By the same token, a comparison of the three migrant streams shows that a different selection process was at work in each town (see Table 2.9). Although most fathers were agricultural or industrial workers and artisans in all three groups, only the Viganais included many children from professional, bourgeois, and other white collar families. Villefort's migrants were more rural than the others, and only they included a large proportion of rail and transport workers' children. Most migrants from Langogne were from the town's poorer laboring and artisan families. Poverty selected migrants from all three towns, but social and educational expectations seem to have played a significant role as well, particularly for the Viganais. The decision to emigrate was doubtless based on myriad factors. "Departures," observes Poussou,

> are a very complex phenomenon by which poverty, necessity, the desire to better one's condition, the tradition of movement, and the availability of work doubtless play about an equal role in a mélange difficult to unravel.[77]

Without migrants' diaries and letters, it is impossible to know the rationale behind the departures of men and women from Le Vigan, Villefort, and Langogne, although the outlines of their economic motives are clear. Individual biographies help to humanize this collective picture.

TABLE 2.9 Economic Sector of Fathers of Migrants

Occupation of Father at Time of Birth[a]	*Le Vigan*	*Villefort*	*Langogne*
Agriculture	15%	31%	12%
Industry			
(a) production	31	14	27
textiles	(13)[b]	(2)	(5)
building and carpentry	(8)	(6)	(12)
shoe and leather	(10)	(6)	(10)
(b) transportation (including railroad)	2	18	3
(c) services	13	14	25
food and lodging	(7)	(10)	(15)
clothing and toilette	(6)	(4)	(10)
(d) unskilled labor	1	4	19
(e) other	8	4	5
Domestic service	2	0	2
Educated and elites	27	14	4
(a) wholesale commerce	(5)	(4)	(2)
(b) liberal professions	(17)	(10)	(2)
(c) bourgeoisie	(5)	(0)	(0)
Illegitimate	1	2	3
Total	100%	101%	100%
N	164	51	59

a. Fathers not living in given town excluded (i.e., this excludes migrants who were born at their grandparents' home when their parents lived elsewhere). Classification scheme is from the 1861 census.
b. Includes silk stocking makers.

SOURCE: ADG E5 *Etat civil*, Le Vigan; ADL 4E 198 *Etat civil*, Villefort; ADL 4E 180 *Etat civil*, Langogne.

BIOGRAPHIES

Life stories of individual migrants can be reconstructed from the meager traces left by ordinary men and women in birth records, conscript records, census lists, and acts of marriage. These biographies frequently parallel the pattern of the migration streams, serving as examples. Perhaps more important, each communicates a vivid and unique experience of home town, migration, and urban life. Consequently, I will refer to a few members of each group throughout the following chapters whose biographies I have been able to compile.

In the opening pages of Chapter 1, I introduced Henri Donzel from Le Vigan, the Protestant joiner's son who established a family tradition of successful government employment in Nîmes. Now meet his compatriot, Raymond Pouzergue. Raymond was born in a hamlet of Le Vigan in the early 1840s. He worked as a tanner in and around Le Vigan and, in his early twenties, married a woman from a nearby mining community. His first son, Raymond Jules, was born in 1865, and another son, Charles, followed seven years later. When Raymond was in his late thirties or early forties, he, his wife, and young son moved to Nîmes, where a daughter was born. The elder son, Raymond Jules, remained in Le Vigan, working as a shoemaker, until after his marriage and the birth of his first child. He then joined his father and brother in Nîmes in the early 1890s. Raymond and his sons were among the relatively few blue collar members of Nîmes' Protestant consistory — Raymond and Charles being construction day laborers, Raymond Jules a shoemaker. Raymond Jules lived near his father and had four children, three born in Nîmes. When he died at the age of 39 in 1904, his wife and four children moved to a crowded section of the Protestant working-class neighborhood where the wages of the eldest son — 17 at his father's death — supported the family. Charles married a Nimoise in his twenties, and by the age of 34 had two young children at home. Raymond's Nîmes-born daughter became a seamstress when still in her teens. In 1906, Raymond's and Charles's families shared a house on the west edge of town.[78]

Camille Giraud was born in 1866 into a Viganais family that possessed both land and one of the town's spinning mills. Because Le Vigan had no secondary school when he was an adolescent, Camille attended *lycée* in Nîmes, served briefly in the army, and entered law school in Montpellier at about the age of twenty. After law school, in the 1890s, Giraud established his law practice in Nîmes and became engaged to marry. The record of his nuptials at the age of 32 predicts power and comfort, if not wealth: Giraud and his young bride, age 19, agreed beforehand to a marriage contract — a settlement of property and finance which few couples found necessary. Giraud's wife was from a successful family that had moved from Alès to Nîmes, where her father acted as a court attorney and officer of public instruction. Her mother came from one of the Gard's prominent political families. Witnesses to the wedding included Giraud's cousin, the vice-president of the administrative council of the Aveyron, a legal advisor in Nîmes' court of appeals, the city's adjunct mayor, and the ex-president of the bar. In the following six years, the couple had three children. Signs of success and civic leadership adorned the household: Giraud became a member of the Protestant consistory and the municipal council of Nîmes, his family lived in a comfortable neighborhood, Madame Giraud had a cook and a nurse to help with the children, and they were able to donate twenty francs — five days' wages for a male worker — to the annual parish collection for the poor in 1904. Giraud made a bid to represent Le Vigan in the national Chamber of Deputies in 1906, running under the short-lived Noncollectivist Socialist ticket. Despite defeat in this race, Giraud clearly was entering the prime of his life as a member of the municipal and regional elite.

Edouard Roche has been introduced briefly as a café operator from Villefort. His father, a maker of wooden shoes, subsequently moved the family to Alès, in the coal basin, and Edouard worked as a waiter. When he was in his twenties, Edouard's father died and his mother became a café operator — probably taking over the family business. Edouard moved to Nîmes, where he met Henriette Chevret, whom he married in Langogne at the age of 27. By 1906, he was a cafetier and the father of two.

Roche's compatriot, Emile Brun, was also a wooden-shoemaker's son born in Villefort in the early 1870s. As a young man he worked for a baker in the village. After being excused from active army service on the grounds that he was the eldest of seven children, Brun moved to Nîmes in 1896, where he worked for the railroad. Five years later, he married the daughter of a fellow employee. Within a few years his wife, Victorine, died, and Brun went to live with his uncle's family. The uncle, also a cheminot, resided between the railroad repair depot east of Nîmes and the freight station. Brun continued to work for the railroad and to visit home. There he met and married Madeleine Vigoroux, daughter of a railroad retiree. At the time of the wedding, in 1908, Brun's widowed father was no longer making wooden shoes but, at the age of 71, made his living from agriculture alone.

Victor Bouzanquet was born to a village barber in Villefort in the year 1856; he was one of the first children in his parents' long life together. His career as a railroad employee began in his teens with a job as clerk in the Villefort station. Victor married a woman from nearby Vans, in the Ardèche, and eventually moved to Nîmes, where he was promoted to the position of bureau chief. Two brothers followed: Charles, born eighteen years after Arthur, arrived in Nîmes after army service and a stint with the PLM in Montpellier. Charles soon married the daughter of another cheminot from a mountain town near Villefort. The couple rented an apartment in the crowded old city of Nîmes and had a son. Antoine, a single younger brother, moved in with Charles and his young family. In 1906, the three brothers were railroad employees of varying rank in Nîmes, two of whom were married and had children. Their parents remained in Villefort, where

Monsieur Bouzanquet, once a barber, had retired on his income from his position as village postman.

Villefortais peasants' daughter Clémence Janvier married a railroad laborer working in Nîmes in 1902. Although it is likely that she too had worked in Nîmes, no record exists of her premarital employment or residence. The couple moved to the heart of the railroad workers' neighborhood and, by the end of four years of marriage, had produced two sons. Clémence had two younger sisters who followed her to Nîmes and found good positions in a bourgeois neighborhood — good because they were cooks, and thus were better paid and did less onerous work than the solitary maid-of-all-work. The three sisters lived within blocks of each other in 1906. Louisa, six years younger than Clémence, worked in the prosperous household of Camille Giraud from Le Vigan. In the spring of 1907, when she was 25, Louisa returned home to marry a mason in Villefort.

The Chevret sisters, a harnessmaker's daughters from Langogne, moved to Nîmes when single, then married and bore children (see Chapter 1). Later they were joined by their mother and young niece. Their brother, who was a notary's clerk, remained in Langogne. Likewise, the baker's daughter, Anna Sabatier, left Langogne to work in Nîmes in her late teens. There she met a tramways worker, a peasant's son from a village in the Ardèche. The two were wed in 1900 in the presence of the groom's brother and friends from Langogne who lived in Nîmes, and Anna's parents, who had come to town for the wedding. In the following years, Anna raised her two sons while running a grocery behind the central markets of Nîmes. Her father and sisters moved to the city. The father, now retired and widowed, lived with the young couple, and Anna's two sisters worked as domestic servants. Her elder brother, a tax clerk in Langogne, probably remained in the Lozère.

Auguste Mathieu was born to a day laborer in Langogne in the late 1860s. He left home in his teens to become an agricultural worker outside Nîmes; his younger brother, Baptiste, who was also an agricultural laborer, despite his poor health, joined Auguste. By the time the brothers were twenty, their father had died. In November of 1897, Auguste Mathieu and Berthe Fabre — daughter of another day laborer from Langogne and resident of Nîmes — went home to marry; he was 30 and she was 19. They moved to the east side of Nîmes, and Auguste worked as a day laborer. The couple had a daughter. Berthe's elder sister, Marie, lived near the Mathieus. Married to a railroad worker and mother of one child at age 35, Marie may have preceded Berthe to Nîmes. Auguste's brother — still an agricultural laborer in 1906 — lived across town from the two households, single and alone. Berthe's parents and Auguste's widowed mother remained in Langogne.

Urbanization in Eastern Languedoc was considerably more complex than a mass outpouring of rurals for the city. Neither the timing of migration shifts, the new destination, or the identity of migrants reflects an unreasoned movement. On the contrary, each reveals a sensible response to changing local conditions and an effective — if biased — knowledge of the world, particularly the cities of the Mediterranean plain and the coal basin of the Gard. The Viganais, Villefortais, and Langognais seized the kinds of urban opportunities then expanding for rural and small town Frenchmen: railroad, government, and service employment. Those who made the decision to move reflect a self-selection shaped by the options available at home.

This chapter's investigation of the regional context of urbanization has uncovered a set of structures that made the region interdependent. This interdependence changed considerably with the crises in agriculture, silk and wine production, the deindustrialization of the countryside, and the metamorphosis of communications and transport that came with roads and the railroad. The resulting transformations varied systematically, but in each case they were accompanied by an increased scope of human movement, one that gravitated toward the city. In the city lay the other pieces to the puzzle of urbanization, for there waited the opportunities attracting the men and women from Le Vigan, Villefort, and Langogne, opportunities that will complete the picture of cityward migration.

NOTES

1. Fernand Braudel, *La Méditerranée et le monde méditerranéen à l'époque de Philippe II* (Paris: Armand Colin, 1949), 272-274; Emmanuel Le Roy Ladurie, *Les paysans de Languedoc* (Paris: S.E.V.P.N., 1966), 98-102.

2. Ibid., 105; Olwen Hufton, *The Poor in Eighteenth-Century France* (Oxford: Clarendon Press, 1974), 72.

3. The reports on temporary migration to and from the arrondissement of Le Vigan in the Gard in 1811 mentioned that chimney sweeps from the Alps expected no profit from their winter's work: "Having come simply to earn their living, they are happy to come home having done so and carrying a five franc coin," Archives Départementales du Gard (hereafter ADG), series 12M, 24; Abel Chatelain, *Les migrants temporaires en France de 1880 à 1914* (Lille: Publications de l'Université de Lille III, 1976), 83-84, 549, 778; Hufton, *The Poor,* 73; Robert Thinthoin, "Structure

sociale et démographique du Gévaudan au XVIIIe et XIXe siècles," *Revue du Gévaudan* 4 (1958): 121-122.

4. Ibid., 121.

5. Armand Boyer, "Les migrations saisonnières dans la Cévenne vivaroise," *Revue de géographie alpine* 22 (1934), 579-580; Abel Chatelain, *Les migrants temporaries*, 395-398; Louis-Jean Thomas, "L'émigration temporaire dans le Bas-Languedoc et le Roussillon au commencement du XIXe siècle, "*Bulletin de la Société Languedocienne de Géographie*, ser. 1, 33 (1910), 302, 308; Thinthoin, "Structure sociale," 121.

6. Marc Bernard, *Salut, camarades* (Paris: Gallimard, 1955), 214.

7. Thinthoin "Structure sociale," 128; see also 122, 126; Armand Audiganne, *Les populations ouvrières et les industries de la France*, Vol. 2 (New York: Burt Franklin, 1970), 153-154. Jules Barbot, *Le paysan lozérien* (Mende: Privat, 1899), 36; Cissie Fairchilds, *Poverty and Charity in Aix-en-Provence, 1640-1789* (Baltimore, MD: Johns Hopkins University Press, 1976), 103; Maurice Garden, "L'attraction de Lyon à la fin de l'ancien régime," *Annales de démographie historique* (1970), 205-222; Le Roy Ladurie, *Les paysans*, 93-98; Jean-Pierre Poussou, "Note sur la mobilité urbaine," *La population française au XVIIIe et XIXe siècles* (Paris: Société de Démographie Historique, 1973), 535-546; Un Vieux Nimois, "La rue de Nîmes en 1900," *La revue économique de la Chambre de Commerce de Nîmes-Uzès-Le Vigan* 6, no. 50 (1955), 28; Jean-César Vincens and Baumès, *Topographie de la ville de Nîmes et de sa banlieu* (Nîmes, 1802), 12.

8. The population of the department of the Lozère peaked in 1851 at 144,705. G. Gallon, "Le mouvement de la population dans le département de la Lozère au cours de la période 1821-1920," *Bulletin de la Société des Lettres de la Lozère, Chroniques et Mélanges* (1935), 4. The rural population of the Cévennes peaked at about the same time; René Lamorisse, who separates the rural from the coal basin and small town population, used samples from decadal censuses beginning in 1836, finding the highest figure for the rural censuses in 1856 and that for the small town population in 1846; see *La population de la Cévenne languedocienne* (Montpellier: Imprimerie Paysan du Midi, 1975), 75. The timing of these population changes in upland Languedoc coincides with national shifts in population and migration patterns; see Chatelain, *Les migrants temporaires*, 1105-1106.

9. Chatelain, *Les migrants temporaires*, 58-59, 126-129, 400, 756; Paul Marrès, "L'évolution de la viticulture dans le Bas-Languedoc," *Bulletin de la Société Languedocienne de Géographie*, ser. 2, 6 (1935), 43; Thomas, "L'émigration temporaire," 308.

10. Jean Pitié, *Exode rural et migrations intérieures en France* (Poitiers: Norois, 1971), 88-92, 109-123, 143, 159. See also Paul Hohenberg, "Migrations et fluctuations démographiques dans la France rurale, 1836-1901," *Annales: E.S.C.* 29 (1974), 461-97.

11. Step migration (from rural area to small town, from small town to city) is recorded in small-town and regional studies. See, for example, Michel Riou, "L'immigration dans les villes du Vivarais," *Actes du LIVe Congres de la Fédération Historique du Languedoc Méditerranéen et du Roussillon* (1972), 291-308; Alain Rouquette, "Une colonie gévaudaise dans les basses-Cévennes: les lozériens à Anduze sous la IIIe et la IVe Républiques," *Cévennes et Gévaudan* (1974), 415-427; Lamorisse, *La population de la Cévenne*, 179. Chatelain summarizes findings of step migration in *Les migrants temporaires*, 663-666.

Pitié, in his study of Poitu-Charentes (*Exode rural*, 56-57), makes a convincing argument that step migration is not always the most important pattern of movement, because Paris proved more attractive than regional centers. He demonstrates the strong attraction of Paris in the south with case studies of Meyrueis (Lozère) and Castries (Hérault). Ibid., 66-69. Many Lozerians did move to Paris, and to the two great cities of Lyons and Marseille, but it is impossible to discern a migration stream between any one town and the large cities without scrutinizing the census lists of the cities. Other studies suggest that migration streams developed from north of the Lozère and the Aveyron to Paris and from south of these departments to the Mediterranean littoral; see Robert Beteille, *Les aveyronnais* (Poitiers: Imprimerie l'Union, 1974) and Hohenberg "Migrations et fluctuations démographiques." The point here is that urbanization also occurred within eastern Languedoc as people from upland areas moved to the lowlands. The greatest number of people in the Gard from other departments were from the Lozère (17,863 in 1911) and the Ardèche (16,381 in 1911) — far more than from the coastal neighbor, the department of the Hérault (8,393 in 1911); Claude Cheballier, "La population du Gard," *Bulletin de la Société Languedocienne de Géographie*, ser. 2, 5 (1934): 184.

12. Pierre Gorlier, *Le Vigan à travers les siècles: histoire d'une cité languedocienne* (Montpellier: Editions de la Licorne, 1955), 211.

13. Léon Dutil, *L'état économique du Languedoc à la fin de l'ancien régime* (Paris: Hachette, 1911), 453; G. Lautier, "La sériciculture et les industries de la soie dans le pays cévenol," *Bulletin de la Société Languedocienne de Géographie*, ser. 2, 4 (1930), 79-86, 217-225.

14. Ibid., Lamorisse, *La population de la Cévenne*, 222.

15. Raymond Dugrand, *Villes et campagnes en Bas-Languedoc* (Paris: Presses Universitaires Françaises, 1963), 353; Lamorisse, *La population de la Cévenne*, 216-218, 220.

16. Paul Marrès, *Les grands causses*, Vol. 2 (Tours: Arrault, 1935), 93, 95, 101; Michael Roussy, *Evolution démographique et économique des populations du Gard* (Thèse de Droit, Université de Montpellier, 1949), 51.

17. ADG, series 14M, 337, 340, 370, Foires et Marchés.

18. Gorlier, *Le Vigan*, 301, 318.

19. ADG, series E5, Marriage Records, Le Vigan, 1851-1855; François Furet and Jacques Ouzouf, *Lire et écrire*, Vol. 1 (Paris: Editions du Minuit, 1977), 30, 57, 62; Lamorisse, *La population de la Cévenne*, 98. Literacy figures appear in tabular form in Appendix III, Table III.1.

20. Daniel Fabre and Jacques La Croix, *La vie quotidienne des paysans du Languedoc au XIXe siècle* (Paris: Hachette, 1973), 386; Furet and Ouzouf, *Lire et écrire*, 88-93; Gorlier, *Le Vigan*, 304-305, 318.

21. Quoted by Marrès, *Les grands causses*, 400.

22. ADG, series 12M, 24. Report on seasonal migration in the arrondissement of Le Vigan lists "tinkers, pewterers, tinmen, knife grinders, cobblers," among others.

23. Ibid.; Marrès, *Les grands causses*, 400.

24. Lamorisse, *La population de la Cévenne*, 103.

25. Ibid., 179.

26. *The Road* (New York: Scribner's, 1929), 104-105.

27. Ibid., 8-9.

28. Maurice Agulhon, Gabriel Désert, and Robert Specklin, *Histoire de la France rural*, Vol. 3, *Apogée et crise de la civilisation paysanne, 1789-1914* (Paris: Seuil, 1976), 477.

29. In the absence of information about the age structure and sex ratio in Le Vigan, Villefort, or Langogne, it was impossible to calculate more specific demographic rates, such as marital fertility, age-specific fertility, or even general fertility.

30. Net migration was calculated using the following formula:

$$M = PT_2 - PT_1 + B - D$$

M = net migration
P = population
T_1 = time 1
T_2 = time 2
B = births in interval
D = deaths in interval

Net migration figures yield a very crude measure of migration because they are based on civil status records and censuses, both of which are subject to error. Among the censuses, those of 1872-1896 are least reliable, according to Etienne Van de Walle, *The Female Population of France in the Nineteenth Century* (Princeton: Princeton University Press, 1974), 86, 88-89. Thus, intercensal birth-death balances are an unreliable indicator of migration because they do not account for differential mis-enumeration in the censuses. This is particularly true for the Lozère, where censuses are unreliable (Ibid., 218). Used over a period, however, the balances do reveal migration trends. According to van de Walle: "If, however, the balance equation is applied over a fairly long period, it will yield interesting results because then the errors in either census are likely to be small compared to the cumulated effect of migration on the intercensal increase" (Ibid., 198-199).

31. Lamorisse, *La population de la Cévenne,* 102; Syndicat de la Bonneterie, "Origine de la bonneterie Gardoise," *La revue économique de la Chambre de Commerce de Nîmes-Uzès-Le Vigan,* 3-4, nos. 23-32 (1952), 2. *Pébrine* has not been translated into English. It refers to the small black dots that appear on the silkworm larvae and originates from the Provençal word *pebrino,* meaning pepper. *Petit Larousse,* 1960 ed., s.v. "pébrine."

32. Gorlier, *Le Vigan,* 321; Lamorisse, *La population de la Cévenne,* 221-225, 246-247.

33. Ibid., 216-218, 220.

34. Gorlier, *Le Vigan,* 316. The decline in small trades such as cabinetry is reflected in a comparison of the occupations of grooms in the town in 1851-1855 with those of 1901-1905, ADG, series 5E; Greffe du Tribunal d'Instance à Nîmes (hereafter ATN), Marriages, Le Vigan, 1901-1905.

35. Gorlier, *Le Vigan,* 318; see also note 2, Chapter 1.

36. Fabre and La Croix, *La vie quotidienne,* 427-428.

37. *Travels with a Donkey in the Cévennes* (New York: Scribner's, 1905), 78, 68.

38. Jules Chabanon, *Villefort-du-Gévaudan* (Mende: Ignon-Renouard, 1920), 3; A. Pointier, "La route à Langogne," *Revue du Gévaudan* 6 (1960), 180.

39. Fabre and La Croix, *La vie quotidienne,* 361-362; Achille Foulquier, *Notes historiques sur les paroisses des Cévennes* (Mende: n.p., 1907), 360-361; Paul Marrès, "Modernization de la vie rurale cévenol," *Mémoires de l'Académie de Nîmes* (1954), 237; O. Poujol, "Réflexions sur les limites des Cévennes," *Revue du Gévaudan* 16 (1970), 129.

40. Robert Thinthoin, "Le commerce en Gévaudan au XVIIIe siècle," *Revue du Gévaudan* 16 (1970), 86. Thinthoin describes the markets:

> Twice a week, the market of Villefort is abundantly furnished with grains, chestnuts and vegetables, animals and butchered meat. It is also the central point for the commerce of grains coming from the Gard for Le Puy, Les Vans, and the Cévennes which most notably need it. Butter, oil, eggs, wool

from Mount Lozère, salt and coal, vegetables (potatoes, peas, favas and beans) are also sold" [Ibid., 87].

In 1840, a report from the Prefect of the Lozère noted that most roads across the Lozère, including the Villefort-Mende highway, were impassable by wheeled vehicles: Archives Nationales, series F14, 1558, cited by Patrice Higgonet, *Pont-de-Montvert* (Cambridge, MA: Harvard University Press, 1971), 103. Similar remarks are made in Théophile Roussel, "Rapport au préfet au sujet de l'enquête sur l'utilité publique du chemin de fer de Brioude à Alès," *Bulletin de la Société d'Agriculture de la Lozère* 12 (1861), 177.

41. Alain Laurans, "Villefort dans la Diocèse d'Uzès, 1700-1789," (Mémoire de Maitrise, Université Paul Valery, 1974), 44-47. The mines ceased operation about 1770; Foulquier, *Les paroisses des Cévennes,* 360.

42. Lamorisse, *La population de la Cévenne,* 101-102. Lamorisse defines the Cévennes' north border as the crest of Mount Lozère; Ibid., 13.

43. Boyer, "Les migration saisonnières," 579, 581; Chatelain, *Les migrants temporaires,* 126-129, 1101-1108; Lamorisse, *La population de la Cévenne,* 150. Peasant miners were not unique to the Cévennes, as historians of miners in the Tarn and the Loire attest. See, for example, Yves Lequin, *Les ourvriers de la région lyonnaise;* Joan Scott, *The Glassmakers of Carmeaux* (Cambridge, MA: Harvard University Press, 1974); Rolande Trempé, *Les mineurs de Carmeaux, 1848-1914* (Paris: Les Editions Ouvrières, 1971).

44. Armand Cosson, personal communication, April 1980; Barbot, *Le paysan lozérien,* 35.

45. Cited by Laurans, "Villefort," 99.

46. Archives Départementales de la Lozère (hereafter ADL), series 3-0, 893, Villefort: Vicinalité; ADL, series M, 4173, Situation industrielle et commerciale, Villefort, 1880-1887; Laurans, "Villefort," 7, 88; Thinthoin, "Structure sociale," 128-129.

47. ADL, series M, 4173, Situation industrielle et commerciale, Villefort, 2nd trimester, 1880; Laurans, "Villefort," 88.

48. Ibid., 99.

49. ADL, series 4E, 198, Marriage Records, Villefort, 1866-1870; ADL, series T, 3148, Schoolteacher's report, Villefort, 1862 and 1874; Furet and Ouzouf, *Lire et écrire,* 30, 57, 62; Guillaume Gérard, *Notes sur cent ans d'histoire en Lozère* (Mende: Chaptal, 1969), 21; Laurans, "Villefort," 99; Lamorisse, *La population de la Cévenne,* 98. Literacy figures appear in tabular form in Appendix III, Table III.2.

50. Jean Anglade, *La vie quotidienne dans le Massif Central au XIXe siècle* (Paris: Hachette, 1971), 224.

51. Poet Claude Lafont is quoted by Remy Chastel, *La Haute Lozère, jadis et nagère* (Paris: Roudil, 1976), 136.

52. Of the men working for the railroad married in Villefort, 1866-1870, two out of 24 on the construction crew were born in Villefort, whereas two out of three of the station personnel were born in Villefort: ADL, series 4E, 198, Marriage records, Villefort, 1866-1870. Raymonde Caralp-Landon, *Les chemins de fer dans le Massif Central* (Paris: Imprimerie Nationale, 1959), 396; Abel Chatelain, "La main-d'oeuvre et la construction des chemins de fer au XIX siècle," *Annales, E.S.C.* 8 (1955), 504.

53. ADL, series 4E, 198, Death records, Villefort, 1869; Lucien André, "L'épopée du chemin de fer: La Lavade-Villefort," *Almanach Cévenol* (1974), 168; Caralp-Landon, *Les chemins de fer,* 104, 107.

54. Chatelain, *Les migrants temporaires,* 170, 866, 868.

55. ADL, series M, 4131, "Foires et marchés," 1875 and 1893.

56. Eugen Weber, *Peasants into Frenchmen* (Stanford, CA: Stanford University Press, 1976), 210.

57. Louis Secondy, "L'établissement secondaire libre de Langogne au XIXe siècle," *Revue du Gévaudan* 19 (1973), 390.

58. Roussel, "Rapport au Préfet," 174-175, 198; Thinthoin, "Le commerce," 86.

59. ADL, series T, 3148, Schoolmaster's report, Langogne, 1874.

60. Conseil Municipal, Langogne, "Déliberation de la ville de Langogne pour être le chef-lieu d'un département," *Lozère Pittoresque* 4 (1900), 43-44; André Rieutort, "Langogne," (unpublished study, Ecole Normale de Mende, 1960), 65; Thinthoin, "Le commerce," 86.

61. ADL, series E, 80 f 1, 1861 census, Langogne; 41 establishments and 273 people were supported by the textile industry; ADL, series M, 4173, Situation industrielle, Langogne, 1881-1886; Thinthoin, "Structure sociale," 131.

62. Thinthoin, "Structure sociale," 137.

63. ADL, series E80, f 1, 1861 census, Langogne; Thinthoin, "Structure sociale," 133-134. In the commune of Langogne in 1836, there were still about twenty large landowners — as in 1764 — each possessing 22 to 300 hectares, in total half the surface of the commune.

64. ADL, series 4E, 80, marriage records, Langogne, 1866-1870; Gérard Cholvy, "Une chrétienté au XIXe siècle: la Lozère," *Revue du Gévaudan* 18-19 (1970-1973), 379; Furet and Ouzouf, *Lire et écrire,* 30, 57, 62. Literacy figures appear in tabular form in Appendix III, Table III.3.

65. Société Internationale des Etudes Pratiques d'Economie Sociale, *Les ouvriers des deux mondes,* Vol. 2 (Paris: Société Internationale des Etudes Pratiques d'Economie Sociale, 1858), 351.

66. D.M. Blanquet, "De la mendicité dans le département de la Lozère," *Mémoires de la Société des Lettres, Sciences et Arts de la Ville de Mende* 15 (1845-1848), 59; Blanquet, "Discours sur la situation de la Lozère en 1844," *Bulletin de la Société d'Agriculture de la Lozère,* quoted by Cholvy, "Une chrétienté au XIXe siècle," 370; Boyer, "Migrations saisonnaires," 381; Chastel, *La Haute Lozère,* 128; Lamorisse, *La population de la Cévenne,* 150; Rieutort, "Langogne," 15.

67. ADL, series M, 3030, Statistique agricole, *arrondissement* of Mende, 1897-1906; Gerard, *Lozère,* 30; report of Inspecteur des Eaux et Forets, 1910, cited by Rieutort, "Langogne," 33; station records, Ibid., 67.

68. Agulhon et al., *Apogée et crise de la civilisation paysanne,* 442-443; Caralp-Landon, *Les chemins de fer,* 266; Higonnet, *Pont-de-Montvert,* 102; Roussel, "Rapport au Préfet," 177-178.

69. Stevenson, *Travels with a Donkey,* 40-41; Weber, *Peasants into Frenchmen,* 232-233.

70. Journal d'Agriculture Pratique, "Une école de fermières à New York," *Bulletin de la Société d'Agriculture de la Lozère* 50 (1878), 131-136.

71. See Charles Tilly, "Migration in modern European history," in W. McNeill and R. Adams, eds., *Human Migration: Patterns and Policies* (Bloomington: Indiana University Press, 1978), 48-52.

72. Chamson, *The Road,* 171-172.

73. Jules Michelet, *The People* (Urbana: University of Illinois Press, 1973), 76.

74. Stanley Brandes, *Migration, Kinship and Community* (New York: Academic Press, 1975); Chamson, *The Road,* 168-178; Pierre Merlin, *L'exode rural* (Paris: Presses Universitaires Françaises, 1971), 69.

75. In patois, the proverb is "Crabas amont/filhas aval"; in French, "Les chevres vers le haut/les filles vers le bas"; Fabre and La Croix, *La vie quotidienne,* 127.

76. Raymond Dugrand et al., "L'organisation urbaine entre Sète et le Rhône," *Bulletin de la Société Languedocienne de Géographie,* ser. 3, 3 (1969), 398.

77. Jean-Pierre Poussou, "Introduction à l'étude des mouvements migratoires en Espagne, Italie et France méditerranéene au XVIIe siècle," in A. Nouschi, ed., *Les migrations dans les pays méditerranéens au XVIIIème et au début du XIXe* (Nice: Centre de la Méditerranée Moderne et Contemporaine, 1973), 14-15.

78. See note 2, Chapter 1.

3

The City of Nîmes

> For me, my city was not a dead city with some sublime vestiges of the past. It was the living image of a stubborn, tenacious civilization, born by the grace of the great god Nemausus and fertilized by Rome.
>
> — Lucie Mazauric Chamson
> *"Belle Rose, Ô Tour Magne"*

Nîmes' past is a great and noble one, commemorated in the fine Roman monuments that dot the city, and retained in memories still alive at the turn of the century of its heyday as an important silk manufacturer. Nîmes' finest days clearly had passed by the *belle époque*. Yet it boasted new vocations, a specific urban style, and a unique culture. These will be examined here in order to understand the relationship between this city and the immigrants who increased its population by nearly 20,000 in the last twenty years of the nineteenth century. What was the relationship between the city of Nîmes and its rural hinterland? What was the city's geography? What kinds of economic opportunities existed in Nîmes, where factory industry was practically nonexistent at the turn of the century? Finally, what kind of culture greeted newcomers to Nîmes? The answer to these questions will sketch the environment in which newcomers were to live, a picture vital to understanding the migrants' place in Nîmes, because the character of the city determined the economic and social possibilities awaiting them.

At the turn of the century, Nîmes was a bustling town of 80,000 located on the Mediterranean littoral between the Rhone river, some 15 miles to the east, and the city of Montpellier in the Hérault, 25 miles to the west. Twenty miles of plain stretched from Nîmes south to the Mediterranean and the marshy Rhone delta called the Camargue. Around the North side of the city curves the dry, rock-strewn heath, the *garrigue,* which played an important role in the lives of the Nimois.

MAZETS AND THE COUNTRYSIDE

Country houses, called *mazets (petits mas),* were the focal point of Nîmes' broad and profound attachment to the countryside. The mazet typically enclosed one or two rooms under a shedlike roof. It sat on a small parcel of rocky land which was cleared to provide space for cultivation and to construct a dry stone wall. The parcels were so small that they were measured, not by the usual measure of hectares, but in *ares,* spaces of 100 square meters. The mazet included a small piece of property on which the family cultivated a few olive, fig, and almond trees, vines, and perhaps vegetables and flowers. The importance of mazets for Nimois and the affection lavished on them are reflected in the city's folklore and celebrated in poetry written in patois. The most famous mazet belonged to Monsieur Roumieux:

> Le mazet de Maître Roumeiux
> Est un mazet comme il n y en a guère
> . . . .
> Gentiment retapé, blanc comme le lis,
> Couronné de fleurs et de rameaux,
> Dans son enclos, il brave, tranquille,
> Le vent, la pluie et le soleil.[1]

Like the *cabanons* and *bastidous* outside Marseille, the *baraquettes* around Sète and Bézier's *granglettes,* the mazet provided urban people with a pied-à-terre outside the city. Yet the little houses seem to have been most important to the Nimois, particularly during the fifty years preceding 1914. According to a national study of property holding from 1890, Nîmes had an extraordinarily high percentage of homeowners. Because of the mazets, the study concludes, a high percentage of houses in Nîmes — nearly half — were occupied by the owner alone. The proportion for Sète and Montpellier was 31 percent, for Paris 15 percent, and considerably less for industrial Lille, Roubaix, and St. Etienne. It is impossible to know how many mazets surrounded Nîmes, because many were not registered with the tax office, but a close study of them published in 1898 estimates that over 4000 surrounded Nîmes, and other estimates concur.[2]

People of nearly every class — workers, artisans, shopkeepers, clerks, and functionaries — owned mazets. Even the girls' lycée owned a mazet. Lucie Mazauric's middle-class family spent Sundays at her uncle's mazet, and Paul Marcelin's artisan father owned one. Marc Bernard's family was miserably poor, but his brother-in-law, who was a railroad car repairman, was able to buy a mazet. All concur that the mazet was inexpensive, and a 1914 estimate fixes the cost at between 150 and 600 francs. The Marcelin's mazet cost 150 francs in 1867, which they paid in six annual payments.[3]

Paul Marcelin describes the mazet's role in the life of the Nimois in his autobiography, *Souvenirs d'un passé artisanal*. The Marcelin's mazet included about two-thirds of an acre of land (33 ares) on which they cultivated a few fruit trees, including figs and native fruits, vines, and olive trees. Later, they bought two more acres and expanded the number of olive trees to twenty. For the Marcelins and other *mazetiers,* Sunday was the day of relaxation and leisure at the mazet, a day to visit with relatives and friends and play *boules*. On the Mondays after Easter and Pentecost, and Ash Wednesday as well, Nîmes emptied onto the garrigue, where the mazetier could relax in the thyme-scented air. Sundays on the garrigue at the mazet were central to social life in Nîmes. It may have been only a slight exaggeration to say that "to have a mazet is the dream of good Nimois, to go to his mazet is supreme happiness."[4]

For most mazetiers, their little houses were more than a picturesque place to relax. Marcelin estimates that the olive trees, vines, and fig trees provided oil, wine, and confections which, along with the old olive branches cut up for firewood in the fall, were worth nearly one-third of the midcentury worker's salary. The Marcelin's oil came from their own trees, and their fruit and almonds from their trees and from the azeroles native to the garrigue. Wealthy Nimois and prosperous artisans had more leisure at the mazet because they could employ an agricultural worker — a *rachalan* – for at least part of the work. No matter how wealthy the owner, however, the mazet supplemented the family's food.[5]

Sustenance and leisure attached the Nimois to the countryside in many ways. The outlying areas of the city had a rural atmosphere; small apartments and houses alternated with gardens, trees, and the natural vegetation of the garrigue. In the mild climate of the Mediterranean plain, it was possible to plant vegetable gardens from early spring on. The housing in Nîmes — airless in the ancient buildings of the old city, and unhealthy in the suburbs — drove many Nimois outdoors. They were anxious to escape the city on hot summer days, and this became easier, especially for children and old people, when the tramline to the garrigue opened at the end of the nineteenth century. Finally, the poor needed to produce some of their own food to get by. Nimois too poor to buy a mazet scavenged food and trapped rabbits on the garrigue and raised some of their own food in gardens on the edge of town provided by the churches. The result of these connections with the countryside was a culture that perceived itself as outdoors and semi-rural. As a young worker in Paris, Nimois Marc Bernard described himself and his Nimois friends as a "brood of garrigue rabbits" in the capital. In the metro, he wrote: "We go at our mazetier's pace in the crowd which ran through the corridors." And after dinner on the balcony, they sang "Lou mazet de Meste Roumieux."[6]

Some Nimois' attachment to the countryside was the result of ownership of more distant property. According to Raymond Dugrand:

> This link is land rent. Almost all the farm houses *(mas)* of the plain are the property of bourgeois city dwellers. In each commune . . . small tenures remain in the possession of former village dwellers who have gone, sometimes generations before, to dissolve in the urban melting pot. Land rents in Languedoc are the base of town-country relations for the commercial classes and even for salaried workers as well as for the upper bourgeoisie.[7]

As a consequence, Nîmes emptied at the time of the grape harvest in the fall, not only of urban workers who hired themselves out for the harvest, but also of white collar workers gone back to a village to harvest grapes and to make their own wine, and of bourgeois to supervise the winemaking at their property. Some owned land in the mountains; peasants and large landowners from the uplands of Languedoc retained their land when they left the countryside. Many members of the bourgeoisie maintained a village or mountain residence. Consequently, the movement of people to the city made Nîmes a capital of property ownership in the Cévennes and on the plain.[8]

Nîmes shared with its region an earthy and concrete patois. Paul Marcelin's aging mother recommended her flesh to the dogs after death, saying: "Quand seraï morto, poures baïa ma car i chin." Years later, young errand boy Marc Bernard urged his horse up a steep hill, swearing like a trooper: "Trou de Diou de noum de Diou? La mounteras! de ques aquella puta de bestia? Lou foui!" Rural folk hawked their wares in patois, using cries like this one for butter and cheese: "Aven de buro et de boun froumadgoun!"[9] Could the mountain-born newcomer make himself understood in patois? More easily, according to Marc Bernard, than the northerners speaking French. Perhaps this is why, in 1901, Nîmes' striking clerks sang to the owner of the Paris-based department store, La Maison Universelle, in patois — to deride him, to scorn him as an outsider. The young men and women advised Maubé to pack his bag: "Moun paore Maubé, faï ta malo!"[10]

These multifaceted links between Nîmes and its hinterland were often familial or communal. City people maintained contacts with their home villages and towns. During the summers, the bourgeoisie retired to villas and family homes in the country; city students, servants, country-born wives with their children, and workers who were able to vacation visited home. This became easier after the railroad was extended into the Cévennes and north through the Lozère. Even for those born in Nîmes, family contacts with the mountains continued. For example, in 1900 Paul Marcelin's parents, descended from families that arrived in Nîmes in the eighteenth century, received chestnuts from kin in the Cévennes. Societies based on common origins flourished; of the 49 mutual aid societies in Nîmes in 1912, nine were based on origin. Among these were the Union Lozérienne and the Association Amicale des Originaires de l'Arrondissement du Vigan, which aided people at home and in Nîmes.[11] Other groups gathered people from Anduze, the Ardèche, Corsica, the Hérault, Italy, the Aveyron, and the Vaucluse.

These societies and kin connections with the region involved many people in Nîmes, for in 1906 nearly half the city's adults had been born elsewhere, and most migrants came from the region. A quarter of them came from the villages on the garrigue and the plain in the arrondissement of Nîmes. Another quarter came from the upland areas of the Gard toward the Ardèche and the Lozère. Of the neighboring departments, the mountainous Ardèche and Lozère sent the most people to the Gard. In all, nearly 70 percent of Nîmes' migrants came from Eastern Languedoc — the departments of the Gard, the Lozère, the Ardèche, and the Hérault. Another 10 percent came from other neighboring departments: the Bouches-du-Rhône,

Vaucluse, and Drôme in Provence, and the Aveyron to the northwest. Migration was still essentially regional even at the turn of the century, for only 15 percent of the migrants in Nîmes came from beyond bordering departments, and only 7 percent were foreigners, most of these Italians — a group which had settled in Nîmes since the Middle Ages.

URBAN GROWTH AND CHANGING *QUARTIERS*

Like other cities in Southern France, Nîmes was densely settled at the core, and its growth stretched out from its medieval boundary. Mazauric characterizes its physical plan as "the old city, corseted by its belt of boulevards, studded with Roman monuments, the outskirts . . . where residents grouped by affinity and by neighborhood, like the Placette and the Enclos Rey."[12] In the nineteenth century, settlements on the outskirts were built up, crowded, and extended — expansion turned from the garrigue southward on the plain. As the city expanded, some parts grew rapidly, while others stagnated. Neighborhoods specialized as commercial, industrial, and residential spaces.

The town's commerce entered in the dense, triangular old city at the turn of the century (see Map 3.1). In the early morning, braying donkeys announced the arrival of produce at the central market in the north end. The market housed 284 stalls — grocers, butchers, fishmongers, florists, and sellers of cheese, poultry, vegetables, and fruit — and attracted small sellers who set up tables for their wares outside. Juvenal, the city's first department store, faced the market across the tramway tracks, and commerce on a smaller scale was spread throughout the old city. Banking and municipal business, carried on in the large but delapidated town hall, were also centered there.[13]

Nimois of all classes lived in the old city — from elite families of the region who lived in its Renaissance *hôtels* to the most miserable of paupers confined to a single room. Rich and poor often lived in the same house, artisans on the ground floor, bourgeois on the second, and the poor above them. Servants and the very poor inhabited attic rooms. As a child, Marc Bernard visited an impoverished shoemaker in his attic room:

> I arrived in the lane, perhaps the most narrow in the city. I went up a staircase which was monumental, but which grew narrower with

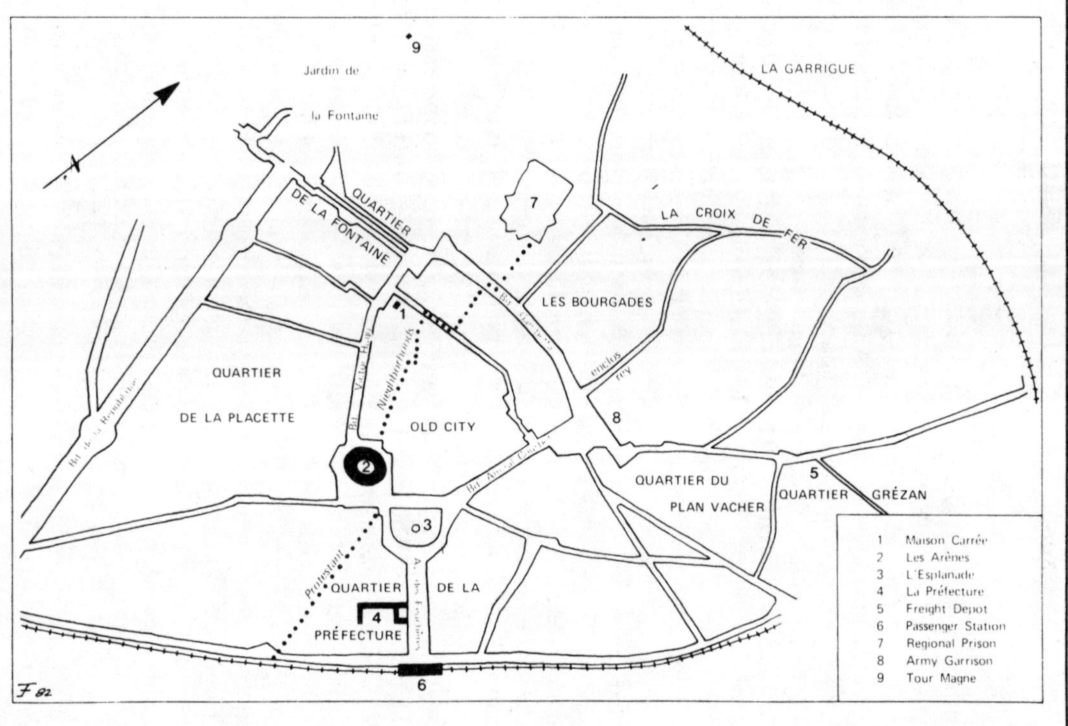

Jardin de
la Fontaine
LA GARRIGUE
QUARTIER
DE LA FONTAINE
LA CROIX DE FER
LES BOURGADES
enclos rey
QUARTIER
DE LA PLACETTE
OLD CITY
Neighborhoods
Bd Victor Hugo
Bd Amiral Courbet
Bd de la République
QUARTIER DU
PLAN VACHER
QUARTIER GRÉZAN
Protestant
QUARTIER DE LA
PRÉFECTURE
Av. des Feuchères
1 Maison Carrée
2 Les Arènes
3 L'Esplanade
4 La Préfecture
5 Freight Depot
6 Passenger Station
7 Regional Prison
8 Army Garrison
9 Tour Magne

Map 3.1: Nîmes

> every story. On the last landing, I found myself facing a wooden staircase as steep as a ladder; a slippery and dirty rope served as a banister.[14]

Wealth and poverty lived side by side. The best preserved of the Renaissance buildings were the preserves of the bourgeoisie and its servants, but parts of the crowded old city housed what Bernard calls "the meanest degrees of misery." Although some of the city's worst slums were demolished to clear space for the central market in the 1880s, the core city still contained the unhealthiest housing in Nîmes at the turn of the century. The old city was no longer growing. The total urban population increased by 52 percent between 1856 and 1906, but the center city grew by only 12 percent, because it was increasingly devoted to commerce.[15] The old city housed the highest proportion of migrants of any part of Nîmes (52 percent), perhaps because it housed the region's aristocrats, their rural-born servants, and the very poor, all of whom were likely to have come from outside Nîmes.

The boulevards and squares surrounding the old city were arteries for the social and commercial life of Nîmes. The largest cafés, hotels, restaurants, and squares lined the boulevards and provided social space in which to see and be seen. Soldiers stationed in Nîmes favored the cafés on the Boulevard Amiral Courbet to the east close to their quarters. The grandest cafés, the Café Tortoni and Grand Café, which boasted six separate rooms, were closer to the park and bandstand south of the city. Prestigious shops and the largest stores lined the boulevards. Political events and social conflict filled the boulevards on occasion. The favored route for parades and demonstrations led participants south down the west side's Boulevard Victor Hugo, around the tip of the triangular old town between the big cafés and the park, and north up the Boulevard Amiral Courbet on the east side (see Map 3.1). Waiters, protesting the conditions of their work and engaged in a long and bitter strike, marched along this route before their most important employers. Celebrants of a Socialist deputy's victory followed the same path in 1906. Thousands paraded around the boulevards and sang by torchlight the night war was declared in August of 1914.[16]

The monuments and squares that stud the boulevards provide meeting places and memorials to Nîmes' past. The most beautiful monument is the Maison Carrée, a finely proportioned Roman temple resembling the Parthenon, built by Emperor Augustus in the first century. It faces the theatre across the Place de la Comédie, once site of the wine market on Monday afternoons. At the foot of the Boulevard Victor Hugo lies the Arena, the central monument of the city and the best-preserved Roman arena in the world. The arena was used for entertainment, holding as many as 20,000 Nimois who attended bullfights and tragedies performed against the dramatic backdrop of the ancient structure. The weekly flour and grain market was held outside in the enormous Place des Arènes. Another important gathering place lay just east of the Arena at the base of the old city: the park called the Esplanade. Its large fountain, bandstand, and trees attracted mothers and children in the afternoons, strollers, and audiences for summer band concerts.

West of the ring of boulevards lies the city's most famous park, the Jardin de la Fontaine. The focal point of the park is the spring, called the *Nemausus,* which was the impetus for the original settlement of Nîmes by the Celts. The lower park includes the "Temple de Diane," a Roman ruin, a *grande allée* decorated with eighteenth-century statuary, and a series of pools, islands, and canals that guided water from the spring toward town. Above this rose an impressive stairway and paths winding among Mediterranean evergreens that ascend to an ancient tower called La Tour Magne. An enormous cypress on the hill provided shade, a view, and a breeze on summer afternoons. Here Nimois could find many features which the Mediterranean plain did not naturally yield — shade, water, and a view toward the sea. Photos of the era show "élégantes" strolling the grand allée, uniformed nurses watching children, and local scholarly societies on excursion. The park was a meeting place for the bourgeois neighborhood on which it bordered.[17]

Six districts, each with a distinct history and character, sprawled out from the old city and boulevards at the turn of the century. The oldest, called *les bourgades,* extended uphill toward the garrigue north of the old city. Baumès and Vincens describe the bourgades as a working-class neighborhood in their 1802 *Topographie médicale.* Textile workers and rachalans, agricultural workers on the garrigue, lived in the area at the beginning of the nineteenth century. One hundred years later, *li bourgadieiro,* as he was called in patois, was still a worker, and his neighborhood was crowded. Of the residents, 44 percent were migrants.[18] In the last half of the nineteenth century, the bourgades housed 12-13 percent of the urban population but increased by only 24 percent, while the city's population grew by 52 percent.

There was little room for more houses or more people in this traditional working-class area.

The Placette to the west was an old working-class neighborhood like the bourgades. Surrounding the small square after which it was named, the Placette was a level area of low buildings bordered by a bourgeois neighborhood to the north. In the eighteenth century, it had been the site of artisans' houses and gardens, but the neighborhood became crowded and built up by textile workers in the first part of the nineteenth century. Silk-weaving families lived in the Placette, and silk-winders worked just to the west, on the borders of the stream called the Cadereau. As the district became more populous, it became less healthy; with crowding, the light and fresh air were reduced, and the unpaved streets turned to muck more quickly in traffic. Moreover, the level topography of the neighborhood limited drainage. By 1856, little room for expansion remained; in the fifty years following the population of the *quartier* expanded less than that of the city.[19] Of the people in this neighborhood, 40 percent were migrants.

The Plan Vacher extended east from the old city. Like other neighborhoods, it housed textile workers and the proletariat of Nîmes in the early nineteenth century, but its vocation soon became the railroad. In 1838 Nîmes' first station opened in this neighborhood, and by 1840 quantities of coal came through Nîmes from Alès on its way to Beaucaire. Four years later, the Nîmes-Montpellier line increased traffic at the eastside terminal, and later the railroad built an important car repair terminal east of Nîmes. The personnel needs of the repair terminal, depots, and trains originating in Nîmes were immense, and most of the work was located in the Plan Vacher and east. According to the 1906 census, 31 percent of railroad workers in Nîmes resided in this neighborhood, and another 34 percent in the other eastside quartiers. Of the residents of the Plan Vacher proper, 39 percent were migrants.

The Plan Vacher and the Grézan, which stretched beyond it to the east, grew with the railroad. Industry also added to the expansion of the east side of Nîmes. In 1906 the head of the tram system replied to a request for a new tramway east of the city:

> This request appears to me to be justified by the number and the importance of the industries on the boulevard Talabot [southeast of town], and particularly by the Grézan agglomeration, with its industries and especially the [railroad] employees, active and retired. . . .

> This neighborhood has developed so enormously in the past fifteen years that many of our citizens who have not visited it for several years would not recognize it.[20]

Between 1856 and 1906, the Plan Vacher grew more than in the city as a whole, and the Grézan beyond it expanded enormously, for it had been virtually uninhabited. Of the residents of south and south-east Nîmes, 46 percent were migrants. At the turn of the century, citizens of the Grézan petitioned the city council for a primary school, letter boxes, and gas and water for their fast-growing neighborhood. Unfortunately, the prosperity of the railroad, the long straight streets of the Plan Vacher, and even new housing did not make for a well-housed population. This was a proletarian area, and an extremely unhealthy one. The streets were unpaved, and the housing deteriorated quickly. The neighborhood's pastor noted that moving from the crowded old city to a suburb like the Plan Vacher did nothing to improve the workers' housing.

> When . . . the jumble of disgusting alleyways which occupy the present site of the market in Nîmes was destroyed . . . that was the right thing to do. But the workers and the paupers who lived there, about whom there was hardly any concern, were compressed into the outlying areas and had to crowd into veritable slums.[21]

Although it was primarily residential, like the bourgades and the Placette, the Plan Vacher was ringed by industry, such as Teyssedre's men's vest manufacture, located on the Boulevard Talabot south of the freight depot.

The Croix de Fer reached northeast into the garrigue from the Plan Vacher. A very old neighborhood at its base, the Croix de Fer was growing to the north. Representatives from the neighborhood bombarded the city council with requests for services to its growing population for a tram line, primary schools, and even a stop on the Nîmes-Alès railway line. The Croix de Fer demanded its own wash house, which was constructed in 1904. A new church, Saint Luc, went up between 1895 and 1912. Growth in this quartier outstripped that in most parts of the city in the fifty years before 1906.[22] Of its residents, 35 percent were migrants.

This was a residential area, removed from Nîmes' commerce and industry. As one went north toward the garrigue, the neighborhood had an increasingly rural character; space between dwellings, the pines of the Mont Duplan, and the surrounding garrigue gave the neighborhood sunshine, fresh air, and the fragrance of thyme and pine. Nimois of all classes lived in the Croix de Fer, although it housed primarily workers. Its poorest inhabitants were crowded near the freight depot and the Route D'Uzès.[23] The housing became less dense and crowded as the old buildings along the Route d'Uzès gave way to smaller apartment buildings, hilltop windmills, and then to villas and mazets on the garrigue.

The last two districts were relatively new and primarily middle and upper class. The *quartier de la Préfecture,* Nîmes' newest neighborhood, heralded the city's development to the south. This began with the installation of rail lines joining Nîmes to Montpellier, which ran south of the city. A large passenger station was built due south of the Esplanade in 1844 and connected to the park by a new boulevard — the wide, tree-lined Avenue Feuchères — anchored in civic importance by the monumental Prefecture (administrative capitol of the department of the Gard), completed in 1855. The Avenue Feuchères was the center of the new neighborhood, and new boulevards running parallel to the railroad tracks defined the parameters of the quartier. Few people lived south of the railroad tracks.

Bourgeois at the core, the neighborhood spread to the east and west, housing middle-class families, doctors, lawyers, government officials, and their servants. The neighborhood wash house was pushed out in 1881 when the River Vistre was covered over, and its quai became the tree-lined Avenue Carnot. Other streets were extended and new ones constructed. This was Nîmes' fastest-growing area; between 1856 and 1906, the population of the quartier tripled.[24] Some 40 percent of the residents of the Préfecture and the area to the southwest were migrants.

The *quartier de la Fontaine* bordered the canal that flowed from the Jardin de la Fontaine into Nîmes. Almost entirely residential and bourgeois in character, its history was not related to commercial or administrative expansion, but to the move of the elite from the old city to the borders of the Jardin de la Fontaine. Beginning in the early nineteenth century with the construction of mansions along the Quai de la Fontaine, the neighborhood filled out and curved around the park. Of its residents, 43 percent were migrants. In the last half of the nineteenth century, expansion here was greater than in many other parts of town. At the same time, the neighborhood became more intensely residential and leisure-oriented. The wash house on the Square Antonin was destroyed and replaced by a circular garden at the end of the canal, decorated in 1874 with a statue of Nîmes' son, the Roman emperor Antonin. The wash house and flower market in the Square d'Assas gave way to another garden financed by private citizens.[25] These squares, the walkways along the canal, and the Jardin de la Fontaine provided the neighborhood with beautiful and luxurious spaces for strolling.

The city of Nîmes, then, was divided into distinct neighborhoods at the turn of the century. At the center was the old city, where people of all classes resided. Laborers and clerical workers dominated the old working-class neighborhoods of *les bourgades* to the north and la Placette to the west. To the east, the Plan Vacher and the Grézan housed many railroad workers. The Croix de Fer spread north into the garrigue, housing primarily working-class families, while the *quartier de la Préfecture* provided housing to the south for middle-class families. The *quartier de la Fontaine* to the northwest was the most exclusive and most aesthetically pleasant area. As we shall see, the geography of Nîmes at the turn of the century was a physical manifestation of both its economic transformation and its unique culture.

ECONOMIC CHANGE AND OPPORTUNITY

The economy of Nîmes was marked by crises and change between 1800 and 1900. In the eighteenth and early nineteenth century, Nîmes was primarily an industrial town, manufacturing textiles and hosiery. One-quarter to one-third of the population worked in the silk industry. Raw silk was reeled off silk worms raised outside the city and in the mountains, and spun into thread. With this thread, frame knitters produced silk stockings, and hand loom weavers made taffeta, silk, and silk-blend cloth, shawls, scarves, and handkerchiefs. As often was the case with preindustrial textile production, the work lent itself to a labor force of mixed ages and sexes. The various tasks of spinning, preparing the warp, reeling the woof, and weaving proper required different degrees of skill and physical strength. Women, often young women from the mountains, did the spinning. The Nimois weaver was usually an adult male assisted by his family, and perhaps an apprentice, in his home.[26]

This pattern of manufacturing continued through 1850, although changes in volume and even in product occurred, with silk crises and competition from other towns. Raw silk was rarely wound in Nîmes after the 1830s, for example, and the production of pure silk cloth decreased. In its place grew the manufacture of woven shawls, rugs, scarves, ties, and handkerchiefs. At midcentury, about half the town's population worked in artisanal manufacturing. Nîmes' 29 shawl manufacturers alone employed over 4000 workers, 40 percent of whom were men, another 40 percent children, and 20 percent adult women. The shawl industry employed a familial and artisanal system of production. Families like that of Françoise Boissière, mother of Paul Marcelin, were typical: Françoise was born in 1838 of two Protestant weavers whose parents had been weavers in Nîmes since 1794.[27] She left school at the age of ten and rose every morning at 5:00 a.m. to work at the loom with her parents and sister in their home. The only leisure for this poor family, buffeted by the crises of the textile industry and impoverished by the meager wages they were able to earn at the loom, was religious services on Sunday. They resided in the Placette, west of the city.

For textile workers like the Boissières, more difficult times came after 1850. Changes in fashion and the successful competition from other industrial centers destroyed the market for Nîmes' textile products. Shawls ceased to be fashionable after 1860, and orders virtually ceased. Silk cloth, taffeta, rugs, and upholstery fabric were produced more cheaply and more competitively elsewhere, as Lyon, northern France, and the United States adopted mechanized looms. By the end of the century, the textile and hosiery industries had virtually disappeared.[28]

In the crisis-ridden economy of the nineteenth century, industrialists reduced their losses by redirecting investments, frequently to the vineyards of the plain. Those with less capital — like the father of Françoise Boissière, whose attempt to become a manufacturer ended in failure — returned to manual labor. Hardest hit were the workers who faced unemployment or salary reductions. They turned to charity and foraged and trapped whatever edibles could be found on the garrigue. Some hosiery and textile workers left Nîmes.[29] Others, however, remained and found new sources of support.

The population of the city grew by one-third between 1880 and 1900. This expansion reflects the change and growth in the city's economy produced by developments whose intertwining and mutually reinforcing effects created new employment opportunities. Phylloxera began to kill grape vines in the Gard in the late 1860s and devastated the entire department in the 1870s. When replanting began, it covered a more extensive area than before, because areas of grain cultivation were given over to vineyards, and the area of cultivation itself was enlarged. Wine production increased all the more because more productive vines replaced the prephylloxera varieties. The Mediterranean littoral became a factory of *vin ordinaire*. Consequently, trends brought on by the epidemic reversed: Wine merchants relocated on the littoral; "a new social class was created," as more people became merchants; banking and retail commerce prospered; and property values increased.[30] The labor force in turn-of-the-century Nîmes reflects the economy created by recovery from the phylloxera epidemic and the new wine industry. Table 3.1 shows that the city had a considerable bourgeoisie; that is, people who enjoyed financial independence and control over their own resources. According to the census of 1906, more than one Nimois in ten fits into this category. Most of these were property owners and rentiers; others were wholesale merchants.

With the prosperity of wholesale wine commerce after 1880 came the demand for skilled workers such as coopers, and for clerical employees in banking and trade. In Nîmes, as elsewhere at the turn of the century, the clerk was "an essential element on the urban social horizon," for by 1906 nearly one worker in five was a *"col blanc"*[31] (see Table 3.1). Most were listed in the census simply as *"employé,"* but others, like the Chevret sisters' niece Rosine, indicated that they were clerks in stores and businesses, banks, the railroad stations, city hall, the Préfecture, and post offices.

The success of the new vineyards lined the pockets of landowners and merchants, for whom luxury trades flowered. The demand for pianos increased, for example. The growth of the urban middle class led to a greater demand for domestic servants. In turn-of-the-century Nîmes, more men and women worked as domestic servants than at any other occupation. Of the town's semi-skilled and unskilled laborers, the largest group were maids, cooks, nurses, valets, manservants, and chauffeurs (Table 3.1). Among these numbered the Chevret sisters from Langogne and the Villefortais Janvier sisters. Moreover, prosperous Nimois supported a large coterie of laundresses and hairdressers; they also kept the city's major cafés in business and supported several domestic servant employment agencies.

With the extension of the railroad, Nîmes was now central to the Paris-Lyon-Mediterranean (PLM) rail company. Rail lines first connected Nîmes with the coalfields of Alès-Grand'Combe to the north and Beaucaire on the Rhone river in the late 1830s, and then with

TABLE 3.1 The Labor Force in Nîmes, 1906

Occupational Status	*Categories Included*	*Important Occupations*	*Percentage of Total*	*N*
Bourgeoisie	property owners, rentiers, owners in commerce and industry, professionals, high-level administrators	property owners and rentiers wholesale merchants administrators professionals in law and medicine	11	150
Petty bourgeoisie	small shopkeepers, other retailers	food dealers cafe operators	6	79
White collar workers	office clerks, sales people, bookkeepers, commercial employees		17	234
Skilled workers	artisans, skilled laborers in industry, transport and food production	shoemakers clothing specialists	25	334
Semi-skilled and unskilled workers	service, railroad and industrial workers, unskilled laborers	servants garment workers railroad workers manual laborers	41	557
Total			100%	1354

SOURCE: ADG 10M 260, 261, 262, *Recensement, Ville de Nîmes, 1906;* systematic sample of individuals in 5 percent of households.

Montpellier in 1844. Nîmes' importance increased most significantly when the PLM made it a crossroad, rather than its competitor Montpellier. In 1867 the northbound line was extended into the Massif Central, completing the link between central France and the Mediterranean littoral. At this junction of north-south lines and the east-west rail network, the PLM located an important repair shop and freight depot.[32] By the turn of the century, nearly 200 trains passed through Nîmes every day.

Heavy rail traffic generated a need for railroad personnel to check the railroad lines, maintain and repair engines, operate the trains, repair the cars, and manage the busy merchandise and passenger depots. A minimum of 2000 Nimois worked at these tasks.[33] Railroad workers could be found throughout the hierarchy of workers in Nîmes: Station employees like Victor Bouzanquet from Villefort figured prominently among white collar workers, and machinists among the skilled workers; one-seventh of the city's semi-skilled and unskilled workers were low-skill PLM workers, such as car repairmen. Railroad employees formed the largest union and mutual aid society in Nîmes. Moreover, the trade engendered by the railroad — the influx of cattle and other products from central France, of wine from the Midi, of Parisian and imported goods — increased the commercial importance of Nîmes. From carters to clerks to merchants, commerce required workers.

Nîmes' administrative functions provided employment for increasing numbers of people in the last years of the nineteenth century. White collar workers in particular named their employer in the 1906 census as the Prefecture, city hall, or the post office (see Table 3.1). Prefectural functions required high-level government administrators and legal professionals. By 1905, the Prefecture employed 103 functionaries like the Donzels, excluding its legal professionals and numerous clerks. The imposing departmental courthouse was the workplace for clerks, government employees with responsible positions, such as the clerk of the court *(greffier)*, lawyers, and judges. The municipality itself employed nearly 800 people at the turn of the century, from ditch-digger to clerk to high-level administrator, because municipal services had grown to meet the needs of the city and changing technology. Roads and postal services had expanded considerably, and gas, electricity, and tramways had been installed.[34] Nîmes was also the regional center for the Protestant and Catholic churches; the Protestant consistory was the most important outside

Paris, and the bishop's residence served as a capital for the diocese. As employers, the churches became less important with the laicization of education after 1880 and the separation of church and state in 1905. The bishop's palace was sold to the city in 1908. Nevertheless, they remained important institutions and continued to employ personnel to meet the spiritual and charitable needs of Nimois.

As a regional center, the city housed institutions that attracted newcomers and employed Nimois. Students came from throughout the department to attend the city's secondary schools. Camille Guiraud, for example, son of a mill owner in Le Vigan, attended the boy's lycée in the early 1880s. By 1900, 200 girls were enrolled in secondary classes, and some 400 boys attended the *Lycée de Nîmes*. The two institutions employed nearly eighty professors. Two normal schools trained the region's teachers, one the former Protestant normal school for women. Men and women from communes throughout the department came to the normal schools and were then assigned to teach in the hinterland. The father of Lucie Mazauric, himself the son of a poor tailor in a little Cevenol town, came to the Ecole Normale des Instituteurs on scholarship and settled in Nîmes at the end of his teaching career. Nîmes' educational institutions in particular expanded under the Third Republic, increasing its attraction for students and providing more employment for teachers. Nîmes' hospitals also received people from other communes in the department. The Hospice d'Humanité, with about 350 beds, and the Hopital Ruffi, with about 300 beds, served the old, infirm, poor, and ill. A more vigorous population of about 3,000 filled the ranks of the two artillery regiments and the infantry regiment garrisoned in Nîmes. In the Vauban-designed fort on the west side of the bourgades was one of the nine regional prisons in France, a men's prison housing up to 1,000 inmates and employing about 70 guards and administrators. By 1906, the boarding students, hospital patients, prison inmates, soldiers, and residents of religious communities numbered 6,073 among the 80,000 Nimois.[35]

Retail commerce prospered as the city expanded. Food sales were most common: independent groceries and specialty shops, rented stalls in the main market, and street hawking. Women, particularly married women, were important in the petty bourgeois community, for they represented nearly one-third of the shopkeepers. For example, Anna Sabatier from Langogne ran a grocery in the old city behind the main market while raising her two sons. Many white collar workers as well worked in stores, according to the census of 1906. Both specialty shops and department stores — the Juvenal, Grand Bazar, and the Paris-owned Maison Universelle — employed large numbers of young men and women as salespeople. Almost from its inception, the mutual aid society and union, Employés de Commerce et de l'Industrie, was a prosperous, active organization soon boasting over 300 members. Numbers and solidarity were such that by 1901 clerks were able to stage large and violent demonstrations against Sunday work.[36] Although most clerical and sales jobs belonged to men in Nîmes at the turn of the century, one in six white collar workers, including clerks, elementary school teachers, postal employees, and salespeople, was a woman.

Finally, two new industries developed in the last quarter of the nineteenth century which employed several thousand workers: the manufacture of shoes and men's clothing. Neither was mechanized or organized on a large scale, so most workers were paid by the piece, not by the hour. In 1904-1905, about 3500 shoemakers were working in Nîmes, most of them at home, making infants and small children's shoes, sometimes working with partners or family members. They formed the largest group of skilled workers in the city (see Table 3.1). Only the leather cutters, who created the material for piecework out of skins and cloth, worked in the atelier. The scale and organization of the Barre and Boisson companies were typical. Eight out of Ulysse Barre's 52 workers, and twelve of the 92 who worked for Boisson, were employed in the shop; the rest worked at home and were paid by the piece. In 1906, Barre was only just preparing to install stitching machinery in his atelier.[37]

The men's clothing industry employed about 1500 workers at the turn of the century. Perhaps twice that many worked in the city's entire garment industry, including the production of women's hats, corsets, and lingerie. The majority of garmentmakers were women and girls, many of whom performed piecework at home. Nearly all the women who were skilled workers in Nîmes, according to the 1906 census, were hatters; vest-, pant-, and shirtmakers; or some other garment specialist. The largest group of female semi-skilled workers, after servants, were the unspecialized garment workers, like the Pouzergue daughter who listed her occupation as *couturière*. The organization of Léopold Landauer's company typified large men's clothing manufacturers. A total of 20 male pressers, 65 couturières, and 15 child apprentices — all girls — labored in the workshop. Another 300 home-based pieceworkers, all of whom were women, were employed by Landauer. Men comprised only 7 percent of Landauer's employees. Smaller manufacturers organized their workers in ateliers. Gaston Portal, for example, employed 40 women in his shop south of the Placette, half of whom sewed on machines, and half of whom made garments by hand.[38]

Nîmes was deindustrialized in the second half of the nineteenth century. Even though two major industries and several smaller industries employed a few thousand workers in 1900, this was a considerably smaller proportion of the population than had once been engaged in manufacturing. Nîmes followed the Mediterranean pattern of deindustrialization and urbanization, in direct contrast to the stereotypical pattern of simultaneous urbanization and industrialization. "In the north and east," writes a historian of the region, "the connection between urbanization and industrialization is startling, it is very clear in the center and on the Atlantic. . . . But this connection . . . seems stripped of all sense on the Mediterranean. There towns and industries seem to be in complete dislocation." While the small towns of the region suffered from crises and consequent emigration, the large regional centers grew steadily in spite of the phylloxera crisis and industrial decline.[39] Transportation, commerce, and services employed many more people than industry in turn-of-the-century Nîmes.

Industry, commerce, and service were all organized on a relatively small scale. Because workers produced goods alone at home or in small workshops and were paid by the piece, Nîmes' industry bears little resemblance to the shoe factories of New England, or to the textile mills of northern France and the English-speaking world. Only the clerks in department stores and government institutions — city hall and the Prefecture — worked with more than a few others. Domestics usually worked alone in a private home. Railroad workers in repair shops and depots, however, worked in a large-scale setting. The level of technology used on the job in Nîmes was not advanced for its time. The typewriter had not yet transformed secretaries' and clerks' work. Machine production, so prevalent in industry elsewhere, was just being introduced in Nîmes. The exception, again, was transportation, for railroad technology was as sophisticated in the Midi as in northern France.

Nevertheless, the economy was a prosperous one at the turn of the century. Although the overproduction of wine caused price crises, these were never so disastrous for the winegrower or for commerce as the phylloxera epidemic. Moreover, the city of Nîmes offered highly differentiated job opportunities at the turn of the century. The woman with relatively few skills could find work as a servant, couturière, or laundress. More training or experience would enable her to work as a cook or garment specialist. For the man with little or no training, the city offered day labor and low-level railroad work. Training as a tailor or shoemaker could gain him entry into the city's industries. The literate worker could find white collar employment as a clerk in business or government. For the educated and wealthy, Nîmes offered opportunities in government, the liberal professions, and wholesale commerce. Yet the working population of Nîmes was differentiated by more criteria than gender, skill, education, and wealth. This was a city of two religions; how religion divided the physical, social, economic, and political space of Nîmes is crucial to understanding the city and its people.

A CITY OF TWO CULTURES

In a country where Protestants were rare, Nîmes was a center of Protestantism. Nearly one-quarter of Nimois counted themselves as Protestants in 1900. This was the largest proportion of Protestants of any city in prewar France, and the largest group in absolute numbers of any city outside Paris. Fed by bitter memories of war and persecution from the Counter-Reformation to the end of Louis XIV's reign, Protestants and Catholics were deeply divided in eighteenth- and nineteenth-century Nîmes. The city of the eighteenth century, the revolution, and the White Terror of 1815 was torn by religious strife. Groups formed along religious-political lines battled in the streets in 1830 and 1848.[40]

By 1870, the society of Nîmes was one of "two antagonistic clans." Mutual hostility declined in the ensuing thirty years as young people attended the same elementary and secondary schools and came into contact daily. By the end of the century, violence between Protestants and Catholics was limited to small-scale fights among young men, and to anti-clerical or anti-Protestant demonstrations. Protestants and Catholics lived in mutual dislike but ignored each other rather than rekindle the antagonisms of three centuries.[41] Moreover, the division of society into two parties applied primarily to the bourgeoisie: "Each having its habitual cafés, meeting places, closed family gatherings, favorite promenades . . . its particular *fournisseurs,* doctors, pharmacies, lawyers, notaries."[42] The middle and upper classes considered religion in its choice of the artisans or professionals it employed. Artisans, on the other hand, such as the devoutly Protestant Marcelin family, chose associates for their competence, not their religion. Workers did not inquire into each other's religion, and the poor took charity from either church. What difference did it make to Marc Bernard's mother, worn by poverty and backbreaking work, whether a gift of food came from a Protestant or a Catholic?[43]

Yet the presence of Protestantism in Nîmes "imprinted in the area a personality which was simultaneously religious, social and political."[44] Distinctions between Protestant and Catholic Nimois corresponded to every social distinction: place of residence, economic activities, and political affiliations. Protestants and Catholics may have had very different lifestyles:

> What relationships would there be between attachment to a religion and consumption patterns? In appearance, none. In reality this would be a misunderstanding of the economical mentality, the horror of waste and cult of saving of Protestant families. . . . One still does not differentiate between rich and poor, even if their buying power is dissimilar, the latter because of their miserable salaries, the former because they do not spend but consume and buy only what is strictly necessary.[45]

This assertion recalls Lucie Mazauric's description of her thrifty mother, who was the daughter of a Protestant manufacturer in the Cévennes. The Protestant Marcelins led austere lives. Monsieur Marcelin, for example, never smoked, spent time in cafés, played cards, or went to the theatre; to drink in excess was "unthinkable" in his household.[46]

Many clubs, most charitable organizations, and even a few unions were composed exclusively of Protestants or Catholics. Despite declining hostility, there was virtually no intermarriage at the turn of the century. The level of religious activity was high among Protestants and Catholics alike, since each feared losing members to the evangelical efforts of the other. Over 6000 men are reported to have received communion at Easter in the 1880s, suggesting that about one-third of the city's Catholics were active communicants — a very high proportion for an urban area. The completion of the Basilica of Saint Baudile near the Plan Vacher in 1882, and of Saint Luc's in 1912, confirms that the church sought to serve a practicing population. Aside from supporting numerous charities and orphanages, Catholic Nimois demonstrated their faith by making pilgrimages to local shrines and to Lourdes. Although they neither constructed new churches nor organized mass pilgrimages, Protestants in Nîmes were also active. The lay community provided personnel, as well as money, for numerous charity works. Moreover, the strength of the Protestant community, which partly lay in its minority status, fostered helping networks between wealthy and poor Protestants.[47]

Neighborhoods were more segregated by religion in 1900 than before. Protestants had shifted from the old city and bourgades to the west side to dominate the quartier de la Fontaine and the Placette, which became the heart of the Protestant community. In 1855, 45 percent of Canton I — the Fontaine, Placette, and areas south of the Placette — was Protestant, as compared to only 16 percent of the city's other cantons. Protestants in Cantons II and III lived on the west edge of those areas in 1876, in the western part of the bourgades, old city, and the quartier de la Prefecture. By the turn of the century, most Protestants — 70 percent — lived west of a line shown on Map 3.1 that runs from the Roman arena to the regional prison.[48] Thus the two Christian communities of the city were oriented toward their cemeteries: the Protestant cemetery on the road leaving town to the northwest and the Protestant Cévennes, and the Catholic cemetery on the road to Catholic Avignon, Provence, and Italy.

Protestant neighborhoods were segregated by class. The Placette housed the poorest families, such as the Pouzergues from Le Vigan — the father and son on the west edge, the young Pouzergue widow and her laborer son in the crowded center. This district, "geographic center of Nimois protestantism, was *the* Protestant working class neighborhood."[49] The surrounding areas housed the petit bourgeoisie and middle class — south of La Fontaine and west of the Prefecture.

The upper middle class and wealthy elite Protestants lived in the heart of La Fontaine, along the city's boulevards, and around the Avenue Feuchères. The eighteen members of the board of directors of the Orpehlinat Coste, the Protestant orphanage, exemplify the Protestant elite, whose addresses reflected their status. Most were retired merchants, industrialists, rentiers, property owners, and pastors. They lived in the Fontaine (six), along the boulevards (five), around the Avenue Feuchères (four), and in the middle-class part of the Prefecture. Only Paul Marcelin's remarkable father, a lampmaker aged 69, did not live at a prestigious address.[50]

The position of Protestants in the economy of Nîmes indicates that they were more powerful than their minority status implies.

Indeed, it was more the economic and social power of the Protestant community than its religious beliefs which threatened Catholics. Protestants dominated the bourgeoisie of Nîmes, primarily because they were usually more active in the economy than were the wealthy Catholic rentiers. Prosperous members of the reformed church were the city's important industrialists and merchants; the same men controlled the banks of the region at the opening of the twentieth century.

Even Protestants and Catholics who were not wealthy often seem to have worked at different kinds of jobs. Analysis of occupations confirms contemporary observations of the *"aisance relative"* of Protestants and their tendency to rank among *"les petits gens, mais non parmi les prolétaires."* This analysis appears in Table 3.2. Catholics were more likely to be industrial workers and artisans. Protestants were more often engaged in commerce, especially as clerks, and were less likely than Catholics to be manual laborers.[51]

Residential and occupational grouping by religion continued to be reinforced by political affiliation at the turn of the century, although both the Protestant liberal tradition and the Catholic royalist tradition had been attenuated. The wealthiest of the reformed faith were less willing to support socialism and turned from the liberal camp as early as 1849. Some supported the "Non-Collectivist Socialist" ticket in 1906. Camille Giraud ran for deputy on this ticket. More important to the city's electoral races, Catholic workers in Nîmes were progressively less willing to provide block support for royalists and other conservatives after 1870. By the end of the century, Radical Socialist Dr. Gaston Crouzet was the town's mayor, and Socialist François Fournier its representative in the national Chamber of Deputies. There were clearly too few Protestants in Nîmes to elect the mayor and deputy without other support. The role of migrants in this political evolution is unclear, for the political beliefs of only three are known. (One is the Protestant Giraud. The other two were Catholic railroad workers from Langogne who, according to personnel records, were rumored to be reactionaries.) It is likely that PLM employees provided the bulk, if not the leadership, for Nîmes' non-Protestant, working-class left, for they were the best organized group of laborers in the city. Deputy Fournier himself was a railroad mechanic from the Gard who had worked for the Socialist party in Paris and Provence. With the information available, it is difficult to disentangle the role of cheminots or migrants, so thoroughly were politics confounded with religious culture.[52]

TABLE 3.2 Protestants in the Economy of Nîmes, 1870-1905

Economic Sector	*Professional Category*	*Protestants category*	*Protestants sector*	*Total Nimois sector*
Agriculture	working landowners	6.8%	7.9%	11.%
	agricultural workers	1.1		
Industry and artisanal production	industrialists and engineers	1.6		
	workers	20.	35.5	51.
	artisans and masters	13.9		
Commerce and transport	merchants	5.8		
	retail sellers	9.2	36.	20.
	commercial employees	21.		
Liberal professionals and functionaries	liberal professionals	3.8		
	functionaries and municipal employees	6.7	10.5	9.5
Rentiers and property owners		9.	9.	8.
Total*		98.9%	98.9%	99.5%

*Missing data account for totals less than 100 percent.

SOURCE: Jean-Daniel Roque, "Nouveaux aperçus sur l'Eglise Protestante de Nîmes dans la seconde moitié du XIXe siècle," *Bulletin de la Société de l'Histoire de Protestantisme* 70 (1974), 69.

Election results from the turn of the century show the Catholic neighborhoods as the most conservative and Protestant neighborhoods as most liberal. For example, in the run-off legislative election of May 1906, the Socialist Fournier faced the Nationalist candidate, Joseph Ménard. Fournier carried the Protestant Fontaine and Placette, with 70 percent of the vote. The majority of voters on the west side of the bourgades, the southwest section and west side of the old city — all relatively Protestant — supported Fournier. In the conservative Croix de Fer and Enclos Rey (a small, traditionally royalist section of the eastern bourgades), where Protestants were most scarce, Fournier commanded only 16 percent of the vote. Elsewhere in the city, about one-third of the voters supported Fournier. He won by a slender margin. The newspaper account of post-election events reflects the neighborhood political affiliations: A celebratory throng of thousands united with the Republican band on the Boulevard Victor Hugo to the west. The unhappy supporters of the defeated Ménard gathered on the Boulevard Amiral Courbet to the southeast. As the celebrants made a tour of the boulevards, they passed under the windows of Ménard's headquarters near the Esplanade. The "aristocrats" emerged on the balcony to hoot and whistle at the visitors. Soon fighting broke out on the Esplanade, and the Republican parade drove the Ménard supporters back to the Boulevard Amiral Courbet with name-calling, rocks, and fists. *Le Petit Midi* described Fournier's victory as *"le triomphe de la Placette."*[53] Thus, neighborhood religion and political persuasion continued to overlap in Nîmes throughout the *belle époque.* The following ditty about the Bourbon pretender to the throne remained the "hymn of the Enclos Rey":[54]

Si Henry V vienne demain
Ah, quelle fête
Ah, quelle fête
Si Henri V vienne demain
. . .
Ah, quelle fête
Mes enfants!

Religion was a basis for group identity in Nîmes, as certain neighborhoods, occupations, and political leanings, if not lifestyles, were associated with Protestants or Catholics. Perhaps the neighbors of the Protestant Pouzergue family in the Placette and the Catholic Roches in the Plan Vacher shared working-class status, but their occupations were quite different, as perhaps their ambitions and political loyalties were, too.

The importance of Protestants in the population of Nîmes had declined in the nineteenth century, down from 30 percent in 1800 to 23 percent in 1900. Many thought this had happened because the Protestants had fewer children than the Catholics, but no evidence supports this idea. Rather, an influx of Catholic migrants from Nîmes' hinterland had decreased the proportion of Protestants in the city; the migrants who pushed the population of Nîmes from 60,000 to 80,000 in the last twenty years of the century included relatively few Protestants. Old migration streams like the one between Le Vigan and Nîmes were replaced by increased migration from the Catholic Lozère. One indication of this trend is the proportion of migrants born outside the Gard. With the exception of migrants from the Protestant Cévennes along the southern border of the Lozère, most migrants in Nîmes from outside the Gard were Catholic. Only 11 percent of the electors to the consistory were born outside the Gard, while 22 percent of the people in Nîmes in 1876 and in 1906 were migrants from beyond this area.[55] Thus, recent migrants were likely to be Catholic. Protestant migrants in Nîmes traveled long-established paths between their home town and the city, while Catholics may have come through more recently established channels.

In this city, divided by class, occupation, and religion, neighborhood characteristics differed on all three counts. Given the parentage of the migrants from Le Vigan, Villefort, and Langogne, and the fact that some Viganais were Protestants, we might expect that the Lozerians lived in the crowded old city and in the Catholic Croix de Fer, and the Viganais in the Protestant Placette and the exclusive Fontaine and Préfecture neighborhoods.

RESIDENCE

In fact, the Viganais were dispersed throughout Nîmes. The majority lived to the east of the neighborhoods where Protestants concentrated, although a sizable proportion resided on the Protestant west side. Some Viganais resided in all four working-class neighborhoods: the Protestant Placette, the old bourgades north of the city, the north edge of the old city, and the proletarian Plan Vacher. Viganais were also scattered in the old city and the bourgeois sections around the Quai de la Fontaine and the Prefecture. Several families lived on the city's wide boulevards and most impressive streets: the Quai de la Fontaine, Boulevard Victor Hugo, Boulevard Amiral Courbet, and the Avenue Feuchères. Map 3.2 illustrates that the Viganais were a group geographically integrated in Nîmes.[56] (In order to clarify residence patterns, maps distinguish the residences of household heads or spouses from those of dependents and servants.) Household heads and spouses from Le Vigan account for most of the Viganais living in Protestant and bourgeois neighborhoods and on the grand avenues. Most servants from Le Vigan lived in the old city, while dependents (children, in-laws, and other relatives) were concentrated in the northern working-class area.

The Villefort group was less widely scattered than the Viganais (Map 3.3). Some resided in Protestant neighborhoods, while the rest were either in the commercial area on the north edge of the old city or in the blue collar Plan Vacher to the northeast. Few lived in the old

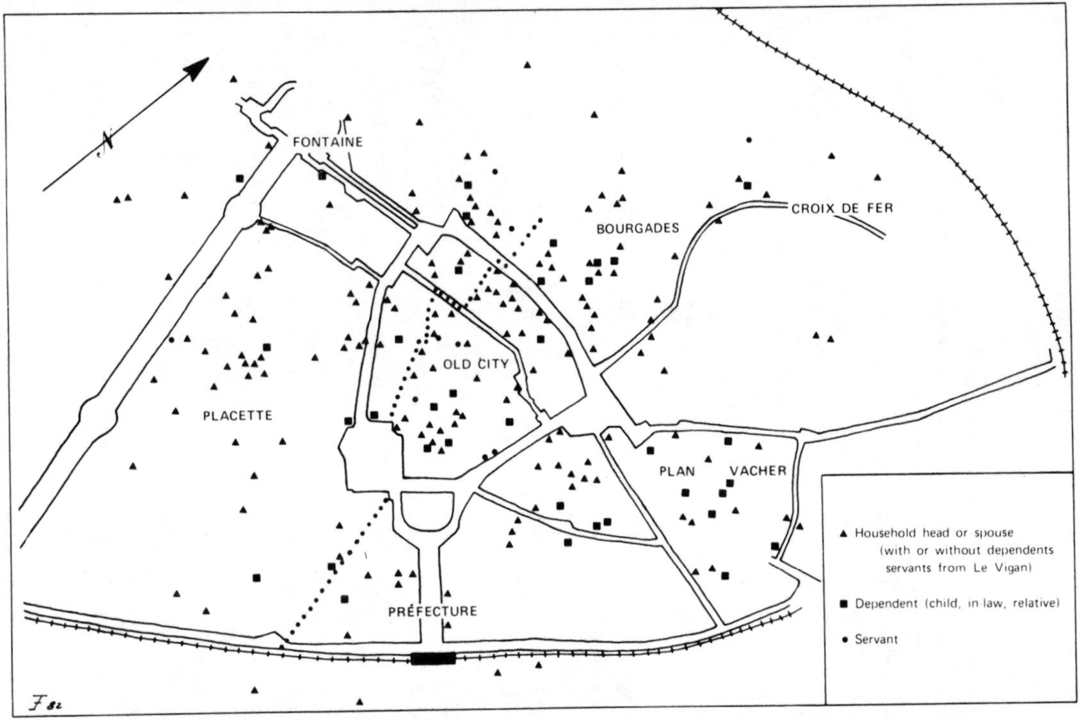

Map 3.2: Viganais in Nîmes, 1906

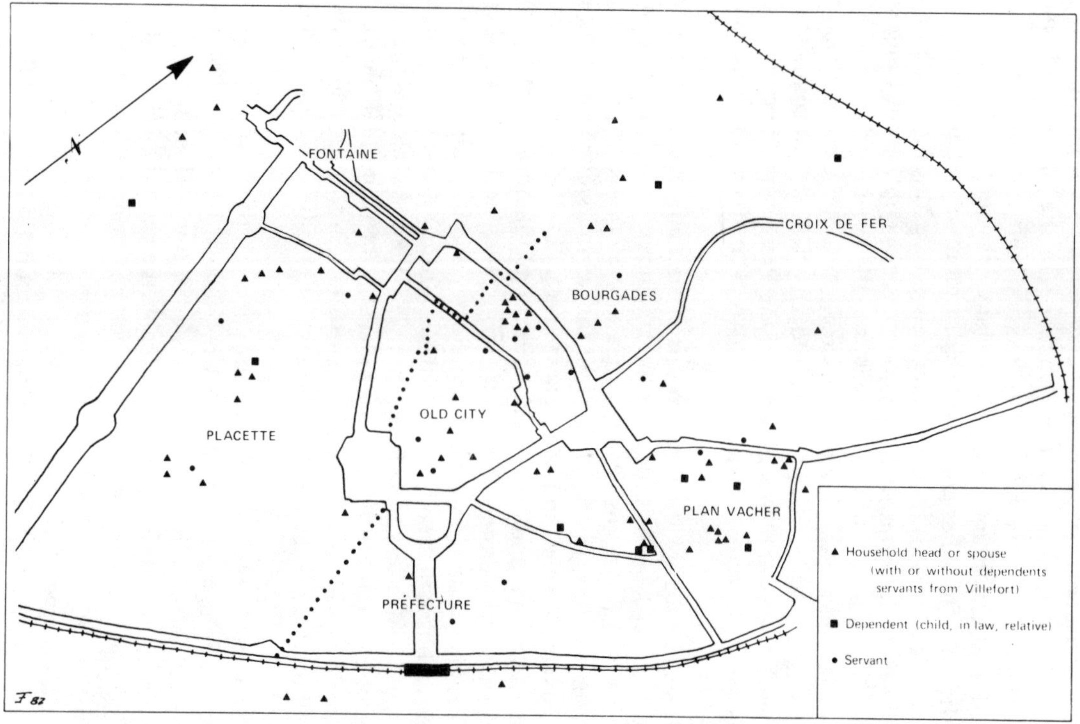

Map 3.3: Villefortais in Nîmes, 1906

city, in bourgeois neighborhoods, or along the prestigious wide avenues. Household heads outnumbered servants considerably in the bourgades, Placette, and Plan Vacher. On the other hand, most Villefortais residing in the middle-class and bourgeois areas of the city were domestic servants, such as the Janvier sisters.

Migrants from Langogne showed a more segregated pattern of geographic clustering than the other groups (see Map 3.4). Although a few lived in the Protestant neighborhoods, people from Langogne primarily resided in the old bourgades to the north, and in two of the poorest areas of town: the narrow streets east of the market, and the Plan Vacher. A few lived in the old city. Those Langognais who resided in the most bourgeois areas of the Prefecture and commercial areas were servants, such as the two who lived on the Avenue Feuchères.

It seems that for the three groups of migrants, rents and employment were at least as crucial in influencing residence as religion or friendship. Life on the grand boulevards was most expensive, and only the wealthy, the hoteliers, and the servants lived on them: the dentists, the jeweler, and a court lawyer from Le Vigan, the domestics from Langogne, and a hotelier's wife from Villefort. Working-class members of the groups lived in the bourgades north of the old city: workers in the shoe and garment industry and day laborers from Le Vigan, white collar and service workers from Villefort, and laborers and service workers from Langogne. The Plan Vacher and the north edge of the old city housed a similar mix of white and blue collar workers, as well as the occasional artisan. On the other hand, high-level bureaucrats, lawyers, and their servants lived near the Prefecture.[57]

Servants' residence was determined by their employers' residence, although they could seek work in a particular neighborhood. Railroad workers lived on the east side of town, close to the freight station and the car repair depot. Finally, the central market attracted food wholesalers and retailers. A butcher from Le Vigan, a baker from Villefort, two grocers, a food merchant, and two café operators from Langogne all lived close to the market. For servants, railroad workers, and food merchants, then, occupation was closely linked with residence.

Protestant religious affiliation seems to have influenced, but not determined, residential patterns. Of 25 families from Le Vigan pos-

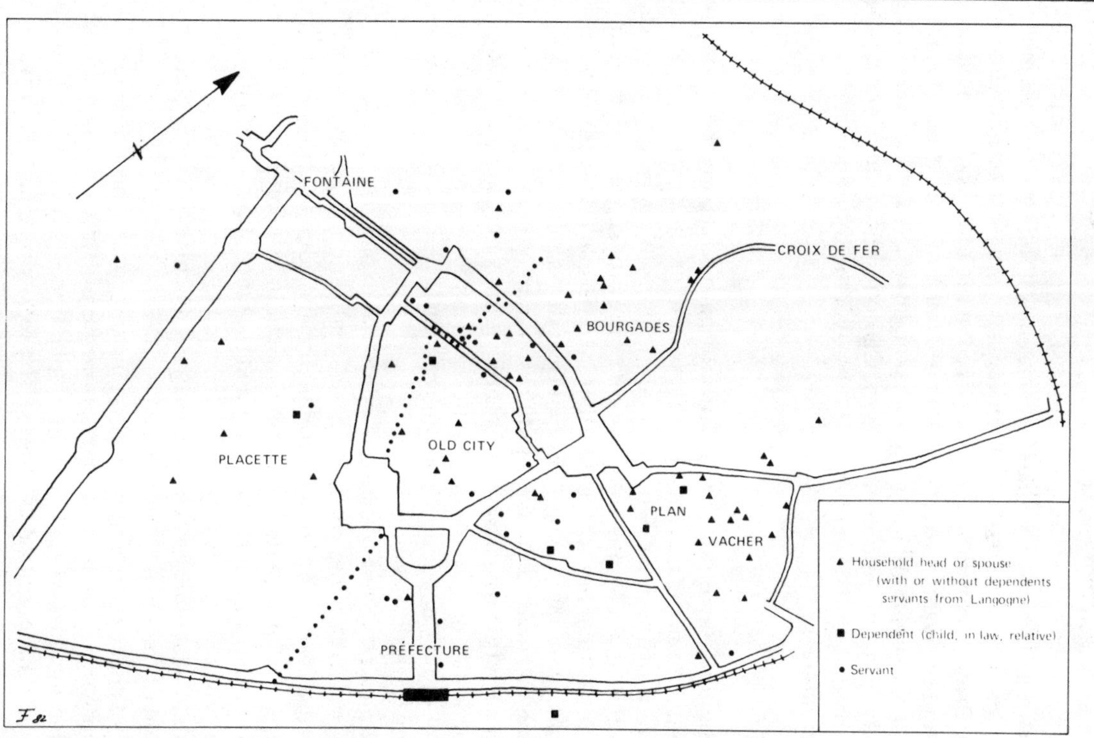

Map 3.4: Langoganais in Nîmes, 1906

itively identified as Protestant, only 15 lived in the area where most Protestants lived.[58] Five were in the Prefecture neighborhood, and five more in the old city, Plan Vacher, and on the southern periphery of Nîmes. Those in the Prefecture were lawyers, with one bureaucrat. Many Protestant railroad workers lived in the Plan Vacher, including one from Le Vigan. When the father of Paul Marcelin, a deacon of the church, was apprenticed to a lampmaker, he worked in the heart of the old city — ironically at the site of Catholic martyrdom during the Reformation — and eventually he took over the shop and spent his life at that address.[59]

Migrants were not segregated into particular neighborhoods or separated from the native-born Nimois; rather, they represented over one-third of the men, women, and children in every quartier. The economic and religious composition of the city suggests that distinctions other than birthplace differentiated people in the city. The residential, economic, social, and political distinctions associated with religion in Nîmes enhance an understanding of the migrants' role in urban society. Protestant and Catholic groups may have offered particular kinds of opportunities and information to newcomers and, devout or not, migrants were implicitly attached to the city's Protestant or Catholic subculture.

Nîmes grew, not because of industrial expansion, but *in spite of* industrial crises and virtual deindustrialization. The vitality of its service sector increased with commerce and administrative business. This particular economic pattern was not unusual in France, for the proliferation of the tertiary sector and the stagnation of industry — or the survival of an industry based on home labor, the small workshop, and small machinery, such as the sewing machine — were common at the end of the nineteenth century.

The changes in Nîmes' geography and society described here — the growth of the neighborhoods on the outskirts of town and the relative increase of the Catholic population — were a direct consequence of in-migration to Nîmes. The following chapters turn to the demographic and familial underpinnings of the migrant community. Whether migrants were young bachelors or parents whose large families replicated rurals' tendency to have many children, their demographic behavior affected urban society and was a fundamental indicator of their place in it. Two questions are central: What was the role of the migrant in the urban family? In addition, where did the groups from Le Vigan, Villefort, and Langogne fit in? In demographic and familial terms, where did these migration streams lead?

NOTES

1. Louis Roumieux, "Lou Maset," in Georges Martin, *Nîmes à la Belle Epoque* (Brussels: Editions Libro-Sciences, 1974), 147.

2. Emile Boutin, "La propriété batie," *Journal de la Société de Statistique de Paris* 32 (1891), 228, 235; L. C. Igolen, "La garrigue et les masets nimois," *Mémoires de l'Académie de Nîmes* ser. 7, 49 (1931-1932), 62, 29; Paul Marcelin, *Souvenirs d'un passé artisanal* (Nîmes: Chastanier, 1967), 32; l'Abbé Achille Sarran, *Les masets nimois* (Nîmes: Imprimerie Générale, 1898), 25, 69.

3. Marc Bernard, *Salut, Camarades* (Paris: Gallimard, 1955), 78; Marcelin, *Souvenirs,* 30-31; Henri Reboul, *L'industrie nîmoise du tissage au XIXe siècle* (Montpellier: Fermin et Montane, 1914), 103, 112; Sarran, *Masets,* 11.

4. Marcelin, *Souvenirs,* 31-32; Sarran, *Masets,* 9.

5. Marcelin, *Souvenirs,* 31-32.

6. Bernard, *Salut, Camarades,* 104, 105, 238; Armand Cosson, "Industrie de la soie et population ouvrière à Nîmes de 1815 à 1848," in G. Cholvy, ed., *Economie et société en Languedoc-Roussillon de 1789 à nos jours* (Montpellier: Université Paul Valéry, 1978), 201; Catherine Martinez, "Commerce et le marché de détail dans une ville moyenne et ses environs. Nîmes," (Thèse de 3e cycle, Université Paul Valéry, 1974), 34; Reboul, *L'industrie nîmoise,* 111-112; Louis Villermé, *Tableau de l'état physique et moral des ouvriers employés dans les manufactures de coton, de laine et de soie* (Paris: Renouard, 1840), 188.

7. Raymond Dugrand, *Villes et campagnes en Bas-Languedoc* (Paris: Presses Universitaires Françaises, 1963), 84.

8. Ibid., 83, 352.

9. Bernard, *Salut, Camarades,* 8; Marcelin, *Souvenirs,* 35; Un Vieux Nimois, "La rue de Nîmes en 1900," *La revue économique de la Chambre de Commerce de Nîmes-Uzès-Le Vigan* 6, no. 50 (1955), 28.

10. Interview, Marc Bernard, Paris, February 10, 1977; *Le Petit Républicain du Midi* (hereafter PR) August 26, 1901.

11. Archives Départementales du Gard (hereafter ADG), series 6M, 4788: Dossiers d'Associations déclarées; PR, 1906, passim; *Guide du Gard* (1912), 128-131.

12. Lucie Mazauric Chamson, "*Belle Rose, Ô Tour Magne*" (Paris: Plon, 1969), 42.

13. *Annuaire du Gard* (1889), 124; Chamson, "*Belle Rose,*" 88-89; Martin, *Nîmes,* 64, 76; Martinez, "Commerce et marché de détail," 182.

14. *Pareils à des enfants* (Paris: Gallimard, 1941), 42.

15. Sample from census shows highest percentage of servants and bourgeois in parts of the old city. Figures for growth are based on comparisons of the urban population by section for 1856 and 1906: ADG, series 10M, 260-262, 1906 census, Nîmes; Ernest Liotard and Charles Liotard, *Annuaire du département du Gard pour l'année 1861* (Nîmes: Clavel-Ballivet, 1861), 838-839. Baumès and Vincens, *Nîmes*, cited in Reboul, *L'industrie nîmoise*, 103; Marcelin, *Souvenirs*, 10-11; Thomas Picard, *Nîmes autrefois, Nîmes aujourd'hui* (Nîmes: Gervais-Bedot, 1901), 156-157; Louis Trial, "Un ennemi de la famille: le logement insalubre," *Revue du Midi* 28 (1900), 947-948.

16. ADG, series 14M 534, Police reports of waiters' strike, 1907; *Le Petit Midi*, May 22, 1906; Bernard, *Salut, Camarades*, 16.

17. Martin, *Nîmes*, 17-19, 74-93; Jean-Paul Volle, "La croissance urbaine de Nîmes," *Bulletin de la Société Languedocienne de Géographie*, ser. 3, 2 (1968), 345-364.

18. Antoine Bigot, *Li bourgadieiro; poesies patoises* (Nîmes: n.p., 1881); Marcelin, *Souvenirs*, 18; Martinez, "Commerce et marché de détail," 34, 181.

19. The Placette grew by 18 percent, the city by 52 percent. Marcelin, *Souvenirs*, 9-10; Reboul, *L'industrie nîmoise*, 101, 102.

20. *Bulletin Municipal* (1906), 220.

21. Trial, "Le logement insalubre," 949-950.

22. The population of the Croix de Fer increased by 82 percent. *Bulletin Municipal* (1906), 220; Ibid. (1907), 162; Ibid. (1908), 214-215; Martin, *Nîmes*, 103; Néaber et cie, eds., *Dictionnaire biographique du Gard* (Paris: Flammarion, 1905), 196; Picard, *Nîmes autrefois*, 171.

23. *Bulletin Municipal* (1907), 162-163; Vidal, "Croissance urbaine," 10.

24. *Bulletin Municipal* (1904), 137; Martin, *Nîmes*, 11-13, 104-106; Henri Mazel, "Nîmes en 1880," *Mémoires de l'Académie de Nîmes*, ser. 7, 52 (1939-1940), 153; Néaber, *Dictionnaire*, 196; Picard, *Nîmes autrefois*, 175-176; Vidal, "Croissance urbaine," 10.

25. Picard, *Nîmes autrefois*, 174-175; Herbert Rouger, "Le vie à Nîmes à la fin du siècle dernier," *La revue économique de la Chambre de Commerce de Nîmes-Uzès-Le Vigan* 7, no. 61 (1956), 14.

26. Cosson, "Industrie de la soie"; Dugrand, *Villes et Campagnes*, 372-391; Léon Dutil, *L'état économique du Languedoc à la fin de l'ancien régime, 1750-1789* (Paris: Hachette, 1911), 453, 461-462; Hector Rivoire, *Statistique du département du Gard*, Vol. 2 (Nîmes: Ballivet et Fabre, 1842), 28-29; Hector Rivoire, "Notice sur l'industrie de la ville de Nîmes," *Mémoires de l'Académie du Gard* (1853), 281, 285; Reboul, *L'industrie nîmoise*, 41.

27. Armand Audiganne, *Les populations ouvrières et les industries de la France*, Vol. 2 (New York: Burt Franklin, 1970), 135; Ministre de l' Agriculture et du Commerce, *Statistique de la France*, Vol. 2: *Industrie* (Paris: Imprimerie Nationale, 1848), 72-73; Reboul, *L'industrie nîmoise*, 66, 76-77; Rivoire, *Statistique*, 28-29; Max Sorre, "La répartition des populations dans le Bas-Languedoc," *Bulletin de la Société Languedocienne de Géographie*, ser. 1, 29 (1906), 129; Syndicat de la Bonneterie, "Origine de la Bonneterie Gardoise," *La revue économique de la Chambre de Commerce de Nîmes-Uzès-Le Vigan* 3, no. 25 (1952), 2.

28. Loss to competition and the reasons for it are constant themes in the reports to the Prefect from the president of Nîmes' Chamber of Commerce, ADG, series 14M, 263, 469, 371, Situation industrielle et commerciale, reports of 1870, 1880, 1889, 1891; Fernand Benoît-Germain, "Commerce et industrie," in Association française pour l'avancement des sciences, ed., *Nîmes et le Gard,* Vol. 2 (Nîmes: Imprimerie Cooperative, 1912), 323-329; Reboul, *L'industrie nîmoise,* 76-77; Rivoire, "L'industrie," 281.

29. Cosson, "Industrie de la soie," 102; Marcelin, *Souvenirs,* 9, 30-31; Rivoire, "L'industrie," 292-293, 287, 296.

30. A. Billange, *Aigues-Vives: Mon village depuis 150 ans* (Paris: Ministère de l'agriculture, 1948), 61; Sorre, "La répartition des populations," 114-118. For post-phylloxera developments, see Rémy Pech, *Enterprise viticole et capitalisme en Languedoc-Roussillon (du phylloxera aux crises de mévent)* (Toulouse: Université de Toulouse-Le Mirail, 1975).

31. Yves Lequin, *Les ouvriers de la région lyonnaise,* Vol. 1 (Lyon: Presses Universitaires de Lyon, 1977), 204.

32. René Brossard, "Les chemins de fer dans le Gard, leurs origines, leur développement," in Association Française pour l'Avancement des Sciences, ed., *Nîmes et le Gard,* 391, 400, 407; Dugrand, *Villes et campagnes,* 419-423.

33. Estimate of employees is from the census sample; the 5 percent sample showed 102 rail employees.

34. ADG, series 10M, 275, Census of civil servants, 1905; *Bulletin Municipal* (1908), 301-303.

35. ADG, series 10M, 260-262, Census of Nîmes, 1906; *Annuaire du Gard* (1880), 486-487; Ibid. (1892), 93-96, 131; Alice Fermaud, "La lycée de jeunes filles de Nîmes," *La revue économique de la Chambre de Commerce de Nîmes-Uzès-Le Vigan* 4, no. 35 (1953), 15-16; *Guide du Gard* (1907), 196-204; Picard, *Nîmes autrefois,* 165-168; J. Reboul and E. Auquier, *Hôtel-Dieu actuel et nouvel hopital à Nîmes* (Nîmes: Gustave Gory, 1901), 24-25.

36. Eugene Benoit, *Association des Employés de Commerce et de l'Industrie de la ville de Nîmes* (Nîmes: La Laboreuse, 1907); *Bulletin Municipal* (1907), 249-250. Reports of the Sunday closing demonstration appear in PR, August and September, 1901; ADG 6M 1224 and 1622, Police reports and demonstration posters; Archives municipales de Nîmes, F7 54, Unions.

37. ADG, series 14M, 534, Strike reports: shoemakers, 1904 and 1906; Benoît-Germain, "Commerce et Industrie," 333-334; Etienne Thérond, "L'industrie nimoise de la chaussure, ses fabrications, ses specialités, ses possibilités," *La revue économique de la Chambre de Commerce de Nîmes-Uzès-Le Vigan* 3, no. 25 (1952), 7.

38. ADG, series 14M, 445, Strike report: Léopold Landauer, 1900; 534, Strike report: Gaston Portal, 1904.

39. Dugrand, *Villes et campagnes* 1, 460.

40. James Hood, "Patterns of popular protest in the French Revolution: the conceptual contribution of the Gard," *Journal of Modern History* 48 (1976), 259-293; Gwynn Lewis, *The Second Vendée* (New York: Oxford University Press, 1978); Leo Loubère, *Radicalism in Mediterranean France: its rise and decline, 1848-1914* (Albany: SUNY Press, 1974), 56 and passim; Jean-Daniel Roque, "Nouveaux aperçus

sur l'église protestante de Nîmes dans la seconde moitié du XIXe siècle," *Bulletin de la Société de l'Histoire du Protestantisme* 120 (1974), 54-63. I am indebted to Mr. Roque's fine work on the Protestant community in Nîmes.

41. ADG, Series 6M, 1224, Police reports of anti-Protestant and anti-clerical meetings and demonstrations; Marcelin, *Souvenirs,* 35-37; Jean-Daniel Roque, "L'église nationale protestante de Nîmes de 1870 à la veille de la séparation des Eglises et de l'Etat" (Mémoire de Maîtrise, Université Paul Valéry, 1969), 176; Herbert Rouger, "Nîmes en 1870; la ville, sa population, sa vie économique," *La revue économique de la Chambre de Commerce de Nîmes-Uzès-Le Vigan* 4, no. 31 (1953), 14; Rouger, "La vie à Nîmes," 14.

42. Ibid.

43. Marcelin, *Souvenirs,* 24; Marc Bernard, *Pareils à des enfants* (Paris: Gallimard, 1941), 138-141.

44. Gilberte Jouverte and Janine Dumas, "La vie religieuse dans le diocèse de Nîmes sous l'épiscopat de Mgr. Besson, 1875-1888" (Mémoire de Maîtrise, Université Paul Valéry, 1972), 160, 168.

45. "Commerce et le marché de detail," 117.

46. Chamson, "*Belle Rose,*" passim; Marcelin, *Souvenirs,* 36.

47. ADG, series 6M, 1224, Railroad police reports of movements of pilgrims. For example, 729 pilgrims from the arrondissements of Nîmes and Alès traveled to Lourdes on July 23, 1902. L'Abbé Etienne Goiffron, *Les hôpitaux et les oeuvres charitables à Nîmes* (Nîmes: Jouve, 1876); Jouverte and Dumas, "La vie religieuse," 82-84, 125, 160-167; Dr. Vauriot, "Assistance publique et privé," in Association française pour l'avancement des sciences, ed., *Nîmes et le Gard,* 520-556.

48. Census figures of 1876 published by confession and census section, *Guide du Gard* (1880), 815; Roque, "Nouveaux aperçus," 63-65.

49. Ibid., 66.

50. ADG, series 6M, 4788, Membership list, Conseil d'Administration de l'Orphelinat Coste.

51. Quotes from Pasteur Babut in 1871 report to the Protestant Consistory (Archives du Consistoire de Nîmes, series B, 91, 98, 151) and Pierre Lestrigent, *Visage de protestantisme français,* 42; both cited in Roque, "Nouveaux aperçus," 55, 70. The information available to Roque for his analysis of Protestants' place in the economy of Nîmes is imperfect; it does not include women and favors wealthy Protestants. Nevertheless, Roque works with extreme care, and the results are unambiguous, as Table 3.2 shows; Ibid., 68-70.

52. ADG, series 5s 7, Chemin-de-fer, personnel, 1886-1896; series 5s 8, Chemin-de-fer, personnel, 1897-1904; Loubère, *Radicalism,* 57, 136-138, 199; Jean-Daniel Roque, "Positions et tendances politiques des Protestants nimois au XIXe siècle," in *Droite et Gauche en Languedoc-Roussillon* (Montpeller, 1975), 231-232; PR, March 8-9 and April 28, 1906.

53. ADG, series 2M, 292, Election results by urban section; *Le Petit Midi,* May 27, 1906.

54. Bernard, *Camarades,* 238; André Siegfried, "Le groupe Protestant cévénol sous la IIIe République," in M. Boegner, ed., *Le Protestantisme français* (Paris: Plon, 1945), 33.

55. Roque, "Nouveaux aperçus," 54, 55, 57; Siegfried, "Protestant cévenol," 33-34.

56. Maps 3.2-3.4 show the residences of each migrant group in 1906. They were plotted by the placement of address (as listed in the census) on the cadastral maps of Nîmes. Some locations on the periphery of town (west of the Cadereau, north of the rue Bonfa, east of Rue Sully, and south of the boulevard Sergent Triaire) have been approximated because street numbers were lacking in the 1906 maps or because the tax map was unavailable.

57. These conclusions are based on calculations of the occupations of migrants from Le Vigan, Villefort, and Langogne in the northern working-class section, section five (Plan Vacher), the southern section, and on the boulevards.

58. The family names and professions of the Viganais suggest that many more than 25 families were Protestant. Certain identification of the 25 families was established by the census of Protestant electors (taken in 1900 and updated in 1904 and 1906), in the Archives du Consistoire de Nîmes, series C53, and the list of donors to the annual collection for the Protestant poor; "Collecte annuelle pour les pauvres," *Bulletin de l'Eglise Reformeée de Nîmes* 18 (1905), 1-11.

59. Marcelin, *Souvenirs,* 10.

4

Migrants and the Urban Population

Youth, Marriage, and Family

> A cousin fell from the sky; the daughter of one of my mother's sisters who came to town.
>
> — Marc Bernard
> *Pareils à des enfants*

Anna Sabatier came to Nîmes from Langogne to work as a domestic. There she met and married a tramway employee from a peasant family in the Ardèche; they had two sons. In a few years Anna's father came to Nîmes to live with his daughter and her young family. They resided on the narrow Rue de la Ferrage in the old city, where Anna operated a grocery behind the central market. Anna's younger sisters also moved to Nîmes to work as servants. Like Anna Sabatier, Emile Brun moved when he was single. At the age of 24 he left Villefort to work for the railroad in Nîmes. He subsequently married the daughter of a fellow worker from Nîmes. His wife died within a few years, and Brun moved in with his aunt and uncle until his second marriage at the age of 33.[1]

The life patterns of Anna Sabatier and Emile Brun share a singular characteristic. When they first arrived in the city, both numbered among those who lived outside of families — the single domestic servant, and the young worker in a rented room. Yet both Anna Sabatier and Emile Brun married, remained in Nîmes, and formed their own families; both stayed on rather than returning to their hometowns. Their initial, relatively marginal living situations were adjustments to their migration as single young people. If the life patterns of Anna Sabatier and Emile Brun were typical of migrants in

Nîmes, only their first few years in the city distinguished them from native-born Nimois in familial terms.

Historically, single migrants, such as the young apprentices and servants who perished in old regime hospitals, have been most marginal to urban society and most susceptible to disease and misfortune, partly because they were alone. Their single status has been associated with the "breakdown" resulting from migration to the city. The unattached migrant was perceived as the most dangerous, vulnerable, or unprincipled. For example, Louis Chevalier emphasizes the single status of the young migrant men in Paris before 1850 in his account of the city's dangerous classes. The *"misère sexuelle"* of single men was associated with the growth of prostitution, itself a predator on poor single women from the countryside. The Nimois shared the perception that single migrants were not the most savory of characters. The head of the municipal employment agency, whose responsibility was young migrants looking for servant jobs, for example, suggestively described his clientele as "girls from eighteen to twenty-five who seem used to all the dangers inherent in their nature and in their profession."[2] Migrants' single status, then, was central both to their role in urban society and to the way they were perceived by others.

Some historical demographers have suggested that young single migrants may have played a key role in depressing fertility and raising mortality. One explanation for low urban fertility hinges on observations that many migrant women were unmarried servants who contributed to low urban nuptiality. The tendency of cities to have more deaths than births — natural decrease — may have hinged on the fact that migrants were disproportionately single and childless. Migrants did not rescue the city from demographic decline by infusing urban areas with reproductive young people, the argument continues; rather, migrants may have reduced the demographic viability of the city because they were less likely to marry and, as a consequence, less likely to have children to compensate for deaths in their own group.[3] This model of urban migration provides the demographic underpinnings of the "breakdown" interpretation of migration to the city, for it bases the city's lack of demographic vitality on the behavior of migrants. The demographic behavior attributed to migrants by the urban migration model, based on their low nuptiality, is essentially the complement to the anti-social and criminal behavior attributed to them.

A number of observations about the single state of European migrants do indeed conform with the urban migration model. Young men often pioneered migration streams, and men and women migrated separately. The men, like the Auvergnat masons in Paris and the Cevenol miners in the coal fields of the Gard, served as laborers, and the women were concentrated in domestic service. Moreover, traditions of circular migration often meant that migrants were only temporary urban residents, even if they returned to the city year after year. The view of migrants as a disfavored urban group in terms of marriage, reproduction, and survival fits with many observations by French historians. The hospital records of the old regime are an important source of information about population movements, and the hospitals were filled with poor, ill, and dying migrants.[4]

Nevertheless, there are reasons to be cautious about this view of migrants' demographic behavior, particularly for migrants in the city at the end of the nineteenth century. Although single males often initiated migration streams, married men and their families subsequently settled in the city. When textile mills offered employment to children and adolescents, families moved together to textile towns. Also, servant women did not always remain single or return home. Indeed, after 1850 migrants became increasingly likely to remain in the city. Finally, the studies concluding that migrants were single were based primarily on data aggregated at the city level which do not distinguish between migrants and natives. Hence, the demographic behavior of migrants is inferred from their status as servants, young journeymen, and soldiers.[5] Because this model rests on differential demographic behavior, it can be tested by an explicit comparison of natives and migrants.

The life patterns of the Nimois illustrated in Figures 4.1 and 4.2 suggest that Anna Sabatier and Emile Brun lived typical lives, because the differences between them and native-born Nimois diminished with age. The male life patterns are summarized in Figure 4.1. As young men (aged 17-29), most native-born Nimois males lived with their parents. They usually spent their middle years (age 30-59) as household heads. After the age of 60, many lived with their grown children. Throughout their lives, then, native men consistently lived with kin: first parents, then their own wives and children — or siblings, in a few cases — and later with their grown children. They were part of a nuclear family throughout their lifetimes. Migrant males, on the other hand, had a different experience. First, they did not live with their parents as young men; most had left their families to head their own households. About half of these men were married, but others lived with other kin or alone in rented quarters. Second, an important minority of young migrants were servants — and sometimes apprentices or boarders — in another household. In contrast with young native-born men, few migrants were part of a nuclear family before the age of 30. The patterns of men's lives, then, differed significantly insofar as natives were more attached to their families of origin in their early years.

The same was true for women. Young women born in Nîmes usually lived with their parents through the age of 29, as Figure 4.2 shows. By the age of 30, household position had changed dramatically, because many women had married. A significant minority, however, resided with other kin, and a growing group headed their own household as the years passed. Native Nimoises over 60 were equally likely to live with a husband, grown children, aged parents, or as head of their own household. Unlike native women, migrant women rarely lived with their parents, seldom lived with kin, and were often servants (see Figure 4.2). Young migrant women usually lived in Nîmes without their parents. In their early years, most were servants or wives, and between the ages of 30 and 59, most migrant women were married. Fewer worked as servants, more were household heads, and a steady but small proportion lived with kin. For those over 60, three possibilities dominated the migrant experience: heading one's own household, living with a spouse, and — most important — living with one's children.

Migrants usually had left their parents to marry, work as servants, or to live independently of their families, while most native men and women remained longer with parents or other kin. Sex differences were important for young people; women were much less likely to live with their parents than men, and migrant women were more likely to work as servants than their male counterparts. Migrants and natives were most similar in their middle years, for marriage and childbearing were the norm for both groups. After the age of 44, similarities between native-born and migrant women continue: the death of parents, then spouses, meant that women increasingly headed their own household. Into old age, many people in both groups lived with their children.

The life patterns of people's household roles in Nîmes suggest that single migrants seemed distinctive. Indeed, migrants were different from native-born Nimois — in youth more than at any other age. Their family situation alone set them apart from the other people of

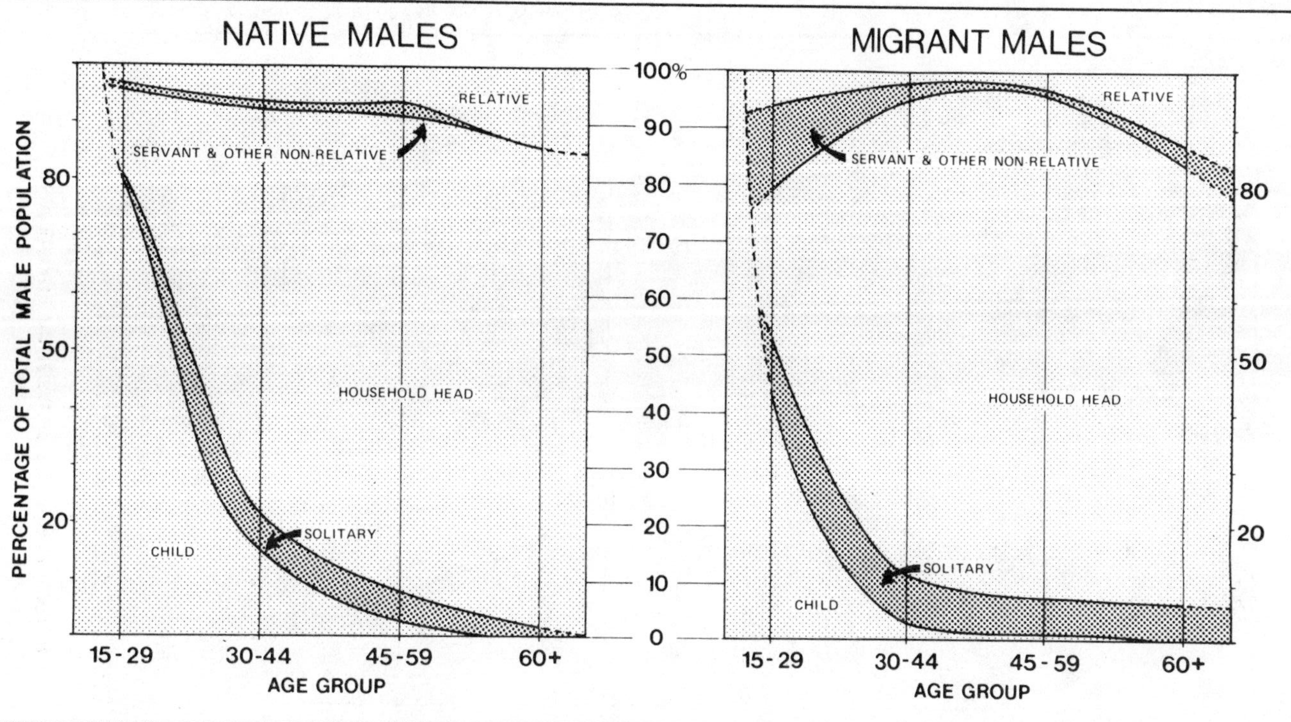

Figure 4.1: Household Position and Age of Males in Nîmes, 1906

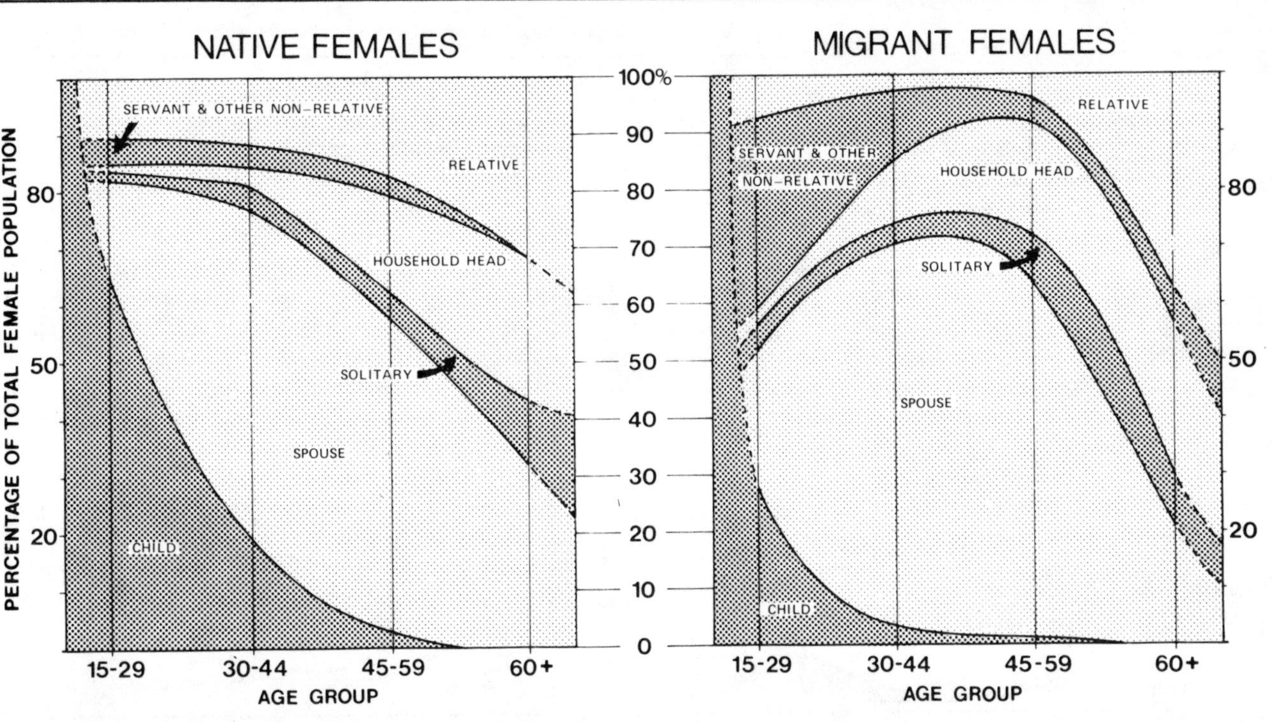

Figure 4.2: Household Position and Age of Females in Nîmes, 1906

the city. For this reason, the youth of Nîmes warrant closer investigation.

YOUTH

On Sunday afternoons, the young paraded in public; they filled the parks, strolled the boulevards, and took in concerts and band recitals performed on the Esplanade. Lucie Mazauric's young male cousins, who had spent their childhood Sundays at the family mazet, stopped spending Sundays in the countryside and stayed in town to stroll the boulevards. So did young women: "My school friends went to the Fontaine on Sundays to parade around, dressed in their best clothing, white gloves and velvet or silk dresses."[6] Sunday was the seamstresses' only day off and the servants' occasion for recreation — also a chance to "slide onto the rough road," observed a priest who promoted walks on the garrigue for one and all.[7] The object was to see and be seen. Middle-class strollers perpetually expressed shock at the finery of servants; young working-class women saw how the bourgeoisie dressed. Marc Bernard describes the impact on many poor young men of seeing the bourgeois face-to-face:

> When we met rich people on the boulevards on Sunday, our elegance was transformed in the wink of an eye. . . . Alone in front of a mirror we were able to look like dandies, but passing near a bourgeois robbed us of all our luster. There was something about them we would never have. Poverty was in our marrow; one look put us in place; we went off with our togs reduced to nothing, as if they had shrunk and barely covered our rumps.[8]

Despite their economic differences, however, middle-class and working-class youth shared this Sunday ritual.

The youth of Nîmes were a visible group. They figured heavily in reports of public life, particularly in partisan affairs. Young people dominated the crowds which triumphantly toured the boulevards after elections. Young men comprised the majority in the gangs that fought out the Republican-Royalist/Protestant-Catholic split on Mont Duplan, and in the crowds that participated in anti-Catholic and anti-Protestant demonstrations. Young people attended the city's cultural events — crowding into public lectures, such as those at the *Université Populaire*.[9]

The clubs that attracted primarily middle-class people — notables, functionaries, small businessmen, and white collar workers —

included large contingents of young people in outing and sporting clubs, musical and theatre clubs, and in such organizations as the Jeunesse Laïque and the Voltigeurs de la Republique. Lucie Mazauric Chamson described the outings of La Société d'Etudes des Sciences Naturelles as occasions on which people walked and sang for hours, "sealing great friendships."[10]

Newspapers reported both the formal social activities of middle-class young people and the crimes and disagreements of poorer youth. Young people committed some of the city's crimes as bicycle thieves, pickpockets, and petty thieves. They took part in barroom brawls and the fights which regularly burst out between soldier and civilian on the Boulevard Amiral Courbet. Young prostitutes were arrested for public argument and resisting arrest. The most frequently reported crime of young people was scaling the wrought-iron fence of the arena to gain free admission to bullfights and other spectacles.[11]

For young people in Nîmes, as in both Europe and America, a socially defined stage of life called adolescence emerged at the end of the nineteenth century. Early adulthood came to be associated with stress, as signs of anxiety and homicidal criminality led the community to adjust its assumptions about youthful innocence and pleasure. In the fall of 1906, Nîmes was shaken by a teenage murder when a brilliant student at the Ecole Normale murdered his brother-in-law and with cold-blooded forethought placed the body on railroad tracks in an effort to disguise the murder as suicide. Disappointment in love prompted girls in their late teens to attempt suicide by jumping into the canal of the Jardin de la Fontaine.[12] A new youth culture emerged in Nîmes by 1900, in which young middle-class people segregated their social life from that of the adults, and yet all classes took part in the citywide ritual of the Sunday afternoon promenade.

With these social changes came changes in young people's residence patterns and labor force participation. Studies of European and American youth have found that people on both sides of the Atlantic lived with their parents longer after the middle of the nineteenth century. The boarding of young people in America, which gave them some autonomy before marriage, declined after 1850. As the apprenticeship of artisans became less common, fewer young men lived with a master or journeyed as the tramping artisans of England, the *compagnons* of France, or the apprentices during the *Wanderjahre* in Germany. Home residence was prolonged as compulsory education laws were passed and years spent in school became more important to one's future. Families who could afford to forego children's wages kept their offspring out of the labor force and in school. As a consequence, young people around 1900 spent their time differently than their parents had in their youth. A prolonged semi-autonomy of living outside the home and working long before the age of twenty was replaced with the more dependent position of residing at home, often attending school.[13]

These changes profoundly divided native-born young people from migrants, for they do not seem to apply to the young migrants leaving small towns and villages for the city. Young migrants often came to the city without their family, and it was common for young people to forge the way for their more firmly rooted elders who would follow later, if at all. This tradition was particularly long-lived for young women working as servants, garmentmakers, and textile workers in urban areas.[14]

For young Nimois, the family was the cornerstone of social life, education, and work. Paul Marcelin recounts life in the Nimois artisanal milieu at the turn of the century, in which the family was united in an effort for success: Monsieur Marcelin was the master artisan, his son an apprentice, and his wife was in charge of the household and shop. Work left little time for leisure.

> Everything was sacrificed to work in this life, an incessant work with no wasted time. The weekly rest . . . was scrupulously observed. But at the mazet on Sundays, with the exception of some hours of relaxation, one still worked.[15]

Any socializing was practically all with the family, "brothers, sisters, nephews," or occasionally with the children's "nursing parents" (wet nurse and spouse). Social occasions were the standard holidays of Christmas, Easter, and Pentecost. Lucie Mazauric reports the experience of an educated, urban middle-class family: Social life consisted of family gatherings, visits *en famille* with parents' intimate friends, and family outings. The exceptions were Sunday walks with schoolmates, with Lucie's mother as chaperone. Family were equally important in the impoverished milieu of young Nimois Marc Bernard. After his father's departure, kin offered the only source of sociability for Madame Bernard: the "banal and grave ceremonies" of Saturday evenings with relatives.[16] The only exception to family-oriented leisure was Marc's Sunday afternoons on the boulevards.

Most young migrants, unlike natives, did not enjoy the familial cornerstone to their work and social life. Under 40 percent of the young migrants lived with their parents; by contrast, over 80 percent of young Nimois lived with at least one parent. In Nîmes, there were four possible patterns of residence for young people: living with parents, with kin, separate lodgings, and domestic service. A small proportion of both native and migrant young people lived with kin. Some people were married and living with a spouse before the age of 25, and others were household heads without a family, usually men living alone or with people to whom they were not related.

Boarding played a minor role for French youth, aside from students boarding at school. There was little boarding with families in Nîmes. (Only 2 percent of the young people were housed as lodgers.) Young men apart from family sometimes lived at their employer's home, or sometimes in a *garni,* a rented room. The garni was the most important form of residence for the young working-class French man in the nineteenth-century city. In large cities, several men shared a room, and often a bed. In the census of Nîmes, garnis were not listed as such but were indicated by lists of single-person households. They were usually attached to a restaurant with which there was a more or less formal arrangement for meals. This form of residence offered the French migrant in the city the same independence from his family as the American boarder, but without the familial structure of American boarding houses.

The arrangements for women were usually more protected than the *garni;* they more often lived with kin. For example, Marc Bernard's cousin Alice came to Nîmes to work and lived with Marc and Madame Bernard until her marriage. Often, women's employment involved a semi-dependent, relatively protected situation, such as that of seamstresses, who worked in a quasi-familial arrangement. Nearly one young migrant in ten was living as an employee or boarder, but nearly one in three was a domestic servant who lived with an employer, or at least in the attic. Most of these were women. In Nîmes, as in other cities of the West, there was a market for domestic servants well into the twentieth century and a dearth of other employment possibilities for single women.[17]

Whether or not young people worked became more closely associated with class during the nineteenth century. Youth from middle-class families became increasingly differentiated from their working-class peers by their school attendance, prolonged into the late teens. It was their early entry into the labor force that set unskilled working-class youth apart from their skilled peers and the middle class. The white collar jobs opening in increasing numbers at the turn of the century required an education. However, families had to forego their child's wages for this education, and many families could not afford to. Requests from parents to the city council of Nîmes for help with their children's educational expenses attest to the difficulty of educating a child.[18] Marc Bernard recounts his family's decision to send him to work rather than to continue his schooling when he was eleven years old:

> The schoolmaster intervened; he proposed that my mother let me take an exam for a scholarship which would allow me to go to secondary school. My cousin once again took charge; What! — my mother would give me up to the school for who knows how many years! — can't even consider it. Thus my fate was decided.[19]

It is impossible to compare the class backgrounds of young people born in the city with those of migrants, because most parents of migrants did not live in Nîmes and the relevant data are therefore not available for comparison. Yet young migrants seem to have come to Nîmes to work, for most of them were employed. When age, sex, and family membership were accounted for, 56 percent of them worked, in contrast to 39 percent of the Nîmes-born. Origin, sex, and employment were all related to living with one's own family for young people. Women were less likely to be in a nuclear family than men, and the employed were less likely to be part of a nuclear family than the unemployed. Origin — migrant or native status — was the most important factor linked with membership in a nuclear family.[20]

In Nîmes, then, the privileged adolescent was primarily city-born. Origin and parentage created three possibilities for young people in Nîmes. The first kind of experience is the one associated with adolescent status — that of cohabitation with family and economic dependence. These young people's parents were able to invest in their education or in home training. Lucie Mazauric belongs to this group, for her parents were able to see that she went to school.

Cohabitation with family in combination with labor force participation is another pattern. This was the case for working-class native youth; that is, for poor young people such as Marc Bernard, who went to work before he was twelve years old, and for young people who migrated with working-class parents. The child of a successful artisan, like Paul Marcelin, could remain in school until the age of sixteen or seventeen, but then apprenticeship and working life began.

The third category of experience belonged almost entirely to migrant youth and is the antithesis of the first type. It was the experience of employed young people like Anna Sabatier and Emile Brun, who did not live with their own family. They lived alone in rented quarters or in another household as employee or servant. The isolation of this experience, in familial and economic terms, was a liability for these young people because they had few economic and human resources upon which to draw.

NUPTIALITY

"They hardly ever marry in Nîmes," mourned Dr. Elie Mazel in 1887. In the period from 1877 to 1886, the marriage rate in Nîmes was lower than that of Paris, Lyon, or even Marseille, "the town of the European continent reputed to be the last in terms of nuptiality."[21] Had Elie Mazel made the same calculations 25 years later, he would have been equally disappointed. The marriage rate had declined further, and there was one divorce for every 19 marriages.[22] The model of urban migration assigns to migrants the responsibility for low nuptiality. To assess this aspect of the model, migrants will be compared with native-born Nimois on two counts: their tendency to be the city's servants and solitary workers, and their levels of nuptiality.

The city's census lists identify the servants, solitary young men, and female household heads — that is, those least likely to be currently married. Most of Nîmes' servants and solitaries were migrants; a full 85 percent of the city's servants were migrants from outside town, and migrants dominated the positions of solitary householder and female household head.[23] On the other hand, migrants were not more likely to be single than were native-born Nimois. Quite the contrary: Migrants were much more likely to be married than were people born in Nîmes. A conservative figure puts the proportion of men currently married at 66 percent for migrant males between the ages of 15 and 49, and a mere 42 percent for males born in Nîmes. Figures for female nuptiality are of greater significance for their bearing on fertility. Of women in their childbearing years (15-49), 53 percent of the women born outside Nîmes and 40 percent of the Nîmes-born were married in 1906. Of women aged 20-44, the most active childbearing years in Nîmes, 56 percent of the migrants and 45 percent of the Nimoises were married. In fact, as Table 4.1 shows, a

TABLE 4.1 Proportion Married, by Sex and Origin

Age	*Males*				*Females*			
	Natives		*Migrants*		*Natives*		*Migrants*	
15-19	0%	(99)	0%	(38)	2%	(100)	2%	(60)
20-24	3	(71)	12	(33)	15	(112)	20	(87)
25-29	36	(75)	51	(45)	42	(90)	51	(98)
30-34	67	(61)	74	(68)	52	(86)	62	(77)
35-39	78	(54)	86	(70)	71	(68)	71	(104)
40-44	65	(60)	86	(71)	66	(64)	77	(86)
45-49	83	(60)	89	(63)	68	(66)	73	(79)
Total	42%		66%		40%		53%	
	x^2, $p < .01$*				x^2, $p < .01$*			
N	(480)		(388)		(586)		(591)	

*Chi square statistic applies to total only.

SOURCE: ADG 10M 260, 261, 262, *Recensement, Ville de Nîmes,* 1906; systematic sample of individuals in 5 percent of households.

greater proportion of migrants than native women were married at practically every age between 15 and 49.

These findings present a challenge to the assumption that because migrants were likely to be servants and young journeymen, they were less likely to be married, relative to native-born city people. In fact, the correlation between a sizable proportion of servants and low nuptiality could be as much a product of the middle class that employed the servants as of the servants themselves.[24] In order to discern the social patterns underlying the differences in nuptiality between native and migrant, the family positions of unmarried adults are compared in order to identify the unmarried people more explicitly. Table 4.2 illustrates the comparison. Among migrant women, servants and female household heads accounted for most of the unmarried (64 percent), although some were living with their relatives or parents. Among Nîmes-born women, on the other hand, the majority of the unmarried lived with their parent(s) (67 percent), while a large proportion (17 percent) were living with a sibling, uncles and aunts, or other relatives. Celibate daughters far outnumbered servants, despite the importance of servant work for young women.[25] Most of the single male natives also lived with their parents (73 percent). Again, unmarried sons living at home outnumbered the unmarried migrant males. Nearly one-third of the native-born adults were unmarried and living at home with their parents (43 percent of the males and 25 percent of the females).

TABLE 4.2 Household Position of People not Married, by Sex and Origin, Ages 15-49 (percentages)

	Males		*Females*	
	Natives	*Migrants*	*Natives*	*Migrants*
Head of Household	9	32	8	22
Child	78	42	67	25
Relative	9	9	17	11
Nonrelative	4	17	8	42
Total	100%	100	100	100
N	279	134	345	273

SOURCE: ADG 10M 260, 261, 262, *Recensement, Ville de Nîmes*, 1906; systematic sample of individuals in 5 percent of households.

More men and women were married as they grew older — the proportion married increased sharply at the age of twenty and continued to increase until the age of forty. Under the age of twenty-five, the great majority of native-born women were at home with their parents, and the majority of single migrant women were servants. Moreover, many native-born Nimois remained single and lived at home into their middle thirties. Thus, it is the great number of single Nimois living with their parents that underlies Nîmes' low marriage rate.

Once married, did Nimois produce more children than migrants?

FERTILITY

The birth rate of Nîmes declined in the last half of the nineteenth century. The number of births fell from about 1,900 per year in the 1850s (when the population was about 54,000) to only about 1,300 births per year after the turn of the century (when the population of Nîmes was over 80,000). The crude birth rate fell by half, from over 34 births per thousand in 1851, to 28 in the 1870s, to 20 in the 1890s, to 16 per thousand in 1906. By then, the index of marital fertility was a low .307.[26]

The decline of fertility in Nîmes coincided with the transformation of the city from an industrial center to a regional transport and commercial center. One result of the transformation of Nîmes' economy was to reduce household production and child employment. The *Enquete industrielle* of 1848 lists 40 percent of the shawl workers as children and 20 percent as women. Yet jobs for children disappeared in the last half of the nineteenth century with the decline of the silk and shawl industries. By 1886, an inspector reporting child labor violations noted that fewer children and female minors were working in Nîmes than ever before because the city had ceased to be an important manufacturing center.[27] In the same period came laws instituting compulsory education and prohibiting child labor.

As a consequence of these social and economic changes — and doubtless of changes in attitudes toward fertility limitation and knowledge about it — the perceived and real costs of children to the Nimois household rose while the benefits of having children declined. The occupational bases for high fertility foundered because children could not bring in a wage as they could in coal-mining or textile towns. Aspirations to white collar work, or at least shop work, kept children in schools and out of the labor force.[28] It is thus reasonable to infer that couples in Nîmes had good reason for making different fertility decisions in 1900 than fifty years earlier, with consequent decreased birth rates and low marital fertility.

The childbearing patterns for natives and migrants could have been very different. For example, women from rural areas could have continued rural patterns of relatively high fertility while living in the city, thus creating a demographically distinct group there. On the other hand, female migrants could have married later than female natives and borne fewer children as a consequence. There are suggestions from a number of sources that migrant women did, in fact, marry late. Theresa McBride's research on domestic servants suggests that the service work so popular among migrant women often caused them to delay marriage. Indeed, according to the city's marriage records, the average age of women marrying for the first time in Nîmes in 1906 was 26.6 for migrant women and 24.9 for Nimoises.

It is nearly impossible to discern whether migrant women in fact had higher or lower fertility than women born in Nîmes. Turn-of-the-century birth records are closed to researchers, and as they cannot be analyzed by birthplace of mother, differential birth rates for native and migrant women cannot be calculated. Even this information would not provide a definitive answer, because a search through small-town and village birth records reveals that women living in the city often returned to their parents' home for childbirth. Consequently, an unknown proportion of children were born to migrant women outside the city. Child-woman ratios calculated from the censuses of this period in southern France are unreliable because children were undercounted. Between 19 percent and 21 percent of the children born in Nîmes between 1900 and 1907 were placed with wet nurses outside the city, but it is impossible to know whether Nîmes-born women or migrant women were more likely to put their children out to nurse.[29] The 1906 census of Nîmes, imperfect indicator that it is, shows a nearly identical number of children in the home for migrant and native wives (1.47 per migrant wife, 1.50 per native wife). Thus, there is no suggestion here that native and migrant women had different levels of fertility.

HOUSEHOLD COMPOSITION

The perception that migrants were disproportionately unmarried has been based on their visibility as single servants and workers, people peripheral to the urban family. This image of migrants as demographically marginal may not rest on marriage patterns alone, but may also be based on the kinds of households and families they formed. For example, they may have been less likely than natives to form extended families because their kin were less likely to be in Nîmes than were those of native-born Nimois. Michael Anderson found this to be the case in Lancashire, where young migrants, single or married, less often lived with their families than natives, for the simple reason that their parents were not present.[30] Likewise, migrants probably formed the majority of solitary households and "no family" groups which did not include a nuclear family — such as two siblings or two unrelated people living together.

When the households of Nimois and migrants are compared, we see that native-born Nimois were more likely to head extended families — and multiple families in a few cases — but by a margin of only four percentage points (18 percent and 14 percent, respectively). Migrants were somewhat more likely than natives to head solitary households, but this difference is one of three percentage points (15 percent and 12 percent). Migrants were only slightly more likely to head "no family" households, such as siblings without parents, or unrelated people living together (5 percent and 4 percent, respectively). The differences between native and migrant households are differences of degree rather than kind: The great majority of households of natives (66 percent) and migrants alike (67 percent) were simple nuclear families, as was true in many other towns.[31] Fewer than one in six households were made up of solitary individuals or included extended families, and fewer than one in twenty were "no family" households.

TABLE 4.3 Household Characteristics by Origin and Age of Household Head

		< 29	*30-39*	*40-49*	*50-59*	*60-98*	*Average*
Percentage of households with:							
one member only	N*	14	11	8	14	14	12
	M**	27	15	12	11	13	15
relatives	N	30	26	31	19	21	25
	M	21	19	15	14	23	18
children	N	44	67	75	66	51	63
	M	41	58	69	69	56	61
Mean household size:	N	2.7	3.8	4.0	3.4	2.9	3.5
	M	2.7	3.2	3.5	3.6	3.0	3.3
Mean number of children	N	.6	1.4	1.8	1.4	.8	1.3
	M	.7	1.1	1.4	1.6	1.0	1.2
N	N	50	90	110	100	105	—
	M	70	137	156	121	115	—

*N = native (total 455)
**M = migrant (total = 599)
SOURCE: ADG 10M 260, 261, 262, *Recensement, Ville de Nîmes,* 1906; systematic sample of individuals in 5 percent of households.

The size of Nimois households — and who lived in them — varied over the life span of the group. Each group absorbed and sloughed off members as circumstances dictated. When the father of Anna Sabatier was widowed and retired, he came from Langogne to join his daughter and her family. The Villefortais cheminot, Emile Brun, lived with his aunt and uncle in Nîmes after the death of his first wife. Marc Bernard's young cousin Alice came to Nîmes to learn her trade as a glovemaker, and she lived with Marc and Madame Bernard until her marriage. When Lucie Mazauric's uncle died, her aunt and cousin joined the Mazauric household.[32]

From individual cases, it seems that accidents of death and unforeseen migrations made families group together randomly. Yet average ages at death and migration created systematic life-cycle changes of family composition. Analyzed by the age of the household head, the composition of households reflect the differences between native and migrant life patterns in Nîmes. The most important points of this analysis are shown in Table 4.3, and the complete figures for household structure appear in Appendix III, Table III.4. Migrants under the age of thirty were more likely to live alone than at any other time of their lives. Other migrants were couples, and another one-fifteenth were couples living with a sibling or a parent. The households of natives under the age of thirty, on the other hand, included a greater variety of relatives and were rarely alone.

When household heads were 30-50 years old, migrants had smaller households than natives, because they were less likely to have children and relatives living with them. While over one-quarter of natives' households had at least one relative living in, fewer than one migrant household in five had any. This is probably because most migrants' relatives did not live in Nîmes. They were less likely to have children, because more migrants lived alone, even between the ages of 30 and 50. It is also feasible that migrants were less likely to have children at home because they bore fewer children, because migrant wives were more likely to put infants out to nurse, and/or because they married later. Unfortunately, there is no way to differentiate between the first two possibilities. The marriage records of Nîmes suggest that migrant males married later, for migrant men married at 30.4 years, while Nîmes-born men married at 27.0 in 1906 (mean age at first marriage).

For native and migrant households alike, solitary and "no family" households became more important as people aged and were widowed. The majority of older people, however, remained in simple nuclear families and lived with their children. Thus, the life of the household was different for native and migrant families, but it differed most significantly for young households, and in a way fitting with a young age of migration. The experience of young households was substantially influenced by the custom of migrants to live in a garni or to rent a room alone. They were also affected by having fewer relatives in Nîmes. For most of the life of the household, differences in size — and even in number of children — were unimportant. Moreover, families were structured in similar ways, although migrant extended families were relatively rare.

MIGRANTS AND URBAN POPULATION PATTERNS

The life patterns, nuptiality, fertility, and households of natives and migrants in Nîmes undermine, rather than corroborate, the stereotype of migrants as single and/or demographically distinct. This may be because the information about Nîmes allows a more complete and clear view of migrants' marriage patterns than do other sources. Doubtless, however, changes in migration patterns which occurred during the nineteenth century help explain why Nîmes does not fit the model. There are indications that temporary migration was less important to young people by the end of the nineteenth century, and that it was replaced by permanent settlement in the city. The implications of this change for urban populations are that migrants became increasingly likely to marry and have children in the city.

Assumptions about the role of urban-born young people in demographic patterns may require substantial adjustment. The connection of Europe's demographic transition, including the fertility decline and increase in marriage rates with urbanization and industrial growth, has encouraged many demographic historians to look to cities as areas of "modern" (early and more universal) marriage.[33] Unexpectedly low urban nuptiality has quite naturally led scholars to turn to the migrants — the young single worker, soldier, and servant — for an explanation. Yet native-born urban people also had good reasons to remain single; many were the middle-class people who employed servants, and who had material and familial constraints on marriage arrangements that working-class people did not.[34]

It is quite possible that some unmarried people stayed at home because they were more dependent on their parents than ever before. Schooling played a much greater role in job and career options than it had fifty years earlier, particularly in a town like Nîmes, where commercial and other white collar employment was relatively important. The postprimary school facilities for both men and women expanded at the turn of the century with the growth of the *lycée,* the *collège de filles,* and normal schools. At this time, stenography attracted more students than any other vocational course offered by the Bourse du Travail.[35] The decrease in jobs for children and young people which accompanied deindustrialization in Nîmes meant prolonged and exacerbated dependence on parents. As a consequence of both trends, young people in Nîmes were likely to stay at home longer in 1906 than ever before.

The obligation to care for aged parents may have been particularly great for urban people, both because they had been supported by their parents and because they had relatively few siblings with whom to share that responsibility. On the other hand, parents of migrants could be cared for by the children who had stayed at home. Among urban children, the situation of Hélène Donzel, who lived with her aging widowed father, her brother and nephew, was not unique. Monsieur Donzel was retired, and the younger men worked at the Prefecture in Nîmes. Despite the family's relative prosperity and high standing in the Protestant community, they had no live-in servant, so it appears that Hélène did much if not all of the cleaning, cooking, and shopping. When Monsieur Donzel died, Hélène was 43 years old. Within months, she wed a twice-married merchant from the Aveyron and left Nîmes.[36]

Opportunity also may have kept more children at home than ever before at the turn of the century, for it was to be found in the cities. The decline of artisanal training gave the urban-born one less reason to leave home. The net result of changing structures of obligation and opportunity may have been to decrease the chances for city people to leave their home town.

The findings about natives and migrants in Nîmes' families and households confirm the importance of low levels of nuptiality to urban demographic structure. Marriage patterns separated natives from migrants more than the kinds of families in which they lived, and perhaps more than the number of children they had. Although the evidence from Nîmes is an insufficient base for judging the impact of internal migration on fertility, the household evidence from the census clearly suggests that nuptiality, not marital (or nonmarital) fertility levels, determined the urban population pattern. The demographic phenomenon to be explained is not simple native-migrant differences, but urban celibacy for both groups.

Some comparisons of migrants with native-born Nimois have employed the very broad categories of people born in Nîmes and those born elsewhere. In one sense, these general categories are particularly appropriate, because they do not cater to the stereotype of the migrant as a poor country bumpkin, or as a social and economic "marginal." On the other hand, it was not high-level bureaucrats and migrants from virtually suburban villages who changed the face of Europe in the nineteenth century.[37] Rather, it was the migrants who left villages and small towns who most changed the patterns of population concentration. It follows that this last kind of migrant is one of the greatest interest to historians and historical demographers. Equally important is the fact that migrants from small towns and villages inform historians' images and ideas about who migrants were and how they behaved. For this reason, it is particularly appropriate to focus on the migrants from Le Vigan, Villefort, and Langogne.

YOUTH, MARRIAGE, AND HOUSEHOLD FOR MIGRANT STREAMS

Just as emigrants from Le Vigan, Villefort, and Langogne were not typical of their towns in terms of social origins, they were not typical in demographic terms. First, most members of all three migrant streams were women. Indeed, there were only four to six men for every ten women in Nîmes from Le Vigan, Villefort, and Langogne. Langogne's group had an especially high percentage of females, with a sex ratio of 43.[38] (This is partly because the census lists exclude the highly male institutionalized population — boarding students at Nîmes' schools and army recruits garrisoned in Nîmes. Such groups were not listed individually, although they were counted in the total population figures.) Women were in the majority in Nîmes among both natives and migrants, but they outnumbered men more among migrants.

It was not unusual for women to migrate or for the city to have a majority of females at the end of the nineteenth century. Women dominated migration streams and urban populations where employment prospects were favorable, which was particularly the case in service-oriented commercial towns like Nîmes. On the other hand, the sex ratio was high in towns where male employment dominated; coal-mining and metal-working centers had high proportions of males.[39] Men outnumbered women in the coal basin to the north of Nîmes, which is where many men from Villefort and Langogne went.

Migrants were young, working-age people. This too is a normal pattern, because most geographical movement occurs at the beginning of one's working life. Most of the emigrants from Le Vigan, Villefort, and Langogne were between 20 and 39. Like other migrants, they usually arrived in their late teens to late twenties and comprised a considerable proportion of the working population.[40] In Nîmes, migrants represented 42 percent of the total population in 1906, and 50 percent of the population over 16.

The population pyramids in Figures 4.3-4.5 illustrate and contrast the size and the sex and age composition of the migrant streams. Figure 4.3 shows that the group from Langogne was very young and mostly female. There was an abundance of young women aged 25-34, and the largest group of men was 30-34 years old. (The large size of the female group aged 25-29 may be due in part to the well-known tendency to report one's approximate age in census returns.)[41] Very few migrants from Langogne were under 15 years of age. The Villefort group was also mostly young and female, as Figure 4.4 illustrates. Most of the women were in their twenties, and only a few of the group were over 64 or under 15. The sex ratio of the Villefortais was 64. The largest group of men were those aged 35-39. Thus, relatively young people dominated the migrant streams from both Langogne and Villefort in Nîmes.

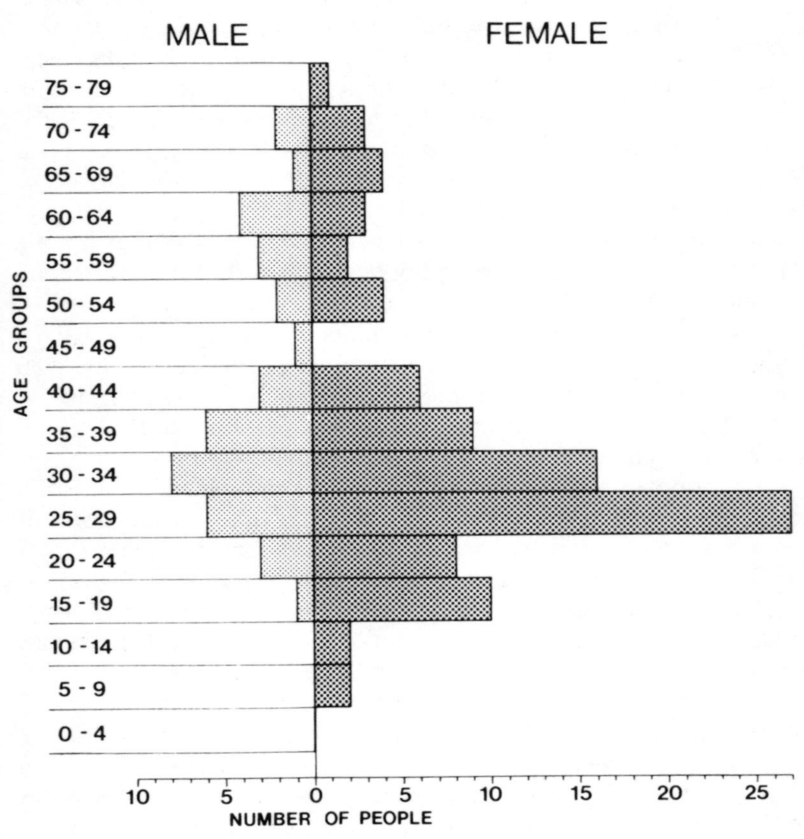

Figure 4.3: Age and Sex of Migrants from Langogne (N = 131)

The Viganais are portrayed in Figure 4.5. This was a larger group than the other two, but like them, the majority were women. (The sex ratio was 59.) Children, and middle-aged and older people were a more important part of the group from Le Vigan than the others. The presence of children suggests that the Viganais may have often come to Nîmes in family groups. On the average, they were older. Those aged 40-59 made up the largest group, and even people over 60 were relatively numerous. This older migrant stream testifies to the long-standing links between Nîmes and Le Vigan.

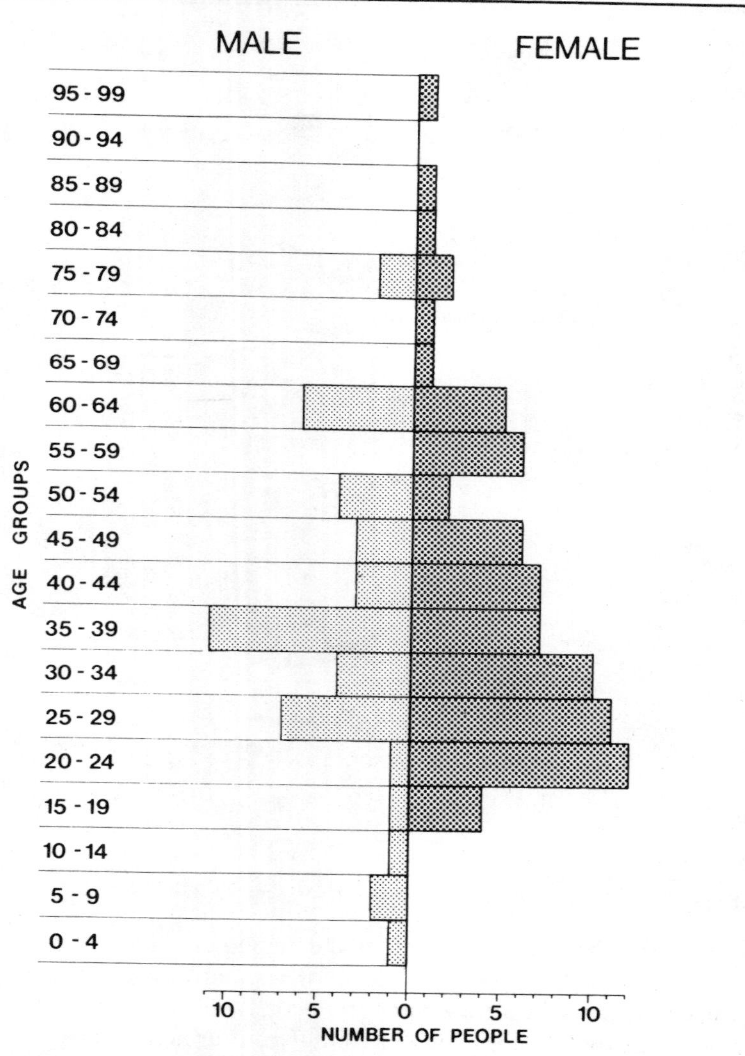

Figure 4.4: Age and Sex of Migrants from Villefort (N = 125)

From the social origins of the three migrant streams — the Viganais, highly professional; the Villefortais, agricultural; and the Langognais, semi-skilled and poor — one would think that the young people in Nîmes from Le Vigan would have lived very different family

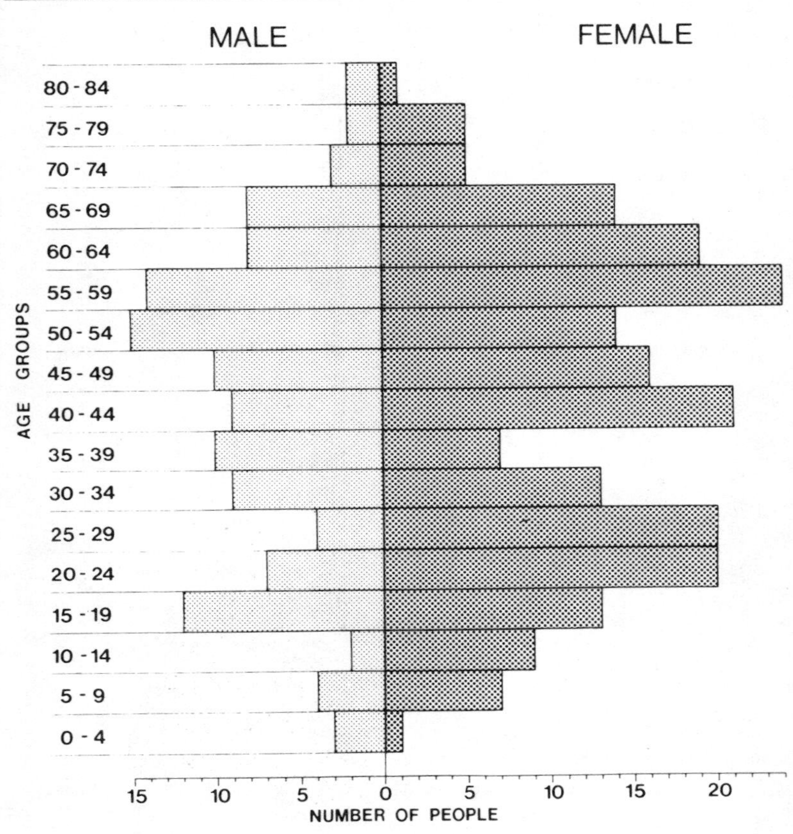

Figure 4.5: Age and Sex of Migrants from Le Vigan (N = 330)

lives from those out of Villefort and Langogne. This is particularly likely because almost all the Villefortais and Langognais in Nîmes under the age of 24 were women. Indeed, Table 4.4 shows that the two groups of young people did live in different urban worlds. While the young Viganais lived with their parents, most young people from the Lozère lived as servants in the households of other families. Further, a much higher proportion of Lozerians worked.

The young Lozerians were almost a caricature of the eighteenth- and early nineteenth-century patterns of young people's migration.

TABLE 4.4 Family Membership, Household Position, and Labor Force Participation, Individuals 15-24

	Le Vigan	*Villefort*	*Langogne*
Percentage in Nuclear Family	75	28	17
Household Position			
Head/Spouse	8	17	14
Child/Relative	77	22	18
Servant/Other	15	61	68
Percentage Employed	58	72	87

SOURCE: ADG 10M 260, 261, 262, *Recensement, Ville de Nîmes,* 1906.

Besides living apart from their parents and working, many — like the Sabatier sisters from Langogne, and the Janvier sisters from Villefort — lived in relatively protected, semi-dependent positions as servants and apprentices. Many Vignais, on the other hand, conformed to the pattern fitting twentieth-century urban adolescence. Most of them lived at home with a parent. Working-class children and widows' children were employed as dressmakers, white collar workers, and laborers. For example, Madeleine Peysson and her two sisters combined their earnings as seamstresses with their father's earnings as a day laborer to support the family. Monsieur Peysson formerly had worked in Le Vigan's defunct wool industry. Children of middle-class people and white collar workers were at home, not employed. Anna Marie Fabre, for example, lived at home with her parents, siblings, grandmother, and a servant. Her father had been the chief clerk in the courthouse of Le Vigan but left government service for the wine trade in Nîmes. Place of origin proves a powerful influence on young migrants' household position. Origins are a more important predictor of family membership than employment status, sex, or age. Family membership, in turn, is highly correlated with labor force participation.[42]

Young migrant women's need for employment and tendency to work as servants made them particularly vulnerable. Long working hours, difficult conditions, vulnerability to sexual advances, and the temptation to turn to prostitution — the problems of domestics — resembled those elsewhere, as local newspapers attest.[43] In one case, a servant en route to the train station was robbed of the precious belongings she planned to take home, by a carter who had offered to help with her burden. An article published in the summer of 1906 entitled "Between Mistress and Lover" describes the misfortunes of a servant from Villefort. She had been seduced with a promise of marriage by an apparently eligible railroad worker and had set up housekeeping with him. Subsequently, he had returned to his usual job assignment and to his wife and family in the coal basin north of Nîmes. Furious and distraught, the woman went to the station where her former lover was employed and made a scene that resulted in police intervention — on behalf of the man. She was scolded and sent back to Nîmes after she promised to mend her ways.[44] The Nimois perceived these women as country bumpkins. To "look like a girl from Langogne" indicated in local slang that a woman looked unsophisticated. Domestics were kept at a distance: "Of course, servants were part of the family," recalled a Nimoise raised in a bourgeois household, "the part that ate in the kitchen and slept in the attic." A servant in another household became pregnant and carried the child without being noticed. She gave birth to her baby during a visit home, only telling her employers about the child after she had returned. The head of the municipal employment agency, through which hundreds of servants found work annually, fulminated against his clientele: "Female domestics, very cumbersome, very troublesome, even embarrassing," he wrote,

> . . . inured to all the dangers inherent in their kind and in their profession, for selfish motives, and in this somewhat idle existence they quickly take up lazy habits. Then they become the familiars of the employment agencies, alternating their professional work with occupations of a different order. . . . Their questions, like their conversations, are generally muddled, and waste a great deal of time.[45]

The experience in youth, the age structure, and the parentage of the migration streams from Le Vigan suggest that the Viganais played a different demographic role in the city than the migrants from Villefort and Langogne. The Viganais seem to be the kind of migrants who would marry, settle in the city, and contribute economically and demographically to Nîmes because they enjoyed their family's protection, they were more likely to be educated for an urban occupation, and they had the background for prosperity as a group. On the other hand, the Lozerians were more commonly poor, young servants and solitary men. They fit the stereotype of migrants that supports the urban migration model — they lacked the protection of their families, and poverty rendered their lives more fragile.

The marriage patterns of the three groups of migrants do not support these suppositions, however, for they all had very similar levels of nuptiality. More important still, the patterns of marriage by age were similar for the Viganais and the Lozerians. Before the age of 25, nearly all were single. Between 25 and 34 the pattern changed, and about 60 percent of the men and 45 percent of the women were married, excluding the group from Villefort. The percentage of married men from Villefort was low — 33 percent — because this group was least able to afford marriage; they were more likely than men from Le Vigan or Langogne to be unskilled and semi-skilled workers in Nîmes and to be sons of *agriculteurs*. Their occupations will be investigated in detail in the following chapter. The relative lack of opportunity in Villefort may account for the high proportion — 71 percent — of married women from that village in Nîmes. That is, Villefortaises may have been particularly likely to stay in the city to marry because returning home was such an unattractive alternative. After the age of 35 the vast majority of all three of these groups were married. Nevertheless, members of all three were also *less* likely to be married than was the total migrant population (Appendix III, Table III.5 lists the nuptiality figures).

What contribution does this information about the migrant streams make to understanding the demographic role of migrants in the city? A focus on the groups confirms one part of the urban migration model, namely that a relatively small proportion of women in the migrant streams were married. This is due, at least in part, to the important role played by domestic service, particularly for women from the Lozère. People in the distant migrant streams studied were less likely to be married than were the total migrants in Nîmes. This suggests that most married migrants were those from the immediate vicinity. Migrants from the *arrondissement* of Nîmes (a radius of about 25 miles around the city) were likely to have settled in Nîmes early in life and to have been similar to the Nimois in terms of life patterns. This speculation is corroborated by the high marriage figures for migrants from Nîmes' immediate hinterland: 72 percent of the men and 60 percent of the women from the arrondissement of Nîmes were married in 1906 — a much higher proportion than for most migrants.

Nevertheless, even domestic servants eventually married. The experiences of the three migrant streams studied here show that the migrant, even the small-town or rural migrant, wed. Marriage after migration and continued residence in the city was common. The life stories of men like Emile Brun and Charles Bouzanquet from Villefort, who married after they had worked for the railroad in Nîmes a few years, corroborate this pattern. Reconstructions of the movements and relationships among women from the Lozère show that often an elder sister such as Anna Sabatier would move to Nîmes, work as a servant, and marry, and that younger sisters would then follow and also find work as servants. At the same time, the proportion of Viganais who moved to Nîmes with their parents shows that families, as well as single people, moved to urban areas. A close look at migrants from different areas, then, undermines the view of the migrant community as a demographic drain on the city.

Thus began the urban lives of Viganais, Villefortais, and Langognais. If they remained in Nîmes to marry, whom did they marry — Nimois, people from their home area, or migrants from other parts of France? Did the women among them marry laborers, or did they find husbands who had railroad jobs or prestigious white collar employment?

> To be sure, the ethnic substrata of lower Languedocian cities had come from the mountains, but until the end of the nineteenth century the descent had been made drop by drop and of necessity the immigrant had dissolved into the urban melting pot. Now, on the contrary, it was a human tide which broke over the lowlands. At the end of the nineteenth century, 202,372 people in lower Languedoc had been born outside the province of which half (47.9%) came from the central Plateau. . . . These men arrived together and lived among themselves. They stayed in contact with their former families. Periodically, they went back to the Causses or the Cévennes. They married a fellow countryman. . . . This montagnard milieu remained profoundly unique and refused to dissolve into the indigenous background. An investigation carried out in Pezenas established that 95% of the immigrants who arrived between 1900 and 1910 married among themselves.[46]

In the case of the small town of Pézenas in lower Languedoc, migrants from the uplands lived apart from the people of the Mediterranean plains. Married or single, migrants did not mix, a situation reminiscent of other migrant and immigrant communities wherein "urban villages" appeared whose population did not dissolve into the new community by intermarriage. In short, what matters is not only

TABLE 4.5 Geographical Origin of Marriage Partners by Sex, 1850 and 1906 (percentages)

	Nîmes	*Neighboring Communes*	*Gard*	*Neighboring Departments*	*Elsewhere in France*	*Outside France*	*Total*	*N*
Grooms								
1850	57	6	16	10	8	3	100%	489
1906	33	6	25	14	18	4	100	102
Brides								
1850	60	5	13	17	5	1	101	496
1906	42	2	21	15	18	2	100	102

NOTE: This tables compares all marriages in 1850 with a 20 percent sample of 1906 marriages. I am grateful to M. Armand Cosson for permitting me to use his analysis of the 1850 marriage records.

SOURCE: ADG E1 *Actes de Marriage, Nîmes,* 1850; ATN *Actes de Marriage, Nîmes,* 1906.

whether or not migrants married, but *whom* they married as well. Did the endogamous marriage patterns of villages and towns like Villefort and Langogne in the early nineteenth century change with urbanization? Was urbanization an integration of people into the city at the intimate level of family life?

Nîmes' marriage patterns show that people of marriageable age were moving longer distances than fifty years before, as was true in the Lozère and Le Vigan[47] (see Table 4.5). Marriage had ceased to be endogamous by the turn of the century. The majority of brides and grooms in Nîmes no longer came from the city, or even from Nîmes and the surrounding communes. More marriage partners came from other areas of the Gard and from neighboring departments. Many came from farther away. Although in 1850 only one in twenty partners came from beyond the departments neighboring the Gard, this proportion had increased to nearly one in five by the turn of the century. Patterns of movement evolved for women as much as for men, a fact that bears emphasizing, because women had migrated shorter distances than men in the past.[48] By the turn of the century, only 44 percent of the brides and grooms married in Nîmes were from either Nîmes or the communes nearby.

Did native Nimois and newcomers intermarry, or did they form segregated pools of marriage partners? The characteristics of couples married in Nîmes in 1906 who settled there after their wedding suggest that natives and migrants met and intermarried freely. Half the native-born grooms married migrant women, and nearly 40 percent of the migrant grooms married Nimoises. The difference between migrants' and natives' marriage partners was not statistically significant.

Couples such as Augustine Gascon and Camille Cardenoux typify Nîmes' marriages in 1906: Cardenoux was a fireman for the railroad from Bagnols-les-Bains near Villefort, and Augustine was born in Nîmes. Fewer than one-quarter of the marriages joined two natives; the majority joined a native with a migrant. The experience of young Pouzergue from Le Vigan, who married a Nimoise, and of Marc Bernard's glovemaker cousin Alice, who married a cheminot from a Nimois family, must not have been uncommon.

On the other hand, marriages in Nîmes often joined two newcomers; witness Sophie Chevret of Langogne and Edouard Roche of Villefort, as well as Charles Bouzanquet of Villefort and his bride from the coal basin. Over one-third of the marriages in Nîmes united two migrants. However, the marriages were not endogamous, like those in Pézenas. The marriage records show that migrants usually did not marry people from home (see Appendix III, Table III.6). Most marriages in Nîmes grew out of meetings in the city. For example, Joseph Raymond from Savoie and Justine Fenouillet from Le Bleymard, near Villefort, were both working in Nîmes at the time of their marriage — he as a carter, she as a cook — and had left parents in their respective home villages. Few marriages ever joined people from the same region, that is, from the same arrondissement within the Gard or from the same department outside the Gard. Men and women from other parts of the Gard were more likely to marry a Nimois than each other. Those from neighboring departments were more likely to marry a Nimois or a Gardois than each other, and migrants from beyond neighboring departments were not likely to marry one another, either. The exception is the Italians, four out of five of whom married a compatriot.

New brides and grooms comprised only a fraction of all the husbands and wives in Nîmes. They were probably more heterogeneous in origin than most couples in the city, for others may have met and married in their home area, or met in Nîmes and returned home to marry. In the census, the married couples of the city offer a more complete sample. Of the 667 couples surveyed, about the same proportion are native and migrant as the marriage partners in Nîmes (44 percent of the wives, and 45 percent of the husbands, were natives). Among these couples, only one-fifth were made up of a migrant and a native, while one-third of the couples were native Nimois. Moreover, of the migrant couples (45 percent of the total), one-fifth were from the same home area — that is, the same department, or the same arrondissement of the Gard. Hence, the resident conjugal couples in

Nîmes were more often married to compatriots than were those marrying in the city (see Table 4.6).

Nevertheless, both marriage records and the census of Nîmes demonstrate that people from different parts of France did meet and marry. The fact that 45 percent of the couples in the city were either native-migrant or migrant-migrant makes a strong case for the mobility of marrying people. Migrants were clearly not in a segregated marriage pool.

The marriage partners of Viganais, Villefortais, and Langognais show that these patterns varied for particular kinds of migrants. About one-third of the Viganais married Nimois, and another 30 percent married people from Le Vigan and the surrounding area. Nearly 40 percent, however, married other migrants who were not from the arrondissement of Le Vigan. Few Villefortais married Nimois — only 12 percent — and fewer than one-third married someone from the Lozère. Rather, most Villefortais married migrants, but not migrants from home. Nearly one-quarter of the Langognais married Nimois, but only one in five married someone from the Lozère. The Langognais pattern, then, was most similar to the Villefortais. The common pattern indicates that there may have been a common migrant marriage pool. Many young migrants, particularly the Villefortais and the Langognais, worked at the same kinds of jobs, lived under similar arrangements, and had similar constraints on their social lives. The young laborer without a family was more likely to meet a servant on her day off than a family-supervised couturière or clerk. The servant, in turn, was more likely to meet a young laborer, the brother of a fellow servant, or a shopkeeper than a business clerk or courthouse records keeper. The Viganais may have been more likely than the others to marry a Nimois or someone from the Protestant Cévennes, because there may have been a Protestant marriage pool based on social relationships and shared interests in Nîmes; Roque's research on the Protestants of Nîmes shows nearly no intermarriage. Viganais were also likely to have a spouse from home, because some married before they moved to Nîmes.

The migration and work experiences of young migrant women did influence their choice of a husband. They were more likely to marry unskilled workers and soldiers garrisoned in Nîmes, while native-born Nimoises were more likely to marry white collar workers and members of the bourgeoisie (figures are given in Appendix III, Table III.7). It seems that the relative paucity of resources for young migrant women in terms of family and economic support caused them

TABLE 4.6 Geographical Origin of Conjugal Couples (percentages)

	Nîmes	*Arrondissement of Nîmes*	*Gard*	*Neighboring Departments*	*Elsewhere in France*	*Outside France*	*Total*	*N*
Partners of men from								
Nîmes	74	9	6	4	3	3	99%	297
Arrondissement of Nîmes	21	42	14	17	3	3	100	94
Department of the Gard	28	13	33	12	9	6	101	69
Neighboring departments	14	11	16	45	8	5	99	99
Elsewhere in France	19	9	10	24	35	3	100	58
Outside France	14	6	12	4	4	60	100	50
Partners of women from								
Nîmes	76	7	7	5	4	2	101	290
Arrondissement of Nîmes	28	42	10	12	5	3	100	93
Department of the Gard	21	16	28	20	7	7	99	81
Neighboring departments	17	16	8	44	14	2	101	102
Elsewhere in France	19	6	13	17	42	4	101	48
Outside France	17	6	8	9	4	57	101	53
Total couples								667

SOURCE: ADG 10M 260, 261, 262, *Recensement, Ville de Nîmes,* 1906; systematic sample of individuals in 5 percent of households.

to fare less well than Nimoises in the marriage market. The story of Justine Fenouillet illustrates the circumstances of a migrant woman's marriage. Justine and her elder brother had come to Nîmes from Le Bleymard in the Lozère — a small village on the windswept highlands between Mende and the Regordane corridor. Their father, a peasant, remained in Le Bleymard. Justine's brother worked as an agricultural laborer on the edge of town, and Justine was a cook. In the early spring of 1906, at the age of 29, Justine married Joseph Raymond, a carter from the Alps who lived in the poorest section of the Placette. Joseph's peasant father did not attend.

Yet migrant brides did not fare so badly when we take into account the support their family was able to give them. Over half their fathers had died by the time of their marriage, compared with 36 percent of the Nimoises' fathers. In all, 13 percent of them came from the families of peasants or agricultural laborers. By contrast, no father of a Nimois bride worked in agriculture, one in eight was a member of the bourgeoisie, and nearly one in ten was a white collar worker. Over one-quarter of the Nimoises' fathers were skilled laborers, while less than one father in five of migrant brides was a skilled laborer.

Moreover, when the entire population of resident wives, native and migrant, is compared, rather than the brides of 1906 alone, the differences in their husbands' status nearly disappear. Thus it appears that marriage as a path of social mobility worked in similar ways for migrant and native-born women.[49] Of the migrant wives in Nîmes, one-third were married to unskilled and semi-skilled laborers; the figure is 30 percent for Nimoises (see Appendix III, Table III.8). Migrant wives were less likely than native-born Nimoises to be married to skilled laborers, but they were slightly more likely to be married to white collar workers and members of the petty bourgeoisie. The differences among the 583 wives in the census sample are not statistically significant. Thus, although patterns of premarital work and leisure were different for migrant and native young women, these differences do not seem to have handicapped migrant women's chances of eventually marrying a white collar or even a bourgeois suitor.

The background and the contacts of the Viganaises shaped the status of their marriage partners, for nearly one-third of the wives from Le Vigan were married to white collar workers. The Viganais pattern offers an important contrast with women from the Lozère, and even with the native-born wives of Nîmes (Appendix III, Table III.9). Approximately one in ten was married to a member of the bourgeoisie, and another 30 percent were married to skilled laborers. By contrast, the great majority of women from Villefort married laborers, and they were more likely to marry semi-skilled and unskilled laborers than skilled workers. None married a member of the bourgeoisie of Nîmes, although nearly one in five Villefortaises did marry a white collar worker, such as a railroad station employee. Almost no Langognaises married white collar workers, and nearly seven in ten married laborers. Nevertheless, a few did marry rentiers and members of the petty bourgeoisie — shopkeepers and cafetiers. As a group, the Viganaises married the most successful men, the Langognaises the next most successful, and the Villefortaises the least successful.

As a consequence, the women from Le Vigan had the largest households to manage. They were the most likely to have servants and the most likely to have relatives — particularly parents — living with them. This is due also to the Viganaises' longer history of residence in Nîmes and to the older age structure; they were more likely to have aging parents in need of housing. (Fewer than one-fifth of the wives born in Le Vigan were under 35 in 1906.) Women from Villefort also managed relatively large households, but it was their children and distant relatives, not servants, who filled their households. Their families were relatively young, and they themselves were younger than the Viganaises; about one-third were under 35. The wives from Langogne were still younger; nearly half under 35, and most of their children were under twelve. They lived in relatively small households because their childbearing years were not yet over. Although some had servants, they did not have many relatives living with them.

The importance of domestic service among women from the Lozère partially explains the fact that, once married, they had few relatives living with them. Sisters or cousins from home lived not with family, but with their employers. The way in which service work may have provided an alternative to living with relatives is suggested by the Sabatier sisters: Anna Sabatier, her husband and two small sons took in Anna's aging father, but her two younger sisters worked as domestic servants and lived with their employers. As the Sabatier family regrouped in Nîmes, then, its members did not live together. The Chevret sisters and the Janvier sisters from Villefort followed the same pattern.

Was the fertility of the women from Le Vigan different from that of the Villefortaises and Langognaises? The census tells us only that the

TABLE 4.7 Household Characteristics by Origin of Household Head

	Migrant Streams			
	Le Vigan	*Villefort*	*Langogne*	*All Migrants*
Percentage of households with:				
one member only	10	27	14	15
extended/multiple family	20	18	13	14
servants	19	0	5	12
relatives	26	30	23	18
children	64	48	60	61
N	129	44	43	599

SOURCE: ADG 10M 260, 261, 262, *Recensement, Ville de Nîmes,* 1906.

average wife from Le Vigan had 1.6 children at home; from Villefort, 1.6; from Langogne, 1.1. Yet it does not tell us how many children they had borne or would ultimately bear, because children living at home did not include those who had moved away, gone to the home village, been sent out to nurse, or who had died. (Young children were also likely to be underreported.) Given the age differences among the women, the number of children at home was about equal. If there were fertility differences, they are not discernible from the census. If there were no differences between the Vignaises and the women from the Lozère, this would suggest that the fertility of urban families reflected their immediate surroundings and employment opportunities, rather than the traditions of their *pays* of origin. The Lozerians had the highest birthrate in France at the turn of the century, and even the crude birth rates of Langogne and Villefort were substantially higher than those of Le Vigan for most of the nineteenth century.

Viganais-headed households usually included only parents and children. Often, however, their families were large, because one in five was an extended family, and one-quarter of them had kin living with them. (A summary of household characteristics is listed in Table 4.7; details are given in Appendix III, Table III.10). If the presence of servants is any indication, the Viganais were very successful, for one in five households employed at least one servant, and some employed two, three, or even four. They were much more likely to have domestics than the Villefortais, Langognais, or those sampled among the other migrant households in Nîmes.

The households formed by the Villefortais offered a stark contrast to those of the Viganais, for while many were simple families, over one-quarter consisted only of a solitary renter, be it in a garni or an apartment. As a consequence of these "solitaries," primarily among Villefort's young men, the average household size and number of children in a Villefort household was small. No Villefortais household had a servant. However, many lived in extended families and had kin living with them — in fact, nearly one-third of the households headed by Villefortais included a relative. Fewer Langognais households had kin living with them, and fewer lived in extended families. Most of them lived in a simple nuclear family including parents and children, with about the same number of children as the Viganais.

The patterns of their households varied according to age and life cycle. The majority of solitaries were young or old, being either newly arrived young people in a garni or rented room, or widowed elderly people living alone. People heading "non-families" were usually over 60. The differences among the households, then, were partly due to age: The Viganais were significantly older than the Villefortais and Langognais; 80 percent of the household heads from Le Vigan were over 40, while just over half the Lozerians were that age.

Several points emerge from a comparison of households. First, the Viganais were successful. The poverty and celibacy of solitary living characterized few among them, and their prosperity is most obvious from the large proportion who had domestic servants. In the next chapter, the occupations on which the Viganais' success rested will be examined.

Second, all three migrant groups were very likely to have kin in their households. Although the total migrant population lived with kin less often than did natives (presumably for lack of family members in town), this was not true of migrant streams: About one-quarter to 30 percent of the householders from Le Vigan, Villefort, and Langogne had a relative living in, in contrast to the sample of all migrant households (among whom less than one in five included a relative). This is partly due to the technical difference between a sample and a population. By contrast, the members of any single migration group are the total population from that origin. Among members of one group, clustering was likely because they were apt to have kin moving to the city who may have traveled with them, joined them later, moved in temporarily while they found their own housing, or who came for an extended visit to try out urban life. Perhaps kin lived together for support and aid; if so, the willingness to provide it was not based on spacious quarters or wealth. Siblings, parents, cousins, and even more distant kin clustered in both the wealthy Viganais households and the less prosperous homes of the Villefortais and the Langognais.

NETWORKS OF MIGRANTS

A fundamental theme of this book is that newcomers in the cities of urbanizing France were not alone; information available to them at home led them to choose the destination of Nîmes, and once in the city they were guided by particular contacts. Friendships, family relationships, and prior contacts supported their move to the city and their search for work and lodging. As a consequence, migration streams — networks of people connecting Le Vigan, Villefort, and Langogne — are at the heart of the study.

The slender but suggestive evidence of the census yields information about friendships and support among members of the migration streams. Many of their households included a young relative. Emile Brun, for example, lived with his aunt and uncle for a few years, and young Bouzanquet moved in with this brother and sister-in-law when he arrived in Nîmes. Retired and widowed parents resided with their children. Migrants, then, lived with kin.

Some lived in the same neighborhoods as their compatriots: the Villefortais in the Plan Vacher, the Langognais in the north end of the old city, and the Viganais on the west side. Within an urban ecology shaped by economic activity and religious affiliation, clustering was evident. It was mediated by the geography of employment, which attracted railroad workers to the Plan Vacher, retail food dealers to the market area, and domestic servants to the bourgeois neighborhoods. In some cases, nevertheless, a shared home town, occupation, and neighborhood provide strong evidence for friendships and continuing relationships among members of the migrant groups. For example, of the eight men from Villefort living in the Plan Vacher neighborhood, five worked for the railroad, five lived in the same building with another man from Villefort, and five were aged 28-43. Young, widowed Emile Brun lived with his uncle, who also worked for the PLM. Louis Jourdan, a rail fireman, lived in the same building. Cafetier Edouard Roche and an older railroad worker lived within a few blocks. Another cheminot and a cook resided six blocks away in a shared building. Old Mandagout, a shoemaker, lived a little farther south; he had been a witness at Emile Brun's first wedding in Nîmes in 1901.[50]

Like most turn-of-the-century cities, Nîmes was a "walking city," so that kin and friends from home could, and did, play a role in each other's lives, whether or not they lived in the same neighborhood. For example, Charles and Anna Bouscarrain from Le Vigan lived in a poor section of the old city with Anna's widowed father. Her cousin Doyat lived across the boulevard in the bourgades. When in 1905 another cousin married a mason on the far west side of town, Charles Bouscarrain acted as a witness. When Anna Sabatier married in Nîmes in 1900, witnesses included fellow Langognais living in the bourgades. Many of these contacts were kin, for even migrants who did not live close to each other often were related. The two Mathieu brothers and three Fabre sisters, for example, all from Langogne, were widely scattered in Nîmes. Sisters lived apart only because they were domestics, which suggests that servants could be less isolated from relatives than one would infer from their living situation. The servant Janvier sisters, for example, had each other and their married sister nearby.

Given the difficulty of establishing kinship relationships among women in the absence of maiden names, any evidence of networks among female kin is particularly striking and suggestive of continuing family ties in the city (see Appendix I). Yet most evidence points to such female kin networks. The stories of the Chevret sisters from Langogne, the Sabatier sisters, and the Janvier sisters are typical. Women from the Lozère often seem to have come to Nîmes in strings of siblings — the eldest sister followed by younger ones, coming in their early to mid-twenties. Male kin, too, joined them in Nîmes.

The friendships reflected in the act of serving as an official to witness the marriage of a compatriot doubtless were nourished at work and leisure — Sunday outings on the garrigue or on the boulevards, holidays, church services, marketing and washing at the *lavoir* for women, and meetings of mutual aid societies for men. There was also the *chambrée:*

> Abroad, our emigrants like to meet together among themselves. . . . Sunday night, in shop back rooms, gatherings take place among compatriots; absent ones, business, and home are spoken of, and one eats home foods, fruit, bacon, saussage, etc. The evening is not complete without a mountain *bourrée* danced to the music of a *cabrette*.[51]

Even in the long workdays and six-day work weeks, people made time for a visit with friends or family members, usually between Saturday and Sunday evening. Formal gatherings, too, such as the annual banquets of the Union Lozérienne and the Amicale des Originaires de l'Arrondissement du Vigan, attracted large crowds for a three-franc banquet and *"grand bal de famille."*

Visits home, visits to Nîmes by compatriots, and temporary employment in Nîmes all contributed to the movement running between Le Vigan, Villefort, and Langogne and the city. The historical record is silent on temporary migrants and visitors, but people of the small towns were vocal about the fact that "everyone was acquainted with Nîmes." The author of the history of Le Vigan noted that several trains a day traveled between the two towns, and that the Viganais would go to Nîmes to shop, to transact court and church business, to attend secondary school, to work, and *"pour servir"* — to work as servants. "Everyone worked in Nîmes at one time or another," recalled a Villefortaise. Contacts and movement so apparent to Nimois and the people of Eastern Languedoc ("Of course, you wouldn't go to the city without some sort of tentacles," reasoned Marc Bernard) can only be dimly perceived.[52] The people residing in Nîmes were only part of the system of migration operating between these three small towns in the hinterland and the city. Others were at home, temporarily, working for a time in the coal basin, serving in the army or, in the case of women particularly, married and moved elsewhere.

How common was it for migrants to operate in such a web of contacts? At the turn of the century, the great majority of migrants in Nîmes were from the Gard and contiguous departments (78 percent); 89 percent of the migrants from any given commune in France were not its sole representative, but shared that origin with at least one other person. Virtually all arrondissements represented in Nîmes (98 percent) were represented by more than one person.[53] The French saw home in broader terms than a single commune. "Study a valley, a cluster of villages," was the advice. This suggests that most migrants in Nîmes, if not relatives or life-long friends with one another, at least had a compatriot in the city.

The study of migration streams has provided no support for the frequently proposed causal link between migration and the dissolution of the social order. All three migrant groups included people who were victims of tragedy or poverty, and people who did not always act within the law, but a focus on the groups of which they were a part suggests the support that may have been available to them. For example, when Viganais Pouzergue, who lived near his father, mother, and brother's family, died at the age of 39 in 1904, family and the Protestant community doubtless came to the aid of the widow and her children. The year of Pouzergue's death, his survivors were unable to contribute to the annual Protestant collection for the poor, probably because they were themselves the recipients of charity. The servant from Villefort, seduced and abandoned by the railroad worker who subsequently returned to his usual assignment and family in Alès, surely figures in that city's police records for disturbing the peace when she pursued her ex-lover. Yet in Nîmes, she had compatriots and perhaps a brother or sister to help her. Emile Brun found solace with his aunt and uncle after his wife's death. These accounts remind us that friendships and family could not shield newcomers from tragedy, poverty, or betrayal, but they were a resource, and for many the only one, in difficult times. The fact that they existed in the city undermines the idea that the migrants' social anchor was dislodged with their departure from home.

Their life patterns, marriages, households, and fertility (as it is dimly reflected in census records) suggest that Anna Sabatier and Emile Brun were typical of newcomers to the city in many ways. First, both came to Nîmes as young, single people, where they lived different lives from other young Nimois, without family and financial resources. The woman worked as a domestic servant and lived on the fringes of a middle-class family; the man lived in a rented room. At this time in their lives, each fulfilled the stereotype of the single migrant. Unlike the stereotypical migrant, though, they married and remained in Nîmes, forming urban families. They lived with kin — Anna Sabatier provided a home for her widowed father, and Emile Brun lived with his aunt and uncle after the death of his first wife. Other migrants, both rich and poor, came to Nîmes along with their families. Both family and single migrants probably had a more positive effect on the population of Nîmes than 70 years before, when fewer migrants were coming to the city and fewer were staying for long. The process of urbanization is this formation of an urban family played out thousands of times over. The migrants' life cycle, in fact, elucidates the process, for it shows the newcomer becoming a demographically productive member of the urban community.

Viganais, Villefortais, and Longognais played specific roles. Cultural and institutional ties brought Viganais of all ages to Nîmes. Like country women since the middle ages, the young women from the Lozère came to Nîmes primarily as servants, but they were very likely to marry if they stayed on in the city. Although domestic service precluded them from living with their families, the presence of their sisters, other kin, and compatriots in Nîmes makes it clear that migration streams did cluster together. Although vulnerable, migrant domestic servants were not alone. Moreover, retired and widowed parents, and siblings, came to join their families. Consequently, the migration streams to Nîmes from Le Vigan, Villefort, and Langogne — as different as they were from one another — all reflect the tendency of migrants to seek each other out, to move together, and to give each other information and support. Whether they came to Nîmes to fulfill the official function of court lawyer or to take one of the city's jobs as a maid-of-all-work, the collective and continuous nature of relationships among migrants is confirmed.

NOTES

1. See note 2, Chapter 1.

2. *Laboring Classes and Dangerous Classes in Paris During the First Half of the Nineteenth Century* (New York: Fertig, 1973); Alain Corbin, *Les filles de noce: misère sexuelle et prostitution (19e et 20e siècles)* (Paris: Aubier Montaigne, 1978); Archives Municipales de Nîmes (hereafter AMN): Series FVII, 55-2, Bureaux de Placement.

3. John Knodel, "Town and country in 19th-century Germany: a review of urban-rural differentials in demographic behavior," *Social Science History* 1 (1977), 356-382; John Knodel and Mary Jo Maynes, "Urban and rural marriage patterns in Imperial Germany," *Journal of Family History* 1 (1976), 129-168; Allan Sharlin, "Natural decrease in early modern cities: a reconsideration," *Past and Present* 79 (1978), 126-138.

4. See, for example, Maurice Garden, "L'attraction de Lyon à la fin de l'ancien régime," *Annales de démographie historique* (1970), 205-220; Emmanuel Le Roy Ladurie, *Les paysans de Languedoc* (Paris: SEVPEN, 1966), 93-98.

5. Evelyn B. Ackerman, *Village on the Seine* (Ithaca, NY: Cornell University Press, 1979), 106; Michael Anderson, *Family Structure in Nineteenth-Century Lancashire* (Cambridge: Cambridge University Press, 1971), 59; Alain Corbin, *Archaïsme et modernité en Limousin au XIXe siècle, 1845-1880* (Paris: Rivière, 1975), 177-221; Theresa McBride, *The Domestic Revolution* (New York: Holmes and Meier, 1976); Louise Tilly, "Occupational structure, women's work and demographic change in two French industrial cities, Anzin and Roubaix, 1892-1906," in J.

Sundlin and Erik Soderlund, eds., *Time, Space and Man* (Atlantic Highlands, NJ: Humanities Press, 1979), 112.

6. Lucie Mazauric Chamson, *"Belle Rose, Ô Tour Magne"* (Paris: Plon, 1969), 195.

7. L'Abbé Achille Serran, *Les masets nimois* (Nîmes: Imprimerie Générale, 1898), 48.

8. Marc Bernard, *Salut Camarades* (Paris: Gallimard, 1955), 97.

9. Newspaper reports following legislative elections, *Le Petit Républican du Midi* (hereafter PR), 1904, 1906, 1908; *Journal du Midi,* February 21, 1902; lecture attendance is noted in PR, January 17, 23, 1906.

10. Mazauric Chamson, *Rose,* 55, 59. The outing clubs, such as those found in the Répertoire des Associations déclarées, ADG, series 6M, 6535, were most certainly out of reach for all but the middle-class youth, because they took time from work and because some excursions were quite expensive. For example, the excursion to Mount Aigoul in the Cévennes advertised in the PR cost 22 francs, which was about one week's pay for a worker, July 5, 1906. Clubs in the Répertoire included shooting, hunting, fencing, and even a flying group.

11. PR, June 27 and October 6, 8, 22, 1906; *Le Petit Midi* (hereafter PM), March 2, 1906. The practice of climbing over the gates of the Arena was especially popular during bullfights; PR, September 1, 4, 7, 1906.

12. John Demos and Virginia Demos, "Adolescence in historical perspective," *Journal of Marriage and the Family* 35 (1969), 368; Joseph Kett, "Adolescence and youth in nineteenth-century America," in T. Rabb and R. Rotberg, eds., *The Family in History* (New York: Harper Torchbooks, 1971), 99; Theodore Zeldin, *France, 1848-1914,* Vol. 1 (Oxford: Clarendon Press, 1973), 333; PM, February 1 and 18 and October 18, 1906.

13. Anderson, *Family Structure,* 59; John Gillis, *Youth and History: Tradition and Change in European Age Relations, 1770 to the Present* (New York: Academic Press, 1974), 61, 77; Michael Katz, *The People of Hamilton, Canada West: Family and Class in a Mid-Nineteenth-Century City* (Cambridge, MA: Harvard University Press, 1975), 156, 174-178; Joseph Kett, *Rites of Passage: Adolescence in America, 1790 to the Present* (New York: Basic Books, 1977), 5, 169.

14. Anderson, *Family Structure,* 85, 101-106; Gillis, *Youth,* 55, 58; Lynn Lees, "Irish slum communities in nineteenth century London," in S. Thernstrom and R. Sennett, eds., *Nineteenth Century Cities* (New Haven, CT: Yale University Press, 1970), 359-385; Joan Scott and Louise Tilly, "Women's work and family in nineteenth-century Europe," *Comparative Studies in Society and History* 17 (1975), 52-53; Adna Weber, *The Growth of Cities in the Nineteenth Century* (Ithaca, NY: Cornell University Press, 1899), 280.

15. Paul Marcelin, *Souvenirs d'un passé artisanal* (Nîmes: Chastanier, 1967), 36, 13; Chamson, *Rose,* 44-48 and passim.

16. *Pareils à des enfants* (Paris: Gallimard, 1941), 182-186.

17. Katz, *People of Hamilton,* 260; Scott and Tilly, "Women's Work," 38-39.

18. Gillis, *Youth,* 127-131; Kett, *Adolescence,* 5; Ville de Nîmes, *Bulletin Municipal* (1910).

19. Bernard, *Des enfants,* 277.

20. Leslie Page Moch, "Adolescence and migration to Nîmes, 1906," *Social Science History* 5 (1981), 25-51.

21. Mazel compared the marriage rate for Nîmes (7.08) with Paris (9.08), Lyon (8.2), and Marseille (7.5) in "Statistique démographique de la ville de Nîmes comparée (1876-1888)," *Mémoires de l'Académie de Nîmes,* Ser. 7, 10 (1887), 230-231.

22. The rate of marriage in Nîmes, 1904-1908, was 6.85 (Ville de Nîmes, *Bulletin Municipal,* 1904-1908).

23. Of the solitary householders, 62 percent were migrants; of the female household heads, 60 percent were migrants. For an assessment of the inference of marital status from census lists, see Appendix I.

24. Knodel and Maynes ("Urban and rural marriage patterns," 150-151, 157) did not assume that all singles were servants; they compared the female nuptiality of natives and migrants in Berlin and Frankfurt in 1885. In Berlin, native-born women were less likely to be single at ages 45-49; in Frankfurt there was no difference. Michael Anderson observed that the middle-class family may be responsible for high proportions of single people: "Marriage patterns in Victorian Britain: an analysis based on registration district data for England and Wales," *Journal of Family History* 1 (1976), 57.

25. About 10 percent of women in Nîmes aged 15-49 worked as domestic servants, and about 20 percent of the migrant women were so employed. Of the unmarried migrant women aged 15-29, over 40 percent were servants.

26. In 1901, the I_g for all of France was .372. I_g for the Department of the Gard was .361 and for the Department of the Somme, where fertility had declined earlier, I_g was .331. For the Department of the Nord, where fertility declined late and from a high level, the I_g was .478. The index of marital fertility, I_g, compares the total births of women of childbearing years with the number of births that would have resulted if married women had experienced the age-specific fertility rates of married Hutterite women. The number of total legitimate births is taken from the *état civil* of Nîmes; the age structure of the married female population is based on the census sample. Because the age structure of the married female population is based on a census sample, the approximate nature of the measure I_g must be emphasized. An accurate measure rests on (a) the absence of sampling error, (b) correct age-reporting in the census, and (c) a flawless coding of marital status. Yet there are probably errors on all three counts; for example, flawless age-reporting is not characteristic of any census. See Allan Sharlin, "Historical demography as history and demography," *American Behavioral Scientist* 21 (1977), 257; Etienne van de Walle, *The Female Population of France in the Nineteenth Century* (Princeton, NJ: Princeton University Press, 1974), 151-154, 309, 394.

27. ADG, Series M 469, Report of labor violations; Statistique générale, *Industrie: Résultats généraux de l'enquête effectuée pendant l'année 1848* (Paris: Imprimerie Nationale, 1848), 70-76.

28. Michael Haines, *Fertility and Occupation: Population Patterns in Industrialization* (New York: Academic Press, 1979); Louise Tilly, "Occupational structure, women's work and demographic change."

29. Van de Walle, *Female Population of France,* 151; Ville de Nîmes, *Bulletin Municipal* (1901-1906).

30. Anderson, *Family Structure*, 52, 54.

31. Ibid., 44; Michael Anderson, "Household structure and the Industrial Revolution: mid-nineteenth century Preston in comparative perspective," in P. Laslett, ed., *Household and Family in Past Time* (Cambridge: Cambridge University Press, 1972), 200, 222; Katz, *People of Hamilton*, 221.

32. Katz, *People of Hamilton*, 251; Bernard, *Des enfants*, 169, 192; Mazauric Chamson, *Rose*, 77, 173.

33. John Hajnal, "Age at marriage and proportions marrying," *Population Studies* 7 (1953), 111-136; Knodel, "Town and country."

34. Michel Frey, "Du mariage et du concubinage dans les classes populaires à Paris (1846-1847)," *Annales: ESC* 33 (1978), 809-812.

35. Victorien Brugier, *La bourse du travail à Nîmes* (Nîmes: Imprimerie l'Idéale, 1925), 138; Alice Fermaud, "La lycée de jeunes filles de Nîmes," *Revue économique de la Chambre de Commerce du Nîmes-Uzès-Le Vigan* 4, no. 35 (1953), 16-18.

36. See note 2, Chapter 1.

37. For the view that movement from nearby towns into cities *was* crucial, see Michael Anderson, "Urban structure in nineteenth century Lancashire: some insights into two competing hypotheses," *Annales de démographie historique* (1971), 13-26.

38. The sex ratio is the ratio of males to females. A figure greater than 100 indicates a male majority.

39. Mazel, "Statistique démographique," 218; Knodel, "Town and country," 360-361; Adna Weber, *The Growth of Cities in the Nineteenth Century* (Ithaca, NY: Cornell University Press, 1899), 289. The sex ratio of the sample from the census of Nîmes is 83, while it is 74 for the migrants from the sample.

40. Mazel, "Statistique démographique," 222; Knodel, "Town and country," 360-361.

41. Robert J. Myers, "Errors and bias in the reporting of ages in census data," *Transactions of the Actuarial Society of America* 41, Part 2 (1940), 411-415.

42. Moch, "Adolescence and migration."

43. McBride, *Domestic Revolution;* Olwen Hufton, *The Poor of Eighteenth Century France* (Oxford: Clarendon Press, 1974).

44. PR, July 21, 1906.

45. AMN, Series F7, 55-2, "Bureaux de placement."

46. Raymond Dugrand, *Villes et campagnes en Bas-Languedoc* (Paris: Presses Universitaires Françaises, 1963), 463.

47. I am grateful to M. Armand Cosson for permitting me to use his analysis of the 1850 marriage records in Nîmes. M. Cosson is preparing a *thèse d'état* on the working class in Nîmes in the early nineteenth century; see idem., "Industrie de soie et population ouvrière à Nîmes de 1815 à 1848," in G. Cholvy, ed., *Economie et société en Languedoc-Roussillon de 1789 à nos jours* (Montpellier: Université Paul Valéry, 1978), 189-214. He is currently a professor of history at the Lycée Alphonse Daudet in Nîmes.

48. Yves Tugault, *La mésure de la mobilité* (Paris: Presses Universitaires Françaises, 1973), 40-41.

49. Veena Thadani and Michael Todaro, "Female migration in developing countries: a framework for analysis" (Working paper 47, Center for Policy Studies, The Population Council, New York, 1980); McBride, *Domestic Revolution*, 90-95; Nor-

val Glenn et al., "Patterns of Intergenerational mobility of females through marriage," *American Sociological Review* 39 (1969), 638-699.

50. ADG, series 10M, 261, "1906 census, Nîmes"; see note 2, Chapter 1.

51. Jules Barbot, *Le paysan lozérian* (Mende: Privat, 1899), 37; see Maurice Agulhon, "Les chambrées en Basse-Provence: histoire et ethnologie," *Revue historique* 498 (1971), 337-368; Lucienne Roubin, *Chambrettes des Provencaux* (Paris: Plon, 1970).

52. Interview with Pierre Gorlier, Le Vigan, May 17, 1977; interview with Marc Bernard, Paris, February 10, 1977. The importance of temporary stays in Nîmes cannot be discerned from sources of information about migration in France; lack of knowledge about back and forth movement is a frustration shared by many students of migration: Neal Ritchy, "Explanations of migration," A. Inkeles et al., eds., *Annual Review of Sociology* 2 (1977), 363-404; Kevin McQuillian, "Economic factors and internal migration: the case of nineteenth-century England," *Social Science History* 4 (1980), 479-499. For an appreciation of the addition made by such information, see two German studies: David F. Crew, *Town in the Ruhr: A Social History of Bochum, 1860-1914* (New York: Columbia University Press, 1979), 59-74; and Steve Hochstadt, "Migration and industrialization in Germany, 1815-1977," *Social Science History* 5 (1980), 445-468.

53. The notation of shared origins is a common way of discerning migration streams at destination; see Josef Barton, *Peasants and Strangers* (Cambridge, MA: Harvard University Press, 1975), 49-50.

5

Migrants in the Urban Economy

> Behind these grand trends, the history of this long emergence is a painting in half-tints, where the new never substitutes the old, but is added to it. It is by a cumulative process that the region's working class is created . . .
>
> — Yves Lequin,
> *Les ouvriers de la région lyonnaise*

The labor force of Nîmes included service workers, such as waiters, domestic servants, and barbers; railroad employees working in the car repair, passenger, and freight depots of the PLM; manufacturing workers in small ateliers and at home; white collar workers in commerce and administration; and myriad unskilled workers performing such tasks as hauling, construction, and road repair. Thus, workers in Nîmes and similar cities were not members of the factory proletariat which informs many historical studies of the labor force. Most, nevertheless, were wage earners — proletarians in the broadest sense — working in nonfactory settings. For example, many of its industrial laborers worked at home, with their own tools, for the mechanization of the shoemaking industry had barely begun in 1906. The severe crises suffered by the workers of Nîmes robbed them of the control over their labor which is normally implied by the title of artisan and by ownership of one's own tools.[1] And although proletarian, many of the tram, post office, and PLM workers experienced a security unheard of in most industries. The white collar worker, who was so important in Nîmes, ordinarily is excluded from the proletariat. In this context, Yves Lequin's musings on such workers are relevant:

> Outside the proletariat, but close to it, the employee is an essential element of the urban social horizon. A petty bourgeois — even though non-owner — or a proletariat in white collar? Beyond theoretical definitions — all too rigorous — the question is posed.[2]

Geographic mobility played a crucial role in the formation of this labor force, for the growth of Nîmes after 1880 coincided with its evolution into a commercial and administrative center, and with industrial decline and the slow recovery from the devastations of the phylloxera epidemic. The pattern of Nîmes was not unique among French cities, for in many cases "the emergence of the working class is not the simple trace of industrial expansion; far from it."[3] The growth of Bordeaux and Montpellier, for example, did not coincide with the growth of industry. Even in the Lyonnais region, where industry played a more central role, the periods of urban growth did not coincide with those of industrial expansion. "Rather," concludes Yves Lequin, "agriculture led the game," as the multifaceted crises of the end of the century forced many people from villages and small towns to move to the city.[4] Once in the city, many migrants stayed on to settle, form urban families, and become permanent members of the city's work force.

The formation of the urban labor force, studied in regional contexts, was a complex and cumulative process. In the exchanges of resources and people between agriculture and the urban economy, between village and town, and among towns and cities, a part of the regional population moved into the city's labor force. We have already seen how this worked in the case of Nîmes, in its human and economic exchange with the silk-producing subprefecture of Le Vigan and its employment of village people from the uplands of the Lozère. The question that this chapter addresses is how the people of Languedoc — who earlier had dissolved in the urban melting pot drop by drop — became part of the urban labor force as those drops turned to a tide at the end of the nineteenth century.[5]

Yves Lequin's pioneering study of the Lyonnais offers answers in his analysis of the origins of occupational groups within the urban labor force. The same questions can be asked for Nîmes: Which occupations were held primarily by urban-born natives? Which were composed of traditional migration streams? In which occupations were the sons and daughters of peasants and small town people new to the city? Which sectors constituted the "crucible of the new labor force"? The analysis of occupational structure by place of birth reveals the strongholds of the native-born and traditional migration streams, as well as the avenues of entry for newcomers. This illuminates the role of migrants in the evolution of the urban economy. With information about migrants' origins, it becomes possible to examine the connection between migration and social mobility and to untangle the complex of factors associated with occupation, such as training, parentage, and birthplace.[6] Understanding the origin and affiliations of the labor force also elucidates how workers — migrants in particular — found jobs through personal contacts.[7] Finally, analysis of occupation, parentage, and birthplace together addresses the origins of social stratification in a changing labor force infused with migrants.[8]

MIGRATION AND OCCUPATIONAL MOBILITY

Newcomers to the city have been likened to passengers on a three-class train, or to people stepping on an escalator, who will in time rise to the top of the urban hierarchy. For many European cities at the turn of the century, the images of the escalator and the train are complicated by the fact that migrants often came from the countryside or small towns, so that moving into the city involved moving into a labor force quite different from that of home. For example, Wolfgang Köllmann indicates that three separate occupational hierarchies (agrarian, industrial, and the public sector) coexisted in urbanizing Germany, and that a move to the city often meant changing from one hierarchy to another. In France, where many rural people supported themselves by a combination of manufacturing and pastoral or agricultural work, a move to the city often signaled an end to work on the land. Moreover, some kinds of urban jobs — particularly white collar jobs — expanded so greatly during the Third Republic that, with the *Certificat d'Etudes Primaires,* the countryman's son as well as the urban child had a chance to enter this expanding arena. Migrants in Nîimes can help us understand for which groups migration and social mobility went hand in hand.

Occupational histories of 102 men Le Vigan, Villefort, and Langogne have been compiled, each including at least the subject's occupation, age, place of birth, and father's occupation. For some it was possible to find occupation at the age of twenty (from conscription records), at marriage, at children's births (from marriage and birth records), and at the turn of the century (from the census of Protestant electors). All the men from Le Vigan, Villefort, and Langogne about whom it was possible to locate information were included as subjects.[9] Appendix II lists the complete occupational histories, and six sample histories appear in Table 5.1. Table 5.2 summarizes the parentage of the subjects.

TABLE 5.1 Occupational Histories of Individual Male Migrants (Examples From Appendix II)

Occupation in Nîmes, 1906	*Occupation of Father*	*Occupation at Age 20*	*Occupation in 1901*	*Occupation at Other Time*	*Assigned Name*	*Age in 1906*
Bourgeois						
conseiller à la cour	greffier de la justice de paix, LV	étudiant en droit, Paris (1867)	conseiller à la cour	conseiller à la cour (1906)	Donzel, E.	59
Petty bourgeois						
cafetier	enfant naturel, V (1867)	. . .	concièrge	débitant de liqueurs (1906)	Mialthe, E.	37
White collar						
employé de banque	surveillant de la filature, LV (1862)	étudiant, LV (1881)	. . .	ingénieur civil (1893), employé comptoir d'escompte (1901)	Dolladille, J.	46
Skilled labor						
boulanger	meunier, L (1873)	pâtissier, L (1893)	. . .	. . .	Saltet, P.	33
Unskilled and semi-skilled						
cultivateur	journalier, L (1877)	cultivateur, (1897)	. . .	. . .	Mathieu, B.	29
Railroad employees						
PLM	tisserand, V (1878)	boulanger, V (1898)	. . .	employé PLM, manoeuvre (1904)	Janvier, P.	28

SOURCE: See Appendix II.

Histories of migrant members of the bourgeoisie in Nîmes, all from Le Vigan, reveal prestigious parentage, as Table 5.2 shows. Most of the fathers were Le Vigan's elite administrators, legal professionals, and entrepreneurs; the sons became administrators and liberal professionals in the city. Some men, such as lawyers Léopold Laurent and Philippe Revel, followed their father's vocation. Most of this group, however, came from one part of Le Vigan's elite and trained for another profession. For example, Monsieur Tessier was chief secretary at the subprefecture in Le Vigan when his son Antoine was born in 1841. After school, presumably in Montpellier, Tessier became a doctor in Nîmes. Camille Guiraud, whose father was a property owner and silk manufacturer, practiced law in Nîmes. Dramatic intergenerational or life-cycle changes of status were rare in this group. Almost the only example is Henri Donzel, the joiner's son who became a bureau chief at the Prefecture in Nîmes. Most of this group came from financially solid, if not educated families. At the age of conscription, many were in school or training.

Migrants who became shop and café keepers in Nîmes originated in more humble families; with the possible exception of one PLM employee, all had artisans and laborers for fathers (see Table 5.2). Not one of them followed his father's occupation. Sons of day laborers, cobblers, and wooden-shoemakers, they must have had little capital backing for their eneterprises. The Mauméjean brothers, for example, were sons of a day laborer in Langogne. Léopold, the elder, worked as a miner, then moved to Nîmes to run a café about the same time as his brother Arthur. Several had worked as waiters when they were in their twenties.

White collar workers in Nîmes — clerks, accountants, government and bank employees — came from a wide range of backgrounds (see Table 5.2). This is partly because their occupations reflect a wide range of statuses, from business clerks to bank department managers. Of those on the most rewarding career ladders, the majority had fathers who were not manual laborers, but who were themselves white collar workers, innkeepers, and businessmen. Félix Pivarot, for example, whose father was a gendarme in Villefort, worked as a tax clerk for the national government. Yet even laborers could become clerical workers. Pierre Faucher, son of an agricultural laborer and himself a ditch-digger in his early days in Langogne, became a clerk in Nîmes. David Donnadieu, a laborer's son from Le Vigan, also became a clerk.

TABLE 5.2 Summary of Occupational Histories

Occupational Category	*N*	*Hometown*	*Occupations*	*Father's Occupational Category*
Bourgeoisie	14	Le Vigan	legal and medical professionals, entrepreneurs, church, rentiers, *propriétaires*	8 bourgeois 2 while collar (functionaries) 4 skilled laborers
Petit bourgeois	8	Le Vigan (4) Villefort (2) Langogne (2)	*cafetiers* (6) *débitant de tabac*, butcher	4 skilled laborers 2 unskilled laborers 1 PLM employee 1 illegitimate
White collar	19	Le Vigan (13) Villefort (4) Langogne (2)	*employés* (6), functionaries (5), bookkeepers and bank employees (4) commercial employees (3), *géometre*	2 bourgeois 4 petit bourgeois 5 white collar 4 skilled laborers 2 unskilled laborers 2 agriculturalists

Skilled labor	24	Le Vigan (15) Villefort (4) Langogne (5)	building & carpentry (6) (mason, joiner) metal (7) (jeweler, machinist, locksmith) clothing and leather (6), food (5)	16 skilled laborers 2 unskilled laborers 3 white collar 3 agriculturalists
Semi-skilled and unskilled labor	22	Le Vigan (13) Villefort (4) Langogne (5)	services (9) (waiter, cook, servant), laborers (11) (day laborer, ragman) agriculturalists (2)	8 agriculturalists 5 unskilled laborers 6 unskilled laborers 1 petit bourgeois 2 illegitimate
Railroad employees	15	Le Vigan (3) Villefort (8) Langogne (4)	employees of the PLM (8), "PLM" (7)	2 white collar 7 skilled laborers 4 unskilled laborers 2 agriculturalists
Total	102			

SOURCE: ADG 10M 260, 261, 262 *Recensement, Ville de Nîmes*, 1906; ADG E5 *Etat civil*, Le Vigan; ADL 4E 198 *Etat civil*, Villefort; ADL 4E 80 *Etat civil*, Langogne.

Most of the migrant skilled laborers had skilled laborers for fathers, and one-quarter of them adopted their father's vocation. Viganais Arthur Lafont followed his father's profession as a jeweler in Nîmes. Henri Dupuis, a watchmaker from Villefort, was probably trained by his father, as were two carpenters from Le Vigan named Louis Giral and Léon Massadau. Some skilled laborers were the sons of unskilled and agricultural laborers, and a few were sons of white collar workers. Most of those whose conscript records could be found were already working at a trade at the age of twenty.

In terms of parentage, unskilled laborers in Nîmes were the most disadvantaged. They include haulers, ragmen, domestics, cooks, waiters, day laborers, gardeners, and agricultural workers. Three-quarters of them were sons of agriculturalists or unskilled workers. Some were illegitimate; a few had artisan fathers. The largest group of fathers, like Baptiste André of Villefort, were agriculturalists. Monsieur André's sons, Jules and Louis, left Villefort in the 1890s for Nîmes, where Jules worked as a carter and Louis as a day laborer. A third of those whose conscript records could be found were agricultural laborers at the age of twenty. In Nîmes, none had the same occupation as his father.

Railroad workers are treated separately because a large and diverse body of workers gave their occupation as "*employé* PLM" or simply "PLM" (Paris-Lyon-Méditerranée Railroad) to the census taker.[10] Like bureau chief Victor Bouzanquet of Villefort, some had rather high-level jobs. Also like him was Daniel Vidal, who had also begun working for the railroad in his hometown of Langogne at an early age. By his forties, Monsieur Vidal was chief conductor, earning 1650 francs per year. However, many who listed their occupation as simply "PLM" were doubtless low-paid laborers who made up the majority of railroad workers — like Eugène, the husband of Marc Bernard's cousin, who repaired railcars in the depot east of the city.[11]

The parentage of railroad workers was diverse; nearly half their fathers were artisans, and the rest unskilled workers and peasants. Victor Bouzanquet's father was the village barber — and postman — of Villefort. Daniel Vidal's father was a peasant in Langogne. The railroad was an employer that drew adult men from their home towns because many were working at home at age twenty, not as cheminots, but as bakers, carpenters, locksmiths, wheelwrights, or barbers. The father of only one of the fifteen PLM employees had previously worked for the railroad. This was Henri Valette, whose father had worked on the line in Villefort. Valette had worked as a locksmith in Villefort as a young man and had moved to Nîmes in his twenties, where he was promoted from fitter to mechanic.

The parentage of these groups suggests that in many cases, home training and resources played an important role in the men's eventual occupation. It also provides some clues about the link between migration and occupational mobility. For the bourgeois, then, parentage was quite important; it supplied financial and moral support for one's education and professional training. It is doubtful that the lawyers, doctors, and dentists from Le Vigan could have achieved their professional standing without family aid. Given their backgrounds, the bourgeois from Le Vigan rarely entered a new hierarchy when going to work in Nîmes. Although the Viganais had moved from a small town to large city, they operated in occupational structures similar to those of their fathers. Some change in scale and prestige, but no basic change was usually experienced by the professional son of a Viganais court lawyer or bureaucrat.

The same holds true for many migrant skilled laborers. Trained and socialized in an artisanal world, work in Nîmes required the same skills. Their histories suggest that parentage was important for this group, too, for many fathers trained their sons. Both groups experienced little discontinuity in their work lives because they had been training for, if not practicing, their life-long vocation even before the age of twenty.

This was not the case for café operators, unskilled laborers, or railroad workers who had not trained for urban jobs in their home towns. This is particularly true of peasants' sons, who often became unskilled laborers. Few men in these three groups adopted their father's occupation or even the same kind of occupation. Thus, to them the change of location meant entry into a different hierarchy, as well as a change in the size of the work force. For cheminots in particular, this was an advancement, because railroad employment offered more secure employment than most other jobs available to the sons of peasants or laborers.

White collar work, and patterns of mobility into it, seems to be divided into two rough categories for migrants from Le Vigan, Villefort, and Langogne. The sons of administrators, businessmen, and government clerks were employed on a relatively high-reaching career ladder. They worked in a sector similar to that of their fathers but were able to advance to a more prestigious position. On the other hand, the sons of peasants and laborers often worked as clerks. Their *Certificat d'Etudes Primaires* qualified them for white collar employment. Work as an urban store clerk or accountant doubtless spelled a vast change in work routine for the sons of peasants, small-town artisans, and workers. Like the railroad workers, the clerks of Nîmes often had work lives that bore little resemblance to those of their fathers.

For migrants whose family training or economic resources did not prepare them for urban work, some sectors of the labor force seem to have opened with relative ease. The young man who managed to acquire some education could find clerical work. Young rural and small-town laborers could become day laborers, or haulers, or they could follow the old custom — nearly gone, for men, by the twentieth century — of working as domestic servants. The PLM was also a ready employer. A comparison of migrants and native-born Nimois will tell us if these patterns of inclusion were general to all of the city's migrants.

MIGRANTS AND MEN'S WORK IN NÎMES

Over half the men working in Nîmes were migrants in 1906. Their occupations, on the whole, were distinctively different from those of native-born Nimois, as Table 5.3 shows. Migrants were less likely to be skilled workers such as shoemakers, locksmiths, or tinsmiths. They were more likely to be semi-skilled and unskilled workers — the city's carters, day laborers, and unskilled railroad workers. Over one-third of employed migrants fell into the lowest job category, and only about one-fifth worked at skilled trades. Migrants were not excluded from the bourgeoisie or from white collar jobs, however; their representation among rentiers, top administrators, professionals, and business employees was about equal to that of the Nimois.

The life patterns of migrants, the nature of the artisanal community, and the history of Nîmes account for these patterns. First, the training for a stonemason, locksmith, shoemaker, or other artisan was only available where these artisans were located, most often in an urban area. Artisans trained apprentices and hired assistants from the pool of available people. These were more likely to be a youth in Nîmes or an already-trained artisan from out of town than an inexperienced, young rural man. Migrants were less likely than natives to have artisans' skills or to be in Nîmes at a trainable age.

TABLE 5.3 Occupational Status and Origin, Males (percentages)

	Natives	*Migrants*	*Total*
Bourgeois	13	14	14
Petit bourgeois	4	8	6
White collar	22	20	21
Skilled labor	34	24	29
Semi-skilled and unskilled labor	27	34	30
Total	100%	100%	100%
N	451	465	916
x^2, $p < .01$			

SOURCE: ADG 10M 260, 261, 262, *Recensement, Ville de Nîmes,* 1906; systematic sample of individuals in 5 percent of households.

Moreover, the migrant was an outsider to the tight-knit world of the artisan. Artisans lived and worked close to each other; they formed a community. These factors facilitated the hiring of friends, relatives, and offspring. Professions with strong customs and local hiring practices have been called "closed professions" in Marseille, because they were not open to outsiders.[12] The same dynamic found in Marseille also seems to have been present in Nîmes. For example, shoemaking was the most important industry in Nîmes, but in 1906 it was organized into small ateliers and home work, and most of the shoemakers were native Nimois. Of the shoemakers in the census sample, 69 percent were born in Nîmes. Marc Bernard describes the citywide friendship network of shoemakers in his autobiography *Pareils à des enfants,* as he recounts being sent from neighborhood to neighborhood in search of a borrowed tool. The social side of their friendships is seen in the artisans' celebration of "Saint Monday," which often ended with performances at the popular theater on Monday nights.[13]

The crises suffered by industrial workers in Nîmes helped to close the doors of industry to outsiders. From the time of the early slumps in the silk industry, Nimois sought other work and/or scrounged a living from the garrigue in hard times. Those who remained in Nîmes at the turn of the century had adapted their skills to rug production, shoemaking, and the remaining small industries. Their flexibility was like that of the Lyon workers who, in Lequin's words, knew how to do nothing and yet could do everything. And like Lyonnais, they monopolized the industrial jobs remaining in Nîmes.

> More than ever, the factory was part of the familiar world, all the more since the working class was largely generated from itself, there, with the adaption and the budding of urban métiers. . . The proletarians of the large factories of the twentieth century come from there, from those who belonged to the working class for one generation at least, leaving the service occupations to the newcomers.[14]

No such exclusion barred migrants from the bourgeoisie of Nîmes. Bourgeois rentiers and *propriétaires* held their positions by virtue of wealth, on which there was no urban monopoly, particularly because it was often based on rural holdings — family land in the Cévennes, or vineyards on the plain. For example, Camille Guiraud's family was founded on the Cevenol silk industry and land holding. The professional members of the bourgeoisie, such as high-level administrators, doctors, and lawyers, qualified for their position by training and career promotions. Personal contacts may have influenced promotions, or preferences for Nîmes, but training and education played the more central role. As a consequence, administrators and urban professionals were not necessarily Nimois.[15]

White collar work in Nîmes also mixed native-born Nimois with migrants. In the rapidly growing commercial service and administrative sectors of Nîmes, white collar employment expanded, and demand was high. Supply was high, too, for many people, both from Nîmes and its hinterland, were eager to become clerks and government employees. Response was strong to the advertised civil service examinations, and those who received positions, such as female postal clerks, were listed in the local papers. As noted elsewhere, stenography was the most popular class at the *Bourse du Travail.*[16] Migrants found government clerical work particularly desirable because it was easy, assured work and had the status of nonmanual labor:

> Civil service is becoming the supreme ideal of young Cevenols. Easy work, with sure earnings, in a city; is that not tempting for a young man who has before him the prospect of a harsh life with uncertain gains in a remote valley?[17]

Migrants also sought out railroad employment, and here they formed the majority, for in Nîmes well over half the railroad employees came from outside the city. The attraction of the PLM came not in salaries, but in the security of guaranteed employment, a pension, and free travel. Madame Audibert of Le Vigan boasted of these advantages when her son signed on with "the Company." The attraction of the railroad for migrants also originated in its visibility for the village and small-town residents of France, many of whom were touched by the railroad for the first time when the "third network" of lines was built into remote areas during the Third Republic. Railroad construction, and even more, the railroad station, demonstrated the possibility of steady employment and a decent salary to people whose rural futures looked progressively dimmer.[18]

Within these general patterns, the men in the long-lived, broadly based migration stream from Le Vigan show particular patterns of employment, patterns distinct from those of men from Villefort and Langogne. These are summarized in Table 5.4. The economic situation and status level of the Viganais were clearly superior to the Lozerian groups. Not only did nearly one in six belong to the bourgeoisie, but over one-quarter of them held a white collar job. One-third performed skilled artisanal work, but the clearest mark of privilege is the relatively small proportion (24 percent) of Viganais who were semi-skilled and unskilled workers. The Lozerians, on the other hand, appear at the bottom of the occupational hierarchy, where about half of them were service workers, day laborers, and unspecialized railroad workers. About one-fifth of the Villefortais and Langognais worked at white collar jobs, and another fifth at skilled occupations, but virtually none attained bourgeois status. Compared with all other male migrants in Nîmes, the Viganais were more likely to have white collar or skilled jobs, and the Lozerians were more likely to have semi-skilled and unskilled positions.

The bourgeois Viganais were primarily educated professionals, rather than rentiers or *propriétaires*. For example, four of the thirteen bourgeois had legal training, including a court judge and the solicitor general. The white collar Viganais included bank employees and government workers in the post office and Prefecture; these were plum jobs by virtue of their security and prestige. Skilled Viganais worked at a variety of trades, from typesetters to barbers, but most notable among them were shoemakers and tailors — workers in the artisanally organized industry of Nîmes. Those in unskilled positions included servants, day laborers, railroad workers, and waiters, but among them, too, numbered three clothing workers.

Le Vigan's long-lived connections with Nîmes, its role as a subprefecture, and its educational history all acted to feed Viganais into the bourgeoisie and the most desirable white collar jobs. Religion

TABLE 5.4 Occupational Status and Origin, Male Migrants (percentages)

	Migrant Streams			
	Le Vigan	*Villefort*	*Langogne*	*All Migrants*
Bourgeois	14	3	0	14
Petit bourgeois	3	3	11	8
White collar	26	22	21	20
Skilled labor	32	19	21	24
Unskilled and semi-skilled labor	24	53	48	34
Total	99%	100%	101%	100%
N	90	36	29	465

SOURCE: ADG 10M 260, 261, 262, *Recensement, Ville de Nîmes,* 1906.

surely played a role. Protestants from Le Vigan had connections with the reformed bourgeoisie, which had dominated the economy for a century. Second, local and national sources attest to particular Protestant aspirations, a keen interest in white collar work and educational and government employment. "This taste for civil service," observed Roussy of the Cevenol aspirations, "seemed to be more developed in Protestants."[19] Protestants in general, and Viganais Protestants in particular, were able to avoid manual labor in Nîmes. Of the Viganais whose occupational histories could be reconstructed, over one-third of the bourgeois and white collar workers were electors of the Protestant consistory in Nîmes. And of all the electors from Le Vigan, 23 percent were members of the bourgeoisie, while another 48 percent held white collar jobs. Consistory membership was the preserve of adult males with at least three years' residence in Nîmes. Many other Viganais doubtless belonged to the Protestant community and shared its values, but were less active in the church.

Protestantism probably does not explain why skilled and semiskilled Viganais had positions in Nîmes' clothing and shoe industries. Paul Marcelin's account of working life in Nîmes shows that religion was less important in the artisanal sector than in the upper classes. Protestants and Catholics mixed freely in the laboring milieu; in any case, few artisans were church-going Protestants. Only one-fifth of the Viganais artisans listed in Appendix II were consistory electors, and of all the Viganais electors, fewer than 30 percent were blue collar workers. A more plausible explanation of the occupational distribution of Viganais workers lies in their social networks. Cevenols had been workers in Nîmes' industry since its heyday in silk producing. As a consequence, many families like the Marcelins, who had come to Nîmes from the Cévennes as silk workers in the eighteenth century, retained contacts with their Cevenol relatives. The long-standing Viganais presence in Nîmes probably eased their entry into artisanal training and employment, enabling men like shoemaker Pouzergue, who began his career in Le Vigan, to continue shoemaking in Nîmes.

The Villefortais fared less well than the Viganais. Over half were semi-skilled and unskilled workers, among whom many were servants or day laborers. As a group, they specialized in railroad employment, for at least one-quarter of them, like the Bouzanquet brothers and Emile Brun, worked for the railroad. This reflects the importance of the PLM to the history of Villefort, it being the sole large-scale employer connecting the village with Nîmes. The government employed two white collar workers (a court records clerk and a policeman). Four of the seven skilled workers were bakers, recalling the two bakers from Villefort living in Nîmes in the 1860s who went home to marry. A large proportion of men in the semi-skilled and unskilled category, like the André brothers, worked as servants or day laborers. The railroad, domestic service, unskilled labor — these were the specialties of rural men. None worked in Nîmes' garment industry.

The Langognais were found at the bottom of the labor hierarchy as odd jobbers, day laborers, ditch-diggers, and haulers. Four were cheminots, three were servants, and three were *cafetiers*. For example, the Mathieu brothers worked as laborers and agricultural workers in Nîmes; one was probably unemployed due to poor health in 1906. François Jean, an illegitimate child who had earlier been an agricultural worker, worked as a servant. No man from Langogne worked as a civil servant, shoemaker, or tailor, and none was a member of the bourgeoisie.

The parentage of the Lozerians was one factor that pointed them toward the bottom of Nimes' occupational ladder. Many sons of peasants or day laborers arrived in the city with no training for skilled urban jobs. Their families probably had not been able to forego their wages or their labor in order for them to acquire a solid fundamental education. Moreover, services rather than government bureaucracy connected their home towns with Nîmes; that is, traditions of domestic service and the historic railroad connection provided the strongest occupational links. The particular jobs taken by unskilled Lozerians may have depended on their social network, which could help them find a valet's position, get hired on a building site, or in a bakery. Or one could find out from friends when the PLM was hiring. Given the alternatives of day laborer and domestic servant, many men from the Lozère welcomed the prospect of becoming a cheminot.

> In fact, administration or the para-public enterprise, the *grande société de chemin de fer* — the "Company" — is assurance of a security formerly offered by domestic service — and. . . it is possible that this was no secret for certain workers. . . Was there not a trace, along with the evident and dominant rural exodus, of a traditional rural emigration which rather than flee deterioration hoped for an urban promotion, where the public service sector had replaced silk weaving?[20]

The PLM offered free travel, security, and the chance to maintain contact with home. The Bouzanquet brothers of Villefort typify the men who realized these advantages at an early age, signed on, and spent their lives working for "the Company." Thus, while parentage, home town, networks of Protestants, and the historical connections between the Cévennes and Nîmes created avenues for the Viganais into the bourgeoisie, prestigious white collar jobs, and into the closed artisanal milieu, it was the railroad line from the Regordane corridor, traditions of domestic service, and personal connections that brought male Lozerians into Nîmes as cheminots, servants, and day laborers.

MIGRANTS AND WOMEN'S WORK

In the eighteenth and early nineteenth century, men and women in Nîmes had worked side by side producing hosiery, shawls, and textiles from pure silk to novelty fabrics. They worked together, although their tasks were usually different. Women spinners were the mainstay of the city's textile industry. When, on a visit to Nîmes in 1787, Thomas Jefferson sat in admiration before the Maison Carrée, he was surrounded by women who had come to the square to knit stockings and spin.[21] By the end of the nineteenth century, however, the labor force was segregated by sex, and fewer women worked in manufacturing. Industrial change bears primary responsibility for the separation of men and women in the workplace, for those industries in which they had worked together declined in favor of these employing either men or women. Several thousand Nimois worked in the shoe industry, which was nearly 90 percent male. In the city's second industry — men's clothing — over nine out of ten workers were women. Other, smaller sections of the garment industry, such as the manufacture of corsets, hats, and hunting vests, seem to have employed women exclusively. Men and women still produced textiles together in 1906, but only 100 workers were involved.[22]

Nonindustrial occupations were also segregated by sex. The railroads employed only a handful of women among its thousands of bureaucrats, clerks, station workers, machinists, firemen, and repairmen. The service sector employed men as waiters, barbers, and hairdressers, and women as laundresses, nurses, and domestic servants. One only has to recall an opening scene from Zola's *L'Assomoir* to remember that the wash house was a woman's place. And by the end of the nineteenth century, male domestics were only found in the homes of the most prosperous employers, those who could afford a valet or chauffeur in addition to a maid-of-all-work — the usual lone domestic — chambermaid, and cook. In all, 85 percent of Nîmes' domestics were women. The turn-of-the-century city, then, was one in which men and women worked apart. Jobs for females constituted the same "women's work" as elsewhere in Europe: domestic service, garment production, and such services as laundry work.[23]

The choice of jobs for women in Nîmes, as in other cities, was restricted to, and dominated by, low-level occupations. Over 60 percent of the women in Nîmes, as opposed to 30 percent of the men, were semi-skilled and unskilled workers. They were only half as likely as men to be skilled or white collar workers. The most financially successful women were not employed at all, but instead enjoyed the wealth of property, an inheritance, or male kin. The rest were for the most part relegated to manual labor. It is for this reason that the difference between the occupational status of native and migrant women in Nîmes was not statistically significant (see Table 5.5). The majority of female workers in both cases were unskilled and semi-skilled laborers. Although more natives than migrants were skilled workers, differences in the bourgeois, petit bourgeois, and white collar categories were miniscule.

Nevertheless, migrants and native women were not equally likely to do wage work — nor did they have the same jobs. Among single women under the age of 30, migrants were more likely to be employed than were women born in Nîmes.[24] Two-thirds of the young unmar-

TABLE 5.5 Occupational Status and Origin, Females (percentages)

	Natives	*Migrants*
Bourgeois	6	5
Petit bourgeois	5	6
White collar	10	9
Skilled labor	21	12
Unskilled and semi-skilled labor	59	68
Total	101%	100%
N	176	262
x^2, $p > .1$		

SOURCE: ADG 10M 260, 261, 262, *Recensement, Ville de Nîmes,* 1906; systematic sample of individuals in 5 percent of households.

ried migrants worked, in contrast with one-third of the natives. The difference between native and migrant singles is striking, but perhaps less so in light of the tradition of domestic service for rural migrants in French cities. Migrant women usually arrived without parents upon whom to depend; most natives, on the other hand, lived with their parents. However, even migrant daughters who moved to Nîmes with their families were twice as likely to be employed as daughters born in Nîmes! Families who moved, then, often required the wages of their daughters.

Two-thirds of the young single migrants were service workers, and the vast majority of these maids-of-all-work, domestics, cooks, nurses, and chambermaids (see Table 5.6). They also took service jobs that did not require living in: housekeeper, laundress, laundry presser. Native women had a secure grasp on the garment industry, for half of them (compared with one-quarter of the migrants) were garment workers. Most were courturières, but many were skilled specialists who produced hats, vests, shirts, corsets, or men's pants. A few worked in the shoe industry, primarily as stitchers. Native-born Nimoises constituted most of the city's young single clerks and schoolteachers — its female white collar workers. They, like their male counterparts, eschewed service jobs for the city's industry and its white collar occupations. These occupations required more skill, training, and acquaintance with the artisanal networks of the city than did service work. Women who lived their whole lives in Nîmes were better able to obtain these advantages than were women from outside the city.

TABLE 5.6 Occupation and Origin, Unmarried Women Aged 15-29

	Natives		*Migrants*
Shoemaking industry	3%		1%
Garment industry	52		24
24 couturières, 7 vestmakers 3 sewing machine oprs., 2 pantsmakers, other specialists		15 couturières, 6 hatmakers, 2 pantsmakers, 2 corsetmakers, other specialists	
Services	28		68
14 servants, 6 laundry workers, 2 housekeepers		72 domestic servants 2 nurses, 2 housekeepers, governess, hairdresser	
White collar	14		5
8 clerks, 3 teachers		4 clerks, 2 teachers	
Other	4		3
weaver, day laborer, cartonmaker		nun, day laborer, cartonmaker	
Total	101%		100%
N	79		119

SOURCE: ADG 10M 260, 261, 262, *Recensement, Ville de Nîmes,* 1906; systematic sample of individuals in 5 percent of households.

Young women from Le Vigan and the Lozère were at opposite ends of this spectrum. While the vast majority of single women under 30 from Villefort (84 percent) and Langogne (83 percent) were employed, only half (49 percent) of the women from Nîmes worked for wages. Women from the Lozère were excluded almost completely from the garment industry, as well as from commercial, white collar, and shoemaking jobs, as Table 5.7 shows. Nearly all of them, like the Chevret sisters and the Sabatier sisters from Langogne, and the Janvier sisters from Villefort, were servants. On the other hand, single Viganais, like the Peysson sisters, were more likely to work as garmentmakers. This is partly because they could live with their families and had no need for live-in domestic employment. Viganaises also may have worked in the garment industry because friends or relatives could help them get jobs.

TABLE 5.7 Occupation and Origin, Unmarried Migrant Women Aged 15-29

	Le Vigan	Villefort	Langogne
Shoemaking industry	1	0	0
Garment industry	7	1	1
5 couturières, 2 hatmakers		couturière	couturière
Services	9	14	23
6 domestic servants, 2 cooks, hairdresser		10 domestics, 4 cooks	17 domestics, 4 cooks, 1 housekeeper 1 laundry worker
White collar	2	0	1
Other			
pastrymaker, propriétaire	2	1	0
		rentier	
Total	21	16	25

SOURCE: ADG 10M 260, 261, 262, *Recensement, Ville de Nîmes*, 1906.

Parentage, home town, and contacts all tended to send women from Villefort and Langogne into domestic service. They worked before marriage because they came from poor families and few jobs were available for them at home. Once in Nîmes, it was relatively easy to find work. Some women's older sisters already lived in Nîmes and helped the newcomer find a place. It was easy to find a job with the aid of the heavily used municipal employment agency and two private agencies. For the single Lozerian seeking employment, then, the search provided no problems.

Married women faced quite a different situation; their work and rate of employment historically have been different from those of single women, and the wives in Nîmes were no exception to this rule. They were less likely to work for pay. According to the census, only about one-tenth of the wives worked, compared with one-half of the young single women.[25] This is partly because few employment opportunities existed for married women. Nîmes' garment industry, which employed a total of 2-3,000 women, service opportunities, and shops could not begin to provide jobs for its married women, who numbered over 13,000. Strike reports from the garment industry show that employers were fully aware that their employees did not have other options in employment, and that other women easily could be hired in their stead. Facing a strike in the shop, Landauer once declared that he could simply turn to his army of homeworkers if the strikers would not resume work on his terms. And both Martel's corsetmakers and Portal's clothing workers had to accept the fees and salary reductions imposed by their employers, because they had no alternative employment and no financial resources from a strike fund.[26] The standard of adult male wages had risen since mid-century, and fewer wives were forced by necessity to work.[27] Finally, married women could provide their families with valuable services without entering the paid labor force. Paul Marcelin recounts his mother's work as an artisan's wife. She prepared abundant and delicious meals and, he reports:

> one can imagine . . . the effort that she had to expend to take care of the children, manage the household and watch the store. She actually worked twelve or thirteen hours a day, more than we did in the workshop.[28]

Even middle-class women such as Madame Mazauric, wife of the poorly paid municipal museum curator, made a substantial contribution to the family's standard of living through frugality and hard work. Madame Mazauric kept to a tight budget, hired no servants except a cleaning woman, and expected her widowed sister to cook for the household.[29]

Most married women worked at occupations that were exclusively women's work. One-third of them were service workers. Another third were garmentmakers, and nearly one-quarter were in petty commerce. Very few were white collar workers. These occupations were different from those of single women. The service workers among wives were laundresses and concièrges, not domestic servants. More of the garment workers were specialists (hat, vest, pants and lingerie-makers) rather than unspecialized courturières. Moreover, married women were more often in petty commerce than single women, selling groceries, meat, tobacco, rags, second-hand goods, and beverages.

Nearly all of these occupations filled needs unique to married women, because they allowed women to work at home, thus combining their work with meal preparation and child care. Anna Sabatier's work as a grocer, for example, enabled her to care for her sons and aging father while bringing in some money. Industrial work was often done at home, paid by the piece. Léopold Landauer, for example, employed 300 female pieceworkers in their homes to make men's suits. Women also produced mittens, gloves, scarves, bags, and underwear at home.[30]

For those employed outside the home, the work day was long, and cooking and child care posed constant problems. Garment workers in the sweatshops labored from 7:00 a.m. until 7:00 p.m. in the winter and from 6:00 a.m. in the summer, with a 2½-hour break at noon. By the time Marc Bernard's mother arrived home from the wash house where she worked as a laundress, night had fallen and she was too exhausted to cook. Young Marc waited for her in the street until she arranged for the shoemakers downstairs to take him in after school.[31]

Differences in employment were minimal between native-born and migrant wives. In part this is due to the similarity of their husbands' occupational status. Although migrant wives were slightly more likely than native wives to work (12 percent v. 9 percent), the difference in their rates of employment is not statistically significant. They worked in similar occupations, as Table 5.8 shows. Both were most often employed as garmentmakers, and the next largest occupational categories were service work and petty commerce. Here some interesting differences appear: migrants were concièrges — the building caretakers who swept the walk, received mail and messages, and acted as general janitoresses in exchange for lodging. No native woman acted as a concièrge. In Nîmes they were very badly housed, according to Marcelin, who lived across the street from an aging concièrge from Villefort. Lodging was in the basement, lit and ventilated by a single airhole to the street.[32] Like domestic servants, concièrges lived in their employer's dwelling and were partly paid in lodging. Perhaps migrant families recently arrived in Nîmes lived as concièrges for the same reasons that young women lived as domestic servants: to obtain inexpensive housing and some income.

Migrant wives engaged in commerce more than native wives — they were twice as likely as the others to be selling foodstuffs, tobacco, and beverages (see Table 5.8). Two different characteristics of urban life for migrants account for this. First, the single migrant woman employed as a domestic servant in the city was bound to have the baker, butcher, and grocer — and their assistants — as some of her daily contacts when she performed errands for her employer. She was more likely to meet them than the industrial worker or clerk, and she might eventually marry a shopkeeper. Second, migrants often set up shops and cafés in French cities. Fellow migrants often served as

TABLE 5.8 Occupation and Origin, Married Women

	Natives		*Migrants*
Shoemaking industry	7%		0%
Garment industry	28		27
3 couturières, other specialists		5 couturières, 3 vestmakers, 2 hatmakers, other specialists	
Services	24		35
3 laundry workers, servant, nurse, cook, housekeeper		7 concièrges, 5 laundry workers, nurse	
Petty commerce	14		24
2 grocers, burcher, used clothing dealer		4 grocers, 3 barkeepers, baker, butcher, other shopkeepers	
White collar	7		6
2 clerks		clerk, teacher, music teacher	
Rentiers and property owners	10		6
Other	10		2
singer, gardener, day laborer		day laborer	
Total	100%		100%
N	29		49

SOURCE: ADG 10M 260, 261, 262, *Recensement, Ville de Nîmes,* 1906; systematic sample of individuals in 5 percent of households.

employees and clientele, and connections with the home area brought home products to the city. It was relatively easy to set up a shop, because no entry into a *compagnonnage* or professional network was required, and no special training was necessary.

By contrast, of the few married women in the shoe industry, all were born in Nîmes, and most of them worked at home with their husbands making *fafiots* (baby shoes), or stitching. The world of the shoemakers in Nîmes was limited to the native-born and those in traditional migrant streams who intermarried with them.

Differences in occupations between native and migrant wives did not stem from one cause or one characteristic of migrant life which set it apart, but from differences in needs, contacts, and opportunities. These variations in circumstance are reflected in the occupations of working wives from Le Vigan and the Lozère. The garment industry employed those from Le Vigan: a vestmaker, an underwear-maker, a dressmaker. One was a clerk, another a laundress. The Lozerian wives specialized in food sales or helped their husbands in carpentry or painting (see Table III.11, Appendix III).

The general pattern of work for migrant and native married women was remarkably similar. About the same proportion of each group was employed, mostly in the female sectors of garmentmaking, petty commerce, and services. In general, then, marriage was an equalizer. It bestowed upon women a commonality they did not share before marriage: the same family position, along with the constraints and responsibilities that accompanied it. As a consequence, married women avoided employment, and when they had to work they gravitated to occupations that allowed them to stay at home while earning some income.

Poverty took a terrible toll on rural and urban women alike. Chamson describes Anna Combes of Le Vigan in her old age, so marked by poverty and the insecurity of her rural origins that she was unable to avoid a greedy materialism even when "necessity was no longer absolute mistress" of her life. "Better than the wrinkles on her face or her lips, her very hands revealed an immense detachment from life, along with a desperate attachment to all the little things of this joyless existence."[33] Likewise, Marcelin tells of his mother's spiritual poverty, wrought by a childhood of deprivation in a Nimois family ruined by industrial crises and by a lifetime of labor. A religious formalism coexisted with personal convictions bristling with materialism. She would say: "When I am dead, you can give my flesh to the dogs," so doubting was her attitude toward the church's promise of eternal life.[34] Marc Bernard recalls his mother's glee at a Protestant lady's charitable gift of food, glee born of the terrible poverty in which the two of them lived after Monsieur Bernard's departure.

> We made an inventory of the treasure. "Oh, oh, beans! good ones! Chick peas, aïe! you don't like them, too bad for you. Smell the coffee! Lentils, you see, I'd guessed! Now that was a fine lady! We have enough to eat for a week. Tonight we would have had bread and coffee for supper. Good timing. The cookies are nice, hmmm? And a book, on top of the deal. The *New Testament?* Hey, look what we've got here!"
>
> But my mother's fever gave me a sort of malaise; seeing her open the sacks with such greed, it seemed to me we had stolen them, and that

someone would come in to take them back. I didn't like this haste, these trembling hands.

"I would have had to work a whole week to earn enough to buy all these things. And here, the door opens, and it all falls on the table!"

She began to arrange the sacks on a shelf of the sideboard, carrying them pressed to her breast.[35]

Insecurity and poverty took its toll on many. This deprivation was unique neither to rural or urban lives, however; it was part of the precarious existence of the poor in country and city.

"The development of the working class is not an irruption; it was still emerging after three-quarters of a century — since the end of the old regime. Has not the banality of this observation contributed to making its importance forgotten?"[36] In the case of Nîmes, one would think the evolution of the labor force to be obvious, for the change was the hallmark of work during the nineteenth century. The city that Audiganne described in midcentury as almost totally industrial became, fifty years later, the city of store and atelier. This transformation coincided with urbanization.

As a consequence, the melting pot of the labor force which emerged in Nîmes after 1900 was those areas in expansion at the time of the rural exodus — the railroad, manual labor, services. Their place of origin was important to workers in the urban economy, for their position in the labor force was less a reflection of poverty or wealth than a reflection of the processes of migration and job-getting, both of which occurred with the help of contacts, acquaintances, friendships, and kin relationships. Both natives and members of long-lived migration streams such as the one between Le Vigan and Nîmes were "strong worker minorities, firmly rooted in the urban milieu," who included the city's shoemakers and garment workers.[37] Newcomers inserted themselves into the city's industries by virtue of their friendships or, in the case of women, through marriage.

The services were left to the newer migration streams, which reached their fullest expansion at the end of the century. This may be due less to a distaste for industrial work or exclusion from it than to the expansion of attractive new jobs. The marriages of Charles Bouzanquet to a cheminot's daughter from the coal basin, of the Chevret sisters to an upland cafetier and cheminot, of Raymonde

Janvier to a cheminot, and of Anna Sabatier to a peasant's son employed by the tramways suggest that rich connections existed among the country-born service and transport workers, connections that created a new laboring community from the flood of newcomers.

Many Viganais joined the city's bourgeoisie. Power and wealth in Nîmes were not the exclusive prerogative of the city-born, in part because the base for wealth in France remained the land. The descent of land ownership from the Cévennes to the vineyards of the plain accompanied urbanization. The industrial wealth of the Protestant bourgeoisie came from the land, for its base was the silk industry and capital from land rents. Government administration and professional positions, too, garnered urban wealth and power. To achieve these positions, it was not necessary to be a Nimois, for education was the essential factor. Thus, rural wealth could be the source of urban prestige and power, if not because it directly financed a city life, then because it afforded an education to children of rural and small-town elites. Just as wealth and power were not the prerogative of the Nimois, further, the migrant had no monopoly on poverty or powerlessness. The working class of Nîmes suffered as much during the economic crises of the nineteenth century as did the chronically insecure peasants and poor townspeople of the uplands.

The agencies of mobility which made many a peasant's son a cheminot, a clerk or teacher, were the institutions that linked rural, small-town, and urban France: the educational system, civil service, and railroad companies. These institutions also shaped the urban culture into which migrants entered. To those for whom mobility was blocked, the city offered a plethora of odd jobs and casual labor, such as ditch-digging, hauling, and the work to which young Marc Bernard was consigned after elementary school:

> Some days later, I began as an errand boy for a wine commissioner; I was not yet twelve. I made fifteen francs a month. I was an "apprentice," but this word did not have at all the meaning which my mother attached to it.[38]

NOTES

1. Armand Cosson, "Industrie de soie et population ouvrière à Nîmes de 1815 à 1848," in G. Cholvy, ed., *Economie et Société en Languedoc-Roussillon de 1789 à nos jours* (Montpellier: Université Paul Valéry, 1978), 195-197.

2. Yves Lequin, *Les Ouvriers de la région lyonnaise (1848-1914),* Vol. I: *La formation de la classe ouvrière régionale* (Lyon: Presses Universitaires de Lyon, 1977), 204.

3. Ibid., III.

4. Quote from bid., 156; see also p. 266-267; Raymond Dugrand, *Villes et campagnes en Bas-Languedoc* (Paris: Presses Universitaires Françaises, 1963), 445-464; Georges Dupeux, "Immigration urbaine et secteurs économiques: l'exemple de Bordeaux au début du XXe siècle," *Annales du Midi* 85 (1973), 209-211.

5. Dugrand, *Villes et campagnes,* 463.

6. Otis D. Duncan, *The American Occupational Structure* (New York: John Wiley, 1967), 207-241; Wolfgang Köllmann, "The process of urbanization in Germany at the height of the industrialization period," *Journal of Contemporary History* 4 (1969), 70-72; William Sewell, Jr., "Social mobility in a nineteenth-century European city: some findings and implications," *Journal of Interdisciplinary History* 7 (1976), 217-234.

7. Grace Anderson, *Networks of Contact: The Portuguese and Toronto* (Waterloo, Canada: Wilfrid Laurier University, 1974); John S. MacDonald and Leatrice MacDonald, "Chain migration, ethnic neighborhood formation and social networks," *Milbank Memorial Fund Quarterly* 42 (1964); 82-97.

8. Such a formulation does not depoliticize the question of the origins of the urban labor force by concentrating less on proletarianization and proletarian status than the Marxian model. Proletarian status alone may be less helpful to an analysis of the labor force in Nîmes than one which takes into account additional factors, because the labor force of Nîmes does not fit the industrial proletariat described by Marx. Also, by the end of the nineteenth century in France, the rural French were proletarianized more by rural demographic patterns — high fertility, which inspired the emigration of excess children — and by declining revenues from the land rather than by a process resembling the English enclosure acts.

9. The subjects of these histories are not representative of any group and thus do not represent a sample of any given population. On the contrary, the migrants included may share a bias which makes the histories atypical: it is likely that they were better reporters of their age, children's ages, and birthplace, because their records could be traced from census information about them and their families. They may be better educated than migrants whose occupations could not be retraced. Consequently, (a) the bourgeoisie and white collar workers are overrepresented, and (b) unskilled laborers are underrepresented. The strength of the histories is that they are constructed from a variety of sources and thus reconstruct a working life. In order to protect the anonymity of the subjects, I assigned each an alias. The sources for each history are listed in Appendix II.

10. The size of the group can only be estimated at several thousand (in Nîmes). Unfortunately, PLM records of employees in Nimes are uncatalogued, not open to the researcher, and many have not been preserved. For the problem of studying railroad personnel, see Abel Chatelain, "La main d'oeuvre et la construction des chemins de fer au XIXe siècle," *Annales, ESC* 8 (1953), 502. See also Elie Fruit for a general description of the hierarchy of railroad workers, *Les syndicats dans les chemins de fer (1890-1910)* (Paris: Editions ouvrières, 1976), 33-34.

11. Archives Départementales du Gard (hereafter ADG), series 5S 8, Chemin de fer: Personnel, assermentations, mouvement, 1897-1904. For a description of Eugene's grueling and dangerous work, see *Salut, camarades* (Paris: Gallimard, 1955), 59-61.

12. William Sewell, "Social change and the rise of working-class politics in nineteenth century Marseille," *Past and Present* 65 (1974), 101.

13. (Paris: Gallimard, 1941), 36-41; interview with Marc Bernard, Paris, February 10, 1977.

14. Lequin, *Les ouvriers de la* région lyonnaise, 138, 271.

15. In Bordeaux, most high-level bureaucrats came from outside Aquitaine. Georges Dupeux, "Immigration urbaine et secteurs économiques," 216.

16. Victorien Brugier, *La bourse du travail à Nîmes* (Nîmes: Imprimerie l'Idéale, 1925), 138; Eugen Weber, *Peasants into Frenchmen* (Stanford, CA: Stanford University Press, 1976), 328; see also Sune Åkerman, "Swedish migration and social mobility: The tale of three cities," *Social Science History* 1 (1977), 193-195.

17. Michael Roussy, "Evolution démographique et économique des populations du Gard," (Thèse de droit, Université de Montpellier, 1949), 68-69.

18. In all, 59 percent of the PLM employees in the census sample of the municipal population were migrants. This does not include the residents of the outlying area of Courbessac where the repair depot was located. André Chamson, *The Road* (New York: Scribner's, 1929), 147, 171-172; Yves Bravard, "Sondages à propos de l'emigration dans les Alpes du Nord," *Revue de géographie alpine* 45 (1957), 118-120; Elie Fruit, *Les syndicats,* 34; Joseph Jacquet, *Les cheminots dans l'histoire sociale de la France* (Paris: Editions Sociales, 1967), 32-33; Weber, *Peasants into Frenchmen,* 210.

19. Georges Duveau, *Les instituteurs* (Paris: Deuil, 1966), 53-54, 110; Emile Léonard, *Le Protestant français* (Paris: Presses Universitaires Françaises, 1955), 226; Roussy, "Populations du Gard," 69. See also Steven M. Lowenstein, "The rural community and the urbanization of German Jewry," *Central European History* 8 (1980), 218-237.

20. Lequin, *Les ouvriers de la région lyonnaise,* 267-268.

21. I am referring to spatial integration, not the integration of specific occupations. The silk-producing labor force of Nîmes was probably as segregated as any by specific task. Sex-typed occupations have been, and remain, the norm. See Edward Gross, "Plus ça change. . .? The sexual structure of occupations over time," *Social Problems* 16 (1968), 198-207; Julian Boyd ed., *The Papers of Thomas Jefferson,* 19 vols. (Princeton, NJ: Princeton University Press, 1955), Vol. 11: 226; Hector Rivoire, *Statistique du département du Gard,* 2 vols. (Nîmes: Ballivet et Fabre, 1842), Vol. 2: 28-29.

22. ADG, series 14M, 534: Shoemakers' strike reports for 1904 and 1905 estimate that 3500-4000 people were employed in the shoe industry and do not mention female employees. The sample from the 1906 census lists shows that 87.5 percent of the shoemakers were male shoemakers and leather cutters; 12.5 percent were female bootstitchers. ADG, series 14M, 445, strike reports from the clothing industry, 1900; the proportion of female employees is corroborated by Fernand Benoît-Germain, "Commerce et industrie," in Association Française pour l'Avancement des Sciences, ed., *Nîmes et le Gard,* 2 vols. (Nîmes: Imprimerie Coöperative, 1914), Vol. 2: 334; ADG, series 14M, 534, report of weavers' strike, 1906, gives proportion of workers by sex.

23. Joan Scott and Louise Tilly, "Women's work and the family in nineteenth-century Europe," *Comparative Studies in Society and History* 17 (1975), 38-39.

24. This section is based on an analysis of the labor force participation and occupations of single women under the age of 30 from the census sample. Only women under 30 were included in the analysis, because the chances of correctly

assessing marital status were greatest for young women. See Appendix I for a discussion of the inference of marital status from the census lists.

25. The census may have underrecorded the proportion of married women employed, because much of married women's employment was in the "secondary labor force" of the city — the unskilled service sector — intermittent, and unreported; Louise Tilly and Joan Scott, *Women, Work and Family* (New York: Holt, Rinehart & Winston, 1978), 76, 87-88, 125. Also, census takers may have been more careful to note the occupation of the head of a household rather than that of the spouse. Nevertheless, there were other cities in France with an equally low rate of employment for married women. See Louise Tilly, "Occupational structure, women's work and demographic change in two French industrial cities, Anzin and Roubaix, 1872-1906," in J. Sundin and E. Soderlund, eds., *Time, Space, and Man: Essays on Microdemography* (Atlantic Highlands, NJ: Humanities Press, 1979), 114-126.

26. Estimate of number of married women is based on the sample from the census. The strike reports are ADG 14M, 445: Landauer, 1876; Grève de Corsetières, Martel, 1899; ADG, 14M, 534: Grève d'Ouvrières en Confection de Vêtements, La Maison Gaston Portal, 1904.

27. Tilly, "Occupational structure," 113; Jean-Michel Gaillard, "Le mouvement ouvrier dans le Gard (1875-1914)" (Mémoire de Maîtrise d'Histoire, Université de Nanterre, 1969), 4-5; Paul Marcelin, *Souvenirs d'un passé artisanal* (Nîmes: Chastanier, 1963), 8-9; Henri Reboul, *L'industrie nîmoise du tissage au XIXe siècle* (Montpellier: Fermin et Montane, 1914), 103-113; ADG series 14M 534: strike reports list wages above midcentury levels.

28. Marcelin, *Souvenirs*, 9, 11.

29. Lucie Mazauric Chamson, *"Belle Rose, Ô Tour Magne"* (Paris: Plon, 1969), 77, 169, 173.

30. ADG, 14M 445: description of employees is from questionnaire and police reports of strike at Léopold Landauer's sweatshop, April, 1900; Benoît-Germain, "Commerce et industrie," 333.

31. Ibid.; working hours were the cause of a strike at Landauer's shop.

32. Marcelin, *Souvenirs*, 23.

33. Chamson, *The Road* 191, 210; see pp. 207-219.

34. Marcelin, *Souvenirs*, 35.

35. Bernard, *Pareils à des enfants*, 140.

36. Lequin, *Les ouvriers de la région lyonnaise*, 156.

37. Ibid., 221.

38. Bernard, *Pareils à des enfants*, 277.

6

The Process of Urbanization

> We ought therefore to rediscover one basic language for all the cities of the world . . . the uninterrupted confrontation with the countryside, a prime necessity of daily life; the supply of manpower, as indispensable as water to the mill-wheel; the aloofness of the towns, that is to say their desire to be marked off from others; their situation necessarily at the centre of a network of communications; their relation to suburbs, secondary cities, often their servants and even their slaves.
>
> — Fernand Braudel,
> *Capitalism and Material Life, 1500-1800*

This study has connected the economic with the social evolution of Languedoc by examining the experiences of people from three small towns. The first focus was the home area, each in the throes of economic change which, in its unique way, reflected the broad trend of ruralizing the countryside typical of nineteenth-century Europe. Parent and child, man and woman responded differently; many emigrated, some peasant-artisans became peasants exclusively, others changed vocation, and some followed their children to the city. Young women suffered particularly from the demise of rural textile production and were especially likely to seek employment in a city like Nîmes with a strong service sector.

The forces of economic change engendered a response that reflected people's ties of kin and friendship. The wealth of personal ties among migrants in Nîmes leaves no doubt that rich links among compatriots and friends drew uplanders to a particular city. The most crucial connections doubtless existed among kin, for kin aided even the poorest newcomers, and the presence of a relative in the city guaranteed at least one source of aid. Indeed, the "deeply entrenched ideal and institution of the family provided the mechanism by which people were bound together" as they entered urban life.[1]

In the city, important differences became apparent among migrants — between those who moved as single young people and as families, between those who moved under the auspices of an employing organization and those who worked as servants or casual laborers, and between Protestants and Catholics. Geographical origins were but one feature distinguishing the urban people from each other, who in Nîmes were also divided by class, occupation, and religious culture. Some migrants, by virtue of their family, education, and associates, became powerful and wealthy members of the community. Others — also by virtue of their education and associates — were relegated to the city's dead-end jobs, its poorest dwellings, and its least powerful constituencies. The value of the urban destinies of the Viganais, Villefortais, and Langognais lies in the very distinctions among them, distinctions that translate the economic evolution of Languedoc into vivid and varied human experience.

"The turbulence of little towns," observed Georges Dupeux, is "one of the keys to urbanization in France."[2] Le Vigan, Villefort, and Langogne bear out this observation, because the fluctuations of their populations reflect the economic changes that were eventually to produce urbanization. Change was underway long before the rural exodus began, when proto-industry spread throughout prerevolutionary Languedoc, giving rural and small-town people a cash resource to complement their agricultural food production.[3] The people of Languedoc gradually lost this resource as a result, for example, of the long agony of the silk industry in Le Vigan and the decisive deindustrialization of wool- and hide-producing Villefort and Langogne. With crises in local industry and agriculture, uplanders could no longer earn sufficient cash in industry, local crops, or seasonal harvest labor, so they emigrated to urban destinations. A shift to wage-earning at distinctly urban vocations accompanied the move.

The emigration from upper Languedoc at the end of the nineteenth century was primarily confined to the region; uplanders went to coal basin towns and to Montpellier, Nîmes, and Marseille on the Mediterranean plain. This was typical for France, where the regional centers of Lyon, Bordeaux, and Marseille attracted people from the surrounding areas. Paris drew people from a large cross-shaped area extending from the northern plain to the southern Massif Central and from Brittany to Lorraine, but its attraction did not eliminate migration to regional capitals.[4] In fact, by the twentieth century, some cities like Bordeaux and Lyon drew people from a more local sphere because the artisans' national repertoire of destinations and the long-distance wanderings of the unskilled had both faded in the nineteenth century.[5] The sole unique characteristic of migration in Eastern Languedoc is the degree to which Lozerians left their home *département* for the coal fields and cities of the plain.[6]

Destinations were urban, but not industrial. Neither Nîmes nor Montpellier developed large-scale factory industry before World War I; rather, they demanded an explicitly nonindustrial labor force. The dynamics of supply and demand provided a labor force for a service economy: one suited by age, training, and gender to work in commerce, transport, government, service industries, and personal service. Major cities of the nation — Paris, Bordeaux, even Lyon — followed the same pattern; their growth at the end of the nineteenth century did not coincide with periods of industrial expansion.[7] Industrialization and urbanization are firmly wedded in images of change during the nineteenth century, but the image is a faulty one; industrialization and urbanization occurred together in France only in rare cases such as Roubaix — France's capital of textile manufacturing — or metalworking St. Etienne. More commonly, regions and cities lost their traditional industries as urban areas grew.[8] Nationally, the tertiary sector expanded slightly more than the industrial sector between 1850 and 1900.[9]

The dialectic between the economic evolution of Eastern Languedoc and the urbanization of its population may best be illustrated by comparing it with the Lyonnais. Paths to urbanization — like paths to industrialization — varied by region, and explicit comparisons highlight both common processes and factors unique to one region. Yves Lequin's account of the formation of the Lyonnais working class provides an ideal comparison, because it is sensitive to the dynamic relationship between city and hinterland.[10] Here we see the paths of urbanization and industrialization diverge.

Old Regime and early nineteenth-century Nîmes were intimately related to its hinterland by ties of industry, capital, and labor. Peasant and Nimois alike worked in the silk industry, because the mulberry trees that fed the silkworms had literally invaded village, town, and city. The annual rite of winding silk from the silkworms left Intendant Ballainvilliers exclaiming in frustration: "How hard it is to execute the law to the great quantity of people spread in hamlets and the countryside!"[11] Besides silk-winding for the production of silk in Nîmes, rurals of lower Languedoc produced hosiery for the city's merchants, and highlanders made wool in their cottages.[12] Thus the market, raw materials, capital, and labor joined Nîmes with rural and small-town Languedoc, creating an industrial region among the most prosperous in France.[13] With the nineteenth century, silk production became more exclusively the purview of the countryside, and production of silk cloth remained Nîmes' specialty. Lyon, too, was connected with its hinterland by the rural production of cotton, linen, wool, and raw silk. After the revolution, however, silk-weaving — particularly of plain cloth — was put out to suburbs and the countryside.[14]

In the early nineteenth century, both Nîmes and Lyon were, in the words of Lequin, "cities without frontiers" because "they projected their dynamism on often very distant villages."[15] Peasant families produced raw silk, hosiery, and other goods for urban merchants, some working in small-town spinning mills like those in Le Vigan. As a result of rural industry, the upland population prospered. A proto-industrial labor force developed that combined agricultural work with industry: "There were few choices between agricultural and industrial work, but rather all the intermediate situations."[16] In Eastern Languedoc, this labor force included the peasants of the Lozère who worked wool, manufactured wooden shoes, or descended the Regordane corridor to mine coal during the long winters. It included the families who tended mulberry trees and raised silkworms in the Cévennes and upper Gard, as well as the wives and children who worked feverishly to wind silk from the mature cocoons for a few weeks in the late spring. This labor force was not proletarian, although its members periodically engaged in wage labor; it could not survive from agriculture alone. Dependent on the wages of industry or seasonal agricultural labor, it survived in small towns, villages, and hamlets by balancing the cash-earning opportunities of various family members with food production.

Crises affecting sources of cash after midcentury — *pébrine* for silk producers, phylloxera for wine growers, *l'encre* for chestnut producers — crippled the hinterland of both Lyon and Nîmes. With these crises, the industry of Lyon shifted: silk production mechanized and moved from the heart of the city, the chemical industry blossomed, and the machine industry mechanized, grew, and concentrated in Lyon and St. Etienne. Silk cloth production in Nîmes neither mechanized nor concentrated, and as it diminished, Nîmes turned to the production of shawls, then novelty items. The once-important center of silk production and capital of the hosiery trade deindustrialized in the nineteenth century. It is the extreme case of the region:

the customs entrepôt, obtained by great pains in 1853, closed in 1861; twenty years later, wool and silk processing ceased altogether. Then, at the beginning of the twentieth century, the weaving and industrial design sections of the School of Textile Production closed; they dated from 1836.[17]

A service economy based on transportation and commerce grew in the stead of industry, which survived in the attenuated production of clothing and shoes. In the Lyonnais, the growth of services outstripped industry, and services came to play a major role even in the economy of industrial Lyon.[18] In concert with these developments pulsed urban growth as men and women left small town and village for regional centers in the late century "rural exodus." In both Lyon and Nîmes, new migration streams came from a more remote hinterland that provided the city's domestic servants, railroad workers, and day laborers. These new and expanding streams included peasants' children who came to the city to stay.[19].

This massive shift of population from rural uplands to urban areas was due more to changes in the countryside than to the pull of industry. For Lequin, the multiple crises depressing agricultural prices at the end of the century explain the exodus to Lyon. This explanation for the rural exodus slights the economic underpinnings of the deindustrialization of the countryside: the movement of capital out of the uplands.[20] As the rural silk industry and other rural textile and hosiery industries became increasingly unprofitable, the bourgeoisie of Languedoc placed its capital elsewhere. The rural and small-town population suffered from this deindustrialization, which made upper Languedoc even more rural and agricultural. Capital moved to the lowlands, and with it, land ownership.

Nîmes' industry could not retain capital, either. Plagued by the natural disaster of pébrine and competition from the mechanized mills to the north, the textile industry also suffered from a bourgeoisie decreasingly interested in its development. The tempting alternative of investing in the wine industry beckoned to the city's manufacturers. Industrial profits could be easily invested in vineyards, but then they were not used to purchase steam engines or automatic looms. Once archaic technology reduced industrial profits, the temptation became irresistible to move definitively from manufacturing to vineyard management. "It is thus," concludes Raymond Dugrand, "that in a generation, industrialists became absentee wine growers."[21] A regional newspaper crowed: "The vine has become the great industry of the region, at the base of unparalleled wealth." But the future was in truth very bleak, because vineyards killed true industry and upset the existent economic and social equilibrium of lower Languedoc.[22] Shifts of capital explain the deindustrialization of both rural and urban Languedoc. The region would lose control over capital as some members of the bourgeoisie moved to Paris, and outsiders bought silk mills, vineyards, and captured regional banks. The same occurred in Lyon.[23]

Thus Lyon and Nîmes were centers to industrial regions in the eighteenth and early nineteenth centuries, where a proto-industrial labor force divided its efforts between manufacturing and agriculture. With regional specialization and the mechanization of textiles, the parts of the Lyonnais that had sent children into silk manufacturing deployed them to factories in and around Lyon. In lower Languedoc, rural areas slowly deindustrialized, and the city offered little alternative industrial employment. At the end of the nineteenth century, agricultural crises and the impact of deindustrialization resulted in a massive movement of population — a geographical shift from rural area and small town to the city, and a sectoral shift from agriculture and rural manufacturing to urban services and, in the case of Lyon, industry. The fates of the two cities were quite dissimilar, because only Lyon entered the twentieth century as an industrial city, with chemical production and metallurgy to complement its mechanized textile production. By contrast, Nîmes, surrounded by the Midi's "wine factory," became primarily a commercial and administrative center. Yet the histories of the Lyonnais and Eastern Languedoc share the economic impulse of an urbanward shift of capital and a shift of population and employment opportunities.

In the case of the regions of both Nîmes and Lyon, change proceeded not from the development of machine industry, but from the prerevolutionary proto-industrialization of the countryside. This comparison has emphasized changes in the locus of production, patterns of sectoral growth, and consequent population movements. As a result of this emphasis, shifts in continuous processes, rather than discontinuities, take center stage. A focus on continuities makes sense of otherwise puzzling radical changes in human migration and employment. To look at the large-scale changes of the nineteenth century through such a prism has advantages over attempts to understand regional change by industrialization. It is misleading and frustrating to look for the development of factory industry in the case of

Eastern Languedoc, because cottage industry was lost and factory production never flowered.[24] Yet Languedoc's history — proto-industrialization followed by deindustrialization — was probably most common in Europe.

Migration is an instructive prism through which to view the nineteenth century, because it elucidates both the forces behind change and the responses to it — in this case the connections between flows of capital linked with deindustrialization and agricultural crises, and the consequent flows of manpower. Such a focus would be equally valuable in areas where an important factory industry developed, such as Flanders or the Ruhr. A history of migration is a history of the human interaction with the conditions that so thoroughly altered the West between the French Revolution and World War I. In Languedoc, a complex but clearly economic impetus turned regional migration paths toward cities. Because migration patterns trace the human response to large-scale change, they bridge two phenomena, usually treated as separate trends, although they sometimes occurred in concert: the important economic changes of the nineteenth century — concentration of production and capital, deindustrialization of the countryside — and significant social changes, such as the evolution of fertility, family formation, education, and the urban labor force. Migration connects economic and social change with the experiences of historical actors who, with shifting fortunes in rural areas, took up urban vocations, founded urban families, and became part of city life.

NOTES

1. Jack Eblen, "An analysis of nineteenth-century frontier populations," *Demography* 2 (1965), 413.
2. Georges Dupeux, "La croissance urbaine en France au XIXe siècle," *Revue d'histoire économique et sociale* 52 (1974), 187.
3. See Charles Tilly, "Flows of capital and forms of industry in Europe, 1500-1900." (Paper presented to the Eighth World Congress of Economic History, Budapest, August 1982.)
4. Paul Hohenberg, "Migrations et fluctuations démographiques dans la France rurale, 1836-1901," *Annales ESC* 29 (1974), 485-490.
5. Pierre Guillaume, *La population de Bordeaux au XIXe siècle: Essai d'histoire sociale* (Paris: Armand Colin, 1972), 56, 62; Yves Lequin, *Les ouvriers de la région lyonnaise (1848-1914),* vol. 1 (Lyon: Presses Universitaires de Lyon, 1977), 239.
6. Hohenberg, "Migrations et fluctuations démographiques," 490-491.

7. Raymond Dugrand, *Villes et campagnes en bas-Languedoc* (Paris: Presses Universitaires Françaises, 1963), 1; Georges Dupeux, "Immigration urbaine et secteurs économiques: l'exemple de Bordeaux au début du XXe siècle," *Annales du Midi* 85 (1973), 209-211; Lequin, *Les ouvriers de la région lyonnaise*, 122-123.

8. See the maps and essays throughout Pierre Léon, François Crouzet, and Richard Gascon, eds., *L'industrialisation en Europe au XIXe siècle: cartographie et typologie* (Paris: Editions du CNRS, 1972); Frank Tipton, *Regional Variations in the Economic Development of Germany During the Nineteenth Century* (Middletown, CT: Wesleyan University Press, 1976).

9. André Armengaud, "Industralisation et démographie dans la France du XIXe siècle," in Léon et al., eds., *L'industrialisation en Europe*, 188; R. M. Hartwell, "The tertiary sector in the English economy during the Industrial Revolution," in *ibid.*, 213-227.

10. See Louise A. Tilly, "Industrial production and the redistribution of capital and labor in nineteenth century Lombardy," in Michael Hanagan and Charles Stephenson, eds., *Workers and Industrialization: Comparative Studies of Class Formation and Worker Militancy* (New York: Greenwood Press, forthcoming).

11. Quoted in Léon Dutil, *L'état économique du Languedoc à la fin de l'ancien régime (1750-1789)* (Paris: Hachette, 1911), 452.

12. Ibid., 426-428, 483.

13. Dugrand, *Villes et campagnes*, 387.

14. Pierre Cayez, "Une proto-industrialisation décalée: la ruralisation de la soierie lyonnaise dans la première moitié du XIXe siècle," *Revue du Nord* 63 (1981), 95-103.

15. Lequin, *Les ouvriers de la région lyonnaise*, 43.

16. Ibid., 45.

17. Dugrand, *Villes et campagnes*, 401.

18. Lequin, *Les ouvriers de la région lyonnaise*, 118, 185-187; see also Hartwell, "The tertiary sector," in Léon et al., eds., *L'industrialisation en Europe*, 213-227.

19. Lequin, *Les ouvriers de la région lyonnaise*, 121, 238-245.

20. Jean Bouvier, *Le Crédit Lyonnaise de 1863 à 1882* (Paris: SEVPEN, 1961); Pierre Léon, "La région lyonnaise dans l'histoire économique et sociale de la France: une esquisse (XVI-XXe siècles)," *Revue Historique* 237 (January-March 1967), 31-62.

21. Dugrand, *Villes et campagnes*, 401.

22. Ibid., 402.

23. Ibid., 411-415; Bouvier, *Le Crédit Lyonnais;* Léon, "La région lyonnaise."

24. See Yves Lequin, "Les bases d'une cartographie industrielle de l'Europe au XIXe siècle," in Léon et al., eds., *L'industrialisation en Europe*, 35-36.

Appendix I

Evaluation of Sources

CENSUS LISTS

Nominal census lists are a particularly appropriate source for the study of migrants in urban France. First, they list individually all members of the population except people in institutions — prisoners and soldiers living in barracks, for example.[1] Consequently, census lists provide more complete information on the urban population than other sources for migration data in France such as marriage records, apprenticeship contracts, voting rolls, and hospital records. Moreover, the French census for the year 1906 lists the commune of birth for each individual so that the historian can distinguish native-born Nimois from migrants. Philippe Pinchemel, who was one of the first French historians to employ census lists, summarizes the advantages of this source:

> The nominal lists are the only document which present demographic and social phenomena while conserving them in their true milieu, which is the commune; only from these lists can social reality be mapped in its actual location [*implantation*].[2]

As a record of migratory movements in turn-of-the-century France, the 1906 census lists are an unparalleled document.[3]

Yet they do have drawbacks as a source. Census lists only give a snapshot of population at a single time and yield no direct information about when, by what processes, or under what circumstances a migrant arrived in the city. They are also subject to errors in reporting, particularly to errors in age reporting.[4]

The 1906 census lists were copied from census forms filled in for each individual at the household (the *bulletin individuel*). The census lists are therefore a copy of householders' information, and as such are subject to copying error. The communes then sent the individual bulletins to Paris, where they served as a base for machine-tallied aggregate statistics. Despite errors in reporting and copying, the reliability of the French census in the early twentieth century marked an improvement over the series taken in the 1870s, 1880s, and 1890s.[5]

I drew from the census lists of the city of Nîmes a sample of individuals in 5 percent of the households, a total of 3602 individuals in 1082 households. I then gathered information on the total population in Nîmes from Le Vigan, Villefort, and Langogne.

The lists for the year 1906 included the following information for each individual: address, family name, first name, year of birth, commune of birth, relationship to household head, occupation, and employer. Individuals were grouped by household, which were in turn listed by address. Address, family name, first name, year of birth (or age), and relationship to head of household were consistently listed for the individuals surveyed. Married women were often listed under the spouse's family name rather than under their maiden name. Like occupational listings elsewhere, these gave married women's occupation as *"sans profession"* with suspicious frequency. Moreover, the occupations listed were imprecise for white collar workers *("employé")* and railroad workers *("PLM"* and *"employé PLM")*. Unfortunately, aside from "PLM," the name of the employer was listed for residents of only one section of the city.[6] Chapter 4 contains a discussion of these problems.

Commune (township) of birth was listed consistently, but the listings posed many difficulties in identifying birthplace. Commune was often listed without the name of the *département,* which made it difficult to identify those with common names (e.g., Bagnols-sur-Cèze, Gard; Bagnols, Puy de Dome; St-Hippolyte-du-Fort and St-Hippolyte-de-Montaigu in the Gard; and Bastide, St-Etienne). The names of other *communes* were not found in any atlas or geographical dictionary, were misspelled, or illegible. To deal with this problem, the certainty of identification of birthplace was coded, and the study focused on migrants from townships with the unambiguous place names of Le Vigan, Villefort, and Langogne (see Chapter 1, note 24). The birthplace of 1369 of the 1510 migrants from the census sample (91 percent) was identified.

In order to investigate nuptiality patterns, I relied by necessity on measures of the currently married. Because marital status was not listed, it was inferred conservatively from relationship to household head/household position. People who were co-residing with spouses were coded as currently married (whether they were head of household, daughter, son-in-law, and so forth), regardless of relationship to head of household. The vast majority of married males (98 percent) were household heads, and the vast majority of married females (93 percent) were listed as spouses, but a few married people were child, child-in-law, parent, or other relative of household head. Servants were coded as not currently married, as were most other men and women without a spouse present, even if children were present in the household. Because I was only able to identify the currently married, it was impossible to measure the Singulate Mean Age of Marriage (which requires sure identification of the *ever*-married), I_m, or the percentage single at ages 45-49 — all standard measures of nuptiality.

Marital status was inferred with some confidence from these data, because household relationship information is complete and very detailed in the 1906 census lists from Nîmes. The census instructions were emphatic as to the explicit nature of information desired in the column "situation par rapport au chef de ménage":

> Indicate in this column the position of each individual in relation to the household of which he is a part, that is, indicate whether he is the head of it or one of its members, whether he belongs as a relative by blood or by marriage, or merely as a paid employer or servant.[7]

More important, the directions were followed. With few exceptions, the precise relationship of each individual to the household head is specified (relationship to head of household is missing in 8 of 2040 cases of individuals 15-40 years old). Table I.1 lists household position for people ages 15-49 and not currently married, by origin and sex. The majority in each category are household heads and children of household heads. Relatives are primarily siblings of a household head, followed by niece or nephew, mother-in-law, cousin, grandchild, and nonspecified relative. Only the mother-in-law is likely ever to have been married, and she may be widowed, divorced, separated, or deserted.

Many people coded as not currently married were not related to the household head; among these, servants were most important numerically. Other "nonrelatives" were lodgers or workers living with an employer's family. A few were nuns or friends of the family. Although it is impossible to know for certain that servants were currently single, several factors suggest that it is most accurate to code them as single. First, historians Abel Chatelain and Theresa McBride have confirmed the primacy of domestic work as the single migrant female's avenue of entry into the city. Live-in domestic service was incompatible with marriage from both the servant's and employer's point of view.[8] Moreover, the age of servants in Nîmes suggests that most were single: Over half were less than 25 years old, and over three-quarters were under 35 (see Table I.2). Migrants — the vast majority of servants — were particularly young: 58 percent were between 14 and 25 years old. The mean age of (first) marriage for women wed in Nîmes in 1906 was 26.9, so women under 25 were often single. Available information on servants' marriages also suggests that they married late.[9] Finally, the census was based on habitual residence on the night of March 3-4,

TABLE I.1 Household Position of People Not Married, By Sex and Origin, Ages 15-49

	Males		*Females*	
	Natives	*Migrants*	*Natives*	*Migrants*
Head of Household	9	32	8	22
Living with relatives/others	4	7	5	14
Living alone	5	25	3	8
Child	78	42	67	25
Child	78	40	67	25
Foster child	*	2	0	*
Other Relatives	9	9	17	11
Sibling/Sibling-in-law	6	3	10	8
Nephew/Niece	1	2	3	2
Cousin	0	2	*	*
Grandchild	1	1	*	0
Daughter-in-law	0	0	*	0
Mother-in-law	0	0	2	0
Uncle	*	0	0	0
Unspecified relative	*	1	1	1
Nonrelatives	4	17	8	42
Servant	2	7	7	36
Lodger	1	7	*	3
Worker/apprentice/employee	*	2	*	1
Nun/priest	0	0	0	1
Friend	*	1	0	*
Other	0	0	0	*
	100%	100%	100%	100%
N	279	134	345	273

*Less than .5 percent, N = 1.

SOURCE: ADG 10M 260, 261, 262, *Recensement, Ville de Nîmes,* 1906; systematic sample of individuals in 5 percent of households.

1906.[10] As a consequence, it reveals whether urban people were living as married or single people. The model of urban migration is based on the de facto living situation of migrants in the city, regardless of the possibility of a spouse living elsewhere.

Detailed information on household position justifies the coding of servants and other urban residents without a spouse present as not currently married, because household position data are very detailed. But this choice carries a bias: Inferred marital status is likely to exaggerate the size of the unmarried population. Given the household positions of the unmarried population, this exaggeration is more likely to distort data on the migrant population than the native population.

TABLE I.2 Age of Servants, By Origin (percentages)

Age	*Natives*		*Migrants*		*Total*	
0-14	0		0		0	
15-19	7	30	21	58	18	52
20-24	23		37		34	
25-29	23	33	14	19	16	22
30-34	10		5		6	
35-39	10	23	7	16	7	17
40-44	13		9		10	
45-49	13	13	2	4	4	5
50-54	0		2		1	
55-59	0	0	1	2	1	2
60-64	0		1		1	
65-69	0	0	1	1	1	1
70 or older	0		0		0	
	99%		100%		99%	
N	30		112		142	

SOURCE: ADG 10M 260, 261, 262, *Recensement, Ville de Nîmes,* 1906; systematic sample of individuals in 5 percent of households.

BIRTH RECORDS

Birth records are a rich source for the study of migrants because they yield valuable information about the parents and the circumstances of birth. The *acte de naissance* names the father and mother, their ages and professions. If one or the other is missing, the acte explains why (*"enfant naturel," "père momentanément absent"*). If a bastard is legitimized later, that is noted beside the acte. If the parents moved to the commune shortly before the birth, that is sometimes mentioned. The parents' residence is listed, and if it is not the town in question, that is also explained *("en passage," "chez les parents de la mère").* Two witnesses signed every birth act. These were usually nonrelatives — city hall employees or office regulars — but when witnesses included a relative of the newborn, the relationship was specified in the document. Information about parents allows one to identify sibling migrants, and the identification of witnesses enabled me to trace the presence of other relatives in the city.

The acte de naissance is located with the *état civil* in municipal archives, in court records for 100 years after the birth, and in departmental archives thereafter. Thus I found those from before about 1870 in the departmental archives of the Gard and the Lozère, others in court archives in Nîmes, Le Vigan, and Mende, and in the municipal archives of Le Vigan, Villefort, and Langogne. I went to these archives supplied with the name and age of individuals as listed in the Nîmes census of 1906. Permission from the head of the court is required to see the état civil after about the year 1870.

I succeeded in finding 40-50 percent of the birth records (50 percent of the Viganais', 40 percent of the Villefortais', and 44 percent of the Langognais'). In a few cases, I was probably unable to find the birth record because the birth went unrecorded. For example, the birth of Sophie Chevret was not recorded in 1870, although the date and place of her birth were certified at her marriage in Langogne. When Georges Mandagout was born in Villefort in 1846, his birth was not recorded, though it was established in court when he was 21.

Other problems in locating birth records stemmed from inadequate census information about the migrant's name, age, and birthplace. The most serious problem was the lack of maiden names for married women. These were often not listed, and when they were not it was impossible to trace the woman's birth. In a few cases I was able to retrieve the maiden name in the birth record of the woman's offspring — if she had children. (For example, I found the maiden name of the Chevret sisters by this method.) The second difficulty stemmed from common names and nicknames listed in the census. Often several people named Marie, Louise, Louis, or Jean X were born within a few years of each other. It was impossible to tell which was the migrant — the notary's daughter or the laborer's daughter? the shoemaker's son or the shepherd's son? Nicknames similarly impeded identification. For example, there were many female migrants named Fanny in Nîmes in 1906, but no girl was given that name at birth in Le Vigan, Villefort, or Langogne! These problems especially inhibited my success in finding the birth records of female migrants.

Inaccurate age reporting also impeded birth identification. It is well known that people round off their ages, sometimes reduce them, and exaggerate them when they grow old. To compensate for this, I first searched for the birth record in the reported year of birth (or year calculated from age; one or the other was listed in the census). If the individual was not listed, I then searched the records four years before and after the given date.

Finally, sometimes I could not locate the birth record because the migrant was not born in Le Vigan, Villefort, or Langogne. Because problems of name and age reporting confound the issue, it is impossible to tell how often this was the case. I twice located another birthplace for a migrant, and in both cases they were near the reported commune. For example, 65-year-old Adèle Mourgues was born in Bez, a hamlet about 10 kilometers from Le Vigan, but of another commune. She may not have recalled this when the census taker asked for her commune of birth. She had married in Le Vigan 40 years before (in 1866), and it is likely that she thought of herself as being from there. Casimir Daudet, 36, was born 20 kilometers from Villefort in the canton of Bleymard (Cubières). When he was young, his family moved to Altier, 10 kilometers from Villefort and in the same canton. The census-taker reported his origins as Villefort.

Problems in locating birth records posed questions about the use of birth records and census data. Should these birth records be used to discuss parentage of the migrant streams, since only half of them are available? Representativeness is the problem. From the comparison of parents with home town grooms at the end of Chapter 2, it is obvious that the parentage of migrants does not perfectly reflect the society of the home town. However, this would not be expected. Parentage of the migrant streams, however, does reflect plausible parentage of all members of the streams — with agricultural parents somewhat underrepresented. The importance of nonagricultural parents and professionals is reasonable given the migrants' urban destination (see Table 2.11). Thus, the parentage information from the birth records closely corresponds as a best estimate for complete information, and I have used it with that caveat. Should birth records be used to establish sibling and other kin relationships among migrants? Certainly. For this purpose, birth records are utterly valid, and as such they do nothing but enrich our understanding of the migrant streams.

One may also ask whether migrants whose birth could not be confirmed should be counted as members of the migrant streams culled from the census lists. Although there is no parentage information or age and birth confirmation on these people, I decided to include them because it is likely that they were part of the migration stream and considered themselves as such, although their births went unrecorded, names or ages were improperly recorded, or they were born near, rather than in, a particular commune. Since it is most sensible to define a migrant group by birthplace as listed in the census, birth records were used as a complementary source to the census.

NOTES

1. France, Statistique générale, *Résultats statistiques du recensement général de la population,* Vol. 1 (Paris: Imprimerie Nationale, 1908), 2.

2. Philippe Pinchemel, *Structures sociales et dépopulation rurale dans les campagnes Picardes de 1836 à 1936* (Paris: Armand Colin, 1957), 21.

3. See, for example, George Dupeux, "Immigration urbaine et secteurs économiques: l'exemple de Bordeaux au début du XXe siècle," *Annales du Midi* 85 (1973), 209-220.

4. The most thorough evaluation and correction of the nineteenth-century French censuses is that by Etienne van de Walle, *The Female Population of France in the Nineteenth Century* (Princeton, NJ: Princeton University Press, 1974).

5. Jean Noël Biraben, "Inventaire des listes nominatives de recensement en France," *Population* 18 (1962), 309-310; France, Statistique générale, *Résultats statistiques,* 3; van de Walle, *Female Population of France,* 24, 88-89.

6. For the wealth of information available from data on employers, see William Reddy, "Family and factory: French linen weaving in the Belle Epoque," *Journal of Social History* 9 (1975), 102-112.

7. France, Statistique générale, *Résultats statistiques,* 24.

8. Abel Chatelain, "Migrations et domesticité féminine urbaine en France, XVIIIe siècle-XXe siècle," *Revue d'histoire économique et sociale* 47(1969); Theresa McBride, *The Domestic Revolution* (New York: Holmes and Meier, 1976), 34-37, 88.

9. Ibid., 87.

10. France, Statistique générale, *Résultats statistiques,* 3.

Appendix II

TABLE II.1 Occupational Histories of Individual Male Migrants

Occupation in Nîmes, 1906[a]	*Occupation of Father*[b]	*Occupation at Age 20*[c]	*Occupation in 1901*[d]	*Occupation at Other Time*[e]	*Assigned Name*	*Age in 1906*
I. Bourgeois						
avocat	avocat, LV (1852)	—	—	avocat[6]	Revel, P.	52
avocat	docteur en droit, LV (1848)	—	—	inspecteur de *la Confiance* (assurances)[6]	Laurent, L.	58
chef du canal de Beaucaire	conducteur . . . des ponts et chaussées, LV (1844)	employé des ponts et chaussées, LV (1864)	—	ingénieur[6]	Bedoc, J.	62
conseiller à la cour	greffier de la justice de Paix, LV (1847)	étudiant en droit, Paris (1867)	conseiller à la cour	conseiller à la cour[6]	Donzel, E.	59
dentiste	apprêteur de bas, LV (1870)	dentiste, Paris (1890)	dentiste	—	Eymann, J.	36
distillateur	négotiant, LV (1877)	sans prof., LV (1895)	—	distillerie d'essence[6]	Mandagout, E.	29

Occupation in Nîmes, 1906[a]	*Occupation of Father*[b]	*Occupation at Age 20*[c]	*Occupation in 1901*[d]	*Occupation at Other Time*[e]	*Assigned Name*	*Age in 1906*
docteur	séc-en-chef du sous-préfecture, LV (1841)	—	—	docteur en medicine[6]	Teissier, A.	65
étudiant	procureur de la Rép. . . . tribunal du 1er instance, LV (1885)	—	—	—	Pouzergue, M.	21
premier vicaire	ferblantier, LV (1859)	étudiant en théologie, Beaucaire (1979)	—	—	Gerbaud, L.	47
propriétaire	horloger, LV (1864)	élève à l'école Polytechnique, Paris (1883)	—	propriétaire[6]	Triaire, J.	42
rentier	faiseur de bas, LV (1826)	—	retraité	—	Malzac, D.	80

TABLE II.1 Occupational Histories of Individual Male Migrants (continued)

Occupation in Nîmes, 1906[a]	*Occupation of Father*[b]	*Occupation at Age 20*[c]	*Occupation in 1901*[d]	*Occupation at Other Time*[e]	*Assigned Name*	*Age in 1906*
retraité	menuisier, LV (1827)	menuisier, LV (1847)	chef du bureau de la Préfecture en retraite	sec. à la mairie, LV (1964)[2] chef du bureau . . . en retraite[6]	Donzel, H.	79
sans prof.	propriétaire, LV (1866)	sans prof. LV (1883)	avocat	avocat[6]	Guiraud, C.	40
vicaire général	architecte, LV (1839)	étudiant écclésiastic (1859)	—	aumonier[6]	Poujol, J.	67
II. Petit Bourgeois						
boucher	employé, chemin de fer, LV (1883)	—	—	—	Bourru, C.	23
cafetier	sabotier, V (1873)	garçon limonadier, Alès (1893)	—	gérant de cercle (1901)[1]	Roche, E.	33

Occupation in Nîmes, 1906[a]	*Occupation of Father*[b]	*Occupation at Age 20*[c]	*Occupation in 1901*[d]	*Occupation at Other Time*[e]	*Assigned Name*	*Age in 1906*
cafetier	(enfant naturel), V (1867)	—	concièrge	débitant de liqueurs[6]	Mialthe, E.	39
cafetier	journalier, L (1873)	mineur, L (1893)	—	—	Mauméjean, L.	33
cafetier	cordonnier, LV (1870)	limonadier (1890)	—	cafetier[6]	Mazoyer, H.	36
débitant de vins	faiseur de bas, LV (1849)	—	voyageur	—	Clement, C.	57
limonadier	journalier, L (1878)	garçon de café (1898)	—	—	Mauméjean, A.	28
tabacs	cordonnier, LV (1855)	—	employé	liqueurs[6]	Montin, E.	51
III. White Collar						
agent de sureté	maçon, V (1858)	maçon, tailleur de pierres, V (1878)	—	Police (1891)[3] Brigadier de police (1898)[1]	Giraud, A.	48

TABLE II.1 Occupational Histories of Individual Male Migrants (continued)

Occupation in Nîmes, 1906[a]	*Occupation of Father*[b]	*Occupation at Age 20*[c]	*Occupation in 1901*[d]	*Occupation at Other Time*[e]	*Assigned Name*	*Age in 1906*
commis de contributions	gendarme à la résidence de V (1877)	surnuméraire de contributions indirectes, Mende (1897)	—	contributions indirectes, Haute Savoie[3] (1902)	Pivarot, F.	29
commis de postes	maître d'hôtel, LV (1865)	—	—	—	Causse, A.	41
comptable	cordonnier, LV (1844)	instituteur (1864)	—	—	Massebiau, L.	62
comptable	commis négotiant, LV (1862)	comptable au Crédit Lyonnais (1881)	comptable	—	Leyre, S.	44
comptoir d'escompte	maître d'hôtel, V (1870)	sans prof., Alès (1889)	—	chef de titres au comptoir d'escompte (1904)[1] sous-chef de titres au comptoir d'escompte[6]	Mathieu, C.	36
employé	négotiant, LV (1885)	—	—	—	Peyre, F.	21

Occupation in Nîmes, 1906[a]	*Occupation of Father*[b]	*Occupation at Age 20*[c]	*Occupation in 1901*[d]	*Occupation at Other Time*[e]	*Assigned Name*	*Age in 1906*
employé	voiturier, V (1870)	commis aux écritures (1890)	—	employé de commerce (1910)[1]	Moulin, H.	36
employé	sans prof., LV (1846)	—	employé de banque	—	Nougarède, L.	60
employé	cultivateur-fermier, LV (1861)	boulanger, LV (1878)	employé	employé de commerce, LV (1889)[2]	Vivens, S.	45
employé	cultivateur, L (1870)	terrassier, L (1890)	—	—	Faucher, P.	36
employé	sabotier, L (1878)	—	—	employé[6]	Metge, A.	28
employé de banque	surveillant de filature, LV (1862)	étudiant, LV (1881)	—	ingénieur civil (1893)[2] employé comtoir d'escompte (1901)[1]	Dolladille, J.	46
employé de commerce	commis négotiant, LV (1876)	—	—	employé de commerce (1903)[1]	Carrel, G.	30

TABLE II.1 Occupational Histories of Individual Male Migrants (continued)

Occupation in Nîmes, 1906[a]	*Occupation of Father*[b]	*Occupation at Age 20*[c]	*Occupation in 1901*[d]	*Occupation at Other Time*[e]	*Assigned Name*	*Age in 1906*
employé Plombel	journalier, LV (1888)	—	—	—	Donnadieu, D.	18
employé à la Préfecture	sec. à la mairie, LV (1865)	commis de bureau (1884)	employé à la Préfecture	—	Donzel, E.	42
mettreur	postillon, LV (1854)	—	géometre	—	Veyrier, C.	52
sans prof.	cabaretier, LV (1835)	aide . . . aux bureaux de postes, LV (1855)	—	sec. à la mairie, LV (1871)[1]	Jeanjean, H.	71
voyageur	aubergiste, LV (1855)	—	—	—	Berthezène, S.	51
IV. Skilled Labor						
bijoutier	orfèvre, LV (1858)	horloger, LV (1878)	—	horloger, LV (1886)[2] horlogerie[6]	Lafont, A.	48
boulanger	meunier, L (1873)	boulanger-pâtissier, L (1893)	—	—	Saltet, P.	33

Occupation in Nîmes, 1906[a]	*Occupation of Father*[b]	*Occupation at Age 20*[c]	*Occupation in 1901*[d]	*Occupation at Other Time*[e]	*Assigned Name*	*Age in 1906*
boulanger	bridier, V (1855)	boulanger, V (1875)	—	boulanger[6]	Montet, A.	51
charron	maréchal-ferrant, LV (1856)	—	—	charron[6]	Rigal, E.	50
cordonnier	professeur au collège d'Uzès, Uzès (1863)	—	—	—	Julian, L.	43
cordonnier	propriétaire, V (1857)[1]	—	—	cordonnier, V (1873)[1]	Mandagout, G.	60
cordonnier chez Thérond	cocher, LV (1860)	cordonnier (1880)	—	—	Abric, H.	46
cordonnier chez Vialas	commis au greffier du tribunal, LV (1854)	commis (1874)	—	employé[6]	Serre, A.	52
ébeniste chez Rouquette	menuisier, L (1868)	—	—	—	Giral, L.	38

TABLE II.1 Occupational Histories of Individual Male Migrants (continued)

Occupation in Nîmes, 1906[a]	*Occupation of Father*[b]	*Occupation at Age 20*[c]	*Occupation in 1901*[d]	*Occupation at Other Time*[e]	*Assigned Name*	*Age in 1906*
facteur boîtier	charpentier, L (1869)	coiffeur, L (1889)	—	coiffeur, L (1894)	André, E.	37
horloger	horloger, V (1869)	—	—	horloger[6]	Depuis, H.	37
maçon	scieur de long, LV (1865)	cardeur, LV (1885)	—	—	Mazel, L.	41
maçon	mégissier, LV (1872)	maçon (1892)	homme de peine	—	Pouzergue, R.	34
maçon	tisserand, L (1841)	—	—	—	Cardenoux, F.	65
mécanicien	faiseur de bas, LV (1859)	ajusteur mécanicien (1879)	mécanicien	contre-maître[6]	Fabre, L.	47
mécanicien	employé, chemin de fer, LV (1885)	—	—	—	Barry, G.	21
menuisier	menuisier, LV (1872)	menuisier, LV (1892)	—	—	Massadau, L.	34

Occupation in Nîmes, 1906[a]	*Occupation of Father*[b]	*Occupation at Age 20*[c]	*Occupation in 1901*[d]	*Occupation at Other Time*[e]	*Assigned Name*	*Age in 1906*
ouvrier boulanger	propriétaire-cultivateur, V (1883)	—	—	—	Commaigne, L.	23
pâtissier	cardeur, LV (1873)	pâtissier, LV (1893)	—	—	Astier, L.	33
tailleur	tailleur d'habits, LV (1875)	tailleur d'habits, LV (1895)	— —	tailleur d'habits[1] (1905) tailleur[6]	Revel, E.	31
tailleur	faiseur de bas, LV (1835)	tailleur d'habits, LV (1855)	—	tailleur d'habits[2] LV (1875) tailleur[6]	Revel, J.	71
typographe	boulanger, LV (1875)	typographe (1895)	employé	—	Durand, A.	31
sans prof.	tisserand, L (1848)	—	—	cordonnier,[2] (1890)	Cardenoux, L.	58
serrurier	cultivateur, L (1887)	—	—	—	André, V.	19

TABLE II.1 Occupational Histories of Individual Male Migrants (continued)

Occupation in Nîmes, 1906[a]	*Occupation of Father*[b]	*Occupation at Age 20*[c]	*Occupation in 1901*[d]	*Occupation at Other Time*[e]	*Assigned Name*	*Age in 1906*
V. Semi-skilled and Unskilled Labor						
camoinneur	cultivateur, V (1870)	cultivateur, V (1890)	—	sans prof.[1] (1901)	Atger, L.	36
chiffonier	cultivateur, LV (1838)	—	—	—	Soulier, L.	68
concierge	ouvrier mineur, V (1844)	—	—	—	Bautid, J.	62
coupeur d'habits	tailleur d'habits, LV (1863)	sans prof. (1881)	—	tailleur[6]	Serven, P.	43
cuisinier	cultivateur, LV (1861)	cuisinier, LV (1881)	—	—	Labat, H.	45
cuisinier	voiturier, V (1872)	cuisinier, Monaco (1892)	—	—	Bonnet, L.	34
cultivateur	journalier, L (1877)	cultivateur, (1897)	—	—	Mathieu, B.	29

Occupation in Nîmes, 1906[a]	Occupation of Father[b]	Occupation at Age 20[c]	Occupation in 1901[d]	Occupation at Other Time[e]	Assigned Name	Age in 1906
domestique	(enfant naturel), L (1869)	cultivateur L (1889)	—	—	Jean, F.	37
domestique	propriétaire-cultivateur, LV (1845)	roulier (1865)	—	—	Minoret, E.	61
garçon de café	coiffeur, LV (1874)	garçon d'hôtel, LV (1894)	—	garçon d'hôtel[1] (1900)	Granier, E.	32
garçon de café	cultivateur-fermier, LV (1868)	garçon d'hotel LV (1894)	—	—	Conti, A.	38
garçon des salles	tailleur d'habits, LV (1864)	manoeuvre, LV (1884)	—	—	Labat, P.	42
homme de peine	aubergiste, L (1880)	—	—	employé de commerce[1] (1908)	Nogier, A.	25
homme de peine	(enfant naturel), LV (1863)	cordonnier (1883)	—	—	Giral, F.	43

TABLE II.1 Occupational Histories of Individual Male Migrants (continued)

Occupation in Nîmes, 1906[a]	*Occupation of Father*[b]	*Occupation at Age 20*[c]	*Occupation in 1901*[d]	*Occupation at Other Time*[e]	*Assigned Name*	*Age in 1906*
homme de peine	cultivateur, V (1869)	cultivateur, V (1892)	—	—	André, L.	37
jardinier-fleuriste	cultivateur, LV (1856)	—	—	—	Daumas, H.	50
journalier	tisserand, L (1833)	—	—	aubergiste, L[2] (1876) (1880) jardinier [4] (1908)	Archer, P.	73
journalier	cordonnier, LV (1886)	—	—	—	Pouzergue, A.	20
journalier	cardeur, LV (1869)	cultivateur, LV (1889)	—	cultivateur, LV[1] (1893)	Bouscarrain, C.	37
manoeuvre	jardinier, LV (1841)	—	—	—	André, P.	65
sans prof.	journalier, L (1867)	—	—	cultivateur[1] (1897) journalier[2] (1902)	Mathieu, A.	39
sans prof.	cultivateur, LV (1861)	cocher (1881)	cocher	—	Massip, P.	45

Occupation in Nîmes, 1906[a]	Occupation of Father[b]	Occupation at Age 20[c]	Occupation in 1901[d]	Occupation at Other Time[e]	Assigned Name	Age in 1906
VI. Railroad Employees						
employé PLM	maréchal-ferrant, L (1869)	mécanicien, Toulon (1888)	—	maître mécanicien[3] (1891) ajusteur mécanicien[3] (1897)	Maurin, J.	37
employé PLM	perruquier, facteur de ville, V (1875)	—	—	—	Bouzanquet, A.	31
employé PLM	perruquier, facteur de ville, V (1874)	coiffeur, V (1894)	—	homme d'équipe, chemin de fer, Montpellier[3] (1899) employé, chemin de fer[1] (1900)	Bouzanquet, C.	32
employé PLM	cultivateur, L (1864)	employé, chemin de fer (1884)	—	conducteur-en-chef, PLM[5] (1900)	Vidal, D.	42
employé PLM	homme d'affairs de M. Alzon, LV (1853)	menuisier, LV (1873)	—	PLM[3] (1881) employé au PLM[6]	Valette, L.	53

TABLE II.1 Occupational Histories of Individual Male Migrants (continued)

Occupation in Nîmes, 1906[a]	*Occupation of Father*[b]	*Occupation at Age 20*[c]	*Occupation in 1901*[d]	*Occupation at Other Time*[e]	*Assigned Name*	*Age in 1906*
employé PLM	cantonnier, V (1869)	cultivateur, Manduel (Gard) (1889)	—	employé, chemin de fer[1] (1899)	Depuis, H.	37
PLM	fabricant d'allumettes, L (1870)	charron, L (1890)	—	meunier, L[1] (1899) ajusteur, chemin de fer[3] (1900)	Testud, E.	36
PLM	journalier, V (1854)	—	—	—	Boissier, L.	52
PLM	perruquier, V (1856)	employé, chemin de fer, commis, V (1876)	—	chef du bureau, chemin de fer[4] (1900) employé des postes[6]	Bouzanquet, V.	50
PLM	tisserand, V (1878)	boulanger, V (1898)	—	employé PLM[1] (1904) manoeuvre PLM[3] (1904)	Janvier, P.	28
PLM	sabotier, V (1874)	boulanger, V (1894)	—	homme d'équipe PLM[3] (1898) employé PLM[1] (1901, 1908)	Brun, E.	32

Occupation in Nîmes, 1906[a]	*Occupation of Father*[b]	*Occupation at Age 20*[c]	*Occupation in 1901*[d]	*Occupation at Other Time*[e]	*Assigned Name*	*Age In 1906*
PLM	marchand chapellier, LV (1856)	—	—	employé PLM, Lyon, (1886)[2]	Baldy, H.	50
retraité PLM	cultivateur, LV (1848)	—	—	—	Chapot, A.	58
sans prof.	homme d'équipe, V (1871)	serrurier, V (1891)	—	ajusteur, PLM (1899)[3] chauffeur, chemin de fer[1] (1901) mécanicien au PLM[6]	Jourdan, L.	35
sans prof.	journalier, L (1848)	—	—	PLM, L. (1874)[5] conducteur-en-chef, PLM[5] (1888) employé au PLM[6]	Pons, J.	60

NOTE: Location is Nîmes unless otherwise noted.
LV — Le Vigan
L — Langogne
V — Villefort

a. As listed in 1906 census, Nîmes
b. As listed on individual's birth act
c. As listed on individual's conscript record
d. As listed in census of Protestant electors, consistory of Nîmes
e. Sources vary
1. marriage record
2. birth act of offspring
3. conscript record
4. witness, wedding act
5. PLM employment record
6. city directory, Nîmes, 1906

Appendix III

TABLE III.1 Marriage Partners Able to Sign Marriage Acts, Le Vigan, 1851-1906

	Le Vigan 1851-1855	*Gard 1866*	*France 1866*	*Le Vigan 1901-1905*	*France 1901-1905*
% Grooms able to sign	86	80	72	99	97
% Brides able to sign	59	60	55	98	95
N of marriages	157	*	*	177	*

*Number of marriages not listed by Furet and Ouzouf

SOURCE: ADG E5 and ATN, *Etat civil,* Le Vigan; François Furet and Jacquer Ouzouf, *Lire et Ecrire* 2 vols. (Paris: Editions du Minuit, 1977), Vol. 1, 30, 57, 62.

TABLE III.2 Marriage Partners Able to Sign Marriage Acts, Villefort, 1762-1906

	Villefort 1762-1789	*Villefort 1866-1870*	*Lozère 1866*	*France 1866*	*Villefort 1901-1905*	*France 1901-1906*
% Grooms able to sign	54	75	90	72	98	97
% Brides able to sign	18	60	60	55	98	95
N of marriages	424	94	*	*	51	*

*Number of marriages not listed by Furet and Ouzouf

SOURCE: ADL 4E 198 and ATM *Etat civil, Villefort;* Alain Laurans, "Villefort dans la Diocèse d'Uzès, 1700-1789," (Mémoire de Maîtrise, Université Paul Valéry, Montpellier III, 1979), 99; François Furet and Jacques Ouzouf, *Lire et Ecrire* 2 vols. (Paris: Editions du Minuit, 1977), Vol. 1, 30, 57, 62.

TABLE III.3 Marriage Partners Able to Sign Marriage Acts, Langogne, 1787-1906

	Langogne				*Lozère*	*France*	*Langogne*	*France*
	1787-1791	*1833-1837*	*1857-1861*	*1866-1870*	*1866*	*1866*	*1901-1905*	*1901-1906*
% Grooms able to sign	47	65	94	90	90	72	100	97
% Brides able to sign	33	48	45	50	60	55	99	95
N of marriages	*	*	*	114	**	**	135	**

*Number of marriages not listed by Cholvy
**Number of marriages not listed by Furet and Ouzouf

SOURCE: ADL 5E 80 and ATM, *Etat civil,* Langogne; Gerard Cholvy, "Une chrétienté au XIXe siècle: la Lozère," *Revue du Gévaudan* 18-19 (1972-1973), 379; François Furet and Jacques Ouzouf, *Lire et Ecrire* 2 vols. (Paris: Editions du Minuit, 1977), Vol. 1, 30, 57, 62.

TABLE III.4 Household Composition and Structure, By Origin and Age of Household Head

		-29	30-39	40-49	50-59	60-98	Total
Household Composition							
Mean household size:	N*/	2.7	3.8	4.0	3.4	2.9	3.5
	M**	2.7	3.2	3.5	3.6	3.0	3.3
Percentage of households with:							
children	N/	44%	67	75	66	51	63
	M	41%	58	69	69	56	61
relatives	N/	30%	26	31	19	21	25
	M	21%	19	15	14	23	18
servants	N/	2%	10	5	10	11	8
	M	9%	8	12	13	17	12
Household Structure							
Mean number of children	N/	.6	1.4	1.8	1.4	.8	1.3
	M	.7	1.1	1.4	1.6	1.0	1.2
Structure							
solitary	N/	14%	11	8	14	14	12
	M	27%	15	12	11	13	15
no family	N/	0%	1	4	1	10	4
	M	3%	2	3	4	12	5
simple family	N/	62%	67	65	72	65	66
	M	49%	66	74	74	63	67
extended/multiple family	N/	24%	21	24	13	11	18
	M	21%	16	12	12	12	14
Total	N/	100%	100	101	100	100	100
	M	100%	99	101	101	100	101
N	N/	50%	90	110	100	105	455
	M	70%	137	156	121	115	599

*N = native
**M = migrant

SOURCE: ADG 10M 260, 261, 262, *Recensement, Ville de Nîmes,* 1906; systematic sample of individuals in 5 percent of households.

TABLE III.5 Proportion Married, By Sex and Origin, Migrant Streams (percentages)

	Males			*Females*		
Age	*Langogne*	*Villefort*	*Le Vigan*	*Langogne*	*Villefort*	*Le Vigan*
15-24	0%	0	6	6	6	12
25-34	57	33	69	49	71	45
35-49	70	68	83	60	60	57
Total	54%	52	56	40	49	40
N	28	33	61	70	57	110

SOURCE: ADG 6M 260, 261, 262, *Recensement, Ville de Nîmes,* 1906.

TABLE III.6 Geographical Origin of Marriage Partners

Origin of Groom:	*Nîmes*	*Gard*	*Neighboring Departments*	*Elsewhere in France*	*Outside France*	*Total*
Origin of Bride						
Nîmes	19	9	3	3	0	34
Gard	6	6	2	3	1	14
Neighboring Departments	6	2	2	5	0	15
Elsewhere in France	6	2	2	3	1	14
Outside France	0	0	0	0	0	2
Total	37	15	9	14	4	79

NOTE: This table only includes couples who were to settle in Nîmes after the wedding.
SOURCE: ATN *Actes de mariage,* Nîmes, 1906.

TABLE III.7 Occupational Status of Groom, By Origin of Bride (percentages)

Occupational Status	*Native Brides*	*Migrant Brides*	*Total*
Bourgeois	15	11	13
Petit bourgeois	3	4	4
White collar	41	24	32
Skilled labor	29	29	29
Unskilled labor	12	20	16
Soldier	0	9	5
Agriculture	0	2	1
Total	100%	99%	100%
N	34	45	79

NOTE: This tables only includes couples who were to settle in Nîmes after the wedding.
SOURCE: ATN *Actes de mariage,* Nîmes, 1906.

TABLE III.8 Occupational Status of Husband, By Origin of Wife (percentages)

Occupational Status	*Native Wives*	*Migrant Wives*
Bourgeois	13	14
Petit bourgeois	6	9
White collar	19	21
Skilled labor	31	23
Unskilled labor	30	33
Total	99%	100%
N	253	329
x^2, $p > .1$		

SOURCE: ADG 10M 260, 261, 262, *Recensement, Ville de Nîmes,* 1906; systematic sample of individuals in 5 percent of households.

TABLE III.9 Occupational Status of Husband, By Origin of Wife, Migrant Streams (percentages)

Occupational Status	*Le Vigan*	*Villefort*	*Langogne*
Bourgeois	11	0	11
Petit bourgeois	7	4	14
White collar	30	17	7
Skilled labor	30	35	29
Unskilled labor	23	44	39
Total	100%	100%	100%
N	57	23	28

SOURCE: ADG 10M 260, 261, 262, *Recensement, Ville de Nîmes*, 1906.

TABLE III.10 Household Composition and Structure, Migrant Streams and Total Population

	Le Vigan	*Villefort*	*Langogne*	*All Migrants*	*All Nîmes*
Household Composition					
Mean household size	3.5	2.7	3.2	3.3	3.3
Percentage of households with:					
children	64	48	60	61	61
relatives	26	30	23	18	21
servants	19	0	5	12	10
Household Structure					
Mean number of children	1.2	.9	1.3	1.2	1.2
Structure					
solitary	10	27	14	15	13
no family	5	2	5	5	4
simple family	64	53	65	67	67
extended/multiple family	20	18	13	14	16
Total	99%	99%	97%	101%	100%
N	129	44	43	599	1054

SOURCE: ADG 10M 260, 261, 262, *Recensement, Ville de Nîmes*, 1906.

TABLE III.11 Employment, Occupation, and Origin, Married Women, Migrant Streams

	Le Vigan		*Villefort*		*Langogne*	
Employment						
percentage employed	10		9		17	
N employed	7		3		5	
Occupational category						
shoe industry	0		0		0	
garment industry	3	(43%)	0		0	
service	2	(29%)	0		1	(20%)
petty commerce	1	(14%)	2	(67%)	3	(60%)
white collar	1	(14%)	0		0	
miscellaneous	0		1	(33%)	1	(20%)
total	7	(100%)	3	(100%)	5	(100%)
Occupational titles						
garment industry	couturière lingère giletière		. . .		. . .	
service	concièrge laveuse		. . .		femme de ménage	
petty commerce	bouchère		laitière épicière		bouchère épicière marchande de comestibles	
white collar	employée		. . .		. . .	
miscellaneous	. . .		charpentière		peintre	

SOURCE: ADG 10M 260, 261, 262, *Recensement, Ville de Nîmes,* 1906.

Bibliography

I. PRIMARY SOURCES

Archives départementales du Gard

(1) Series E: Etat Civil
- E5: Etat civil, Le Vigan, 1845-1872
- E1: Etat civil, Nîmes, 1845-1872

(2) Series M: Personnel, Police et Administration Générale
- 1M 292 bis: Elections législatives, 1906
- 6M 1224: Police, général: grèves, congrès, réunions politiques, 1890-1902
- 6M 1622: Police, général
- 6M 4788: Associations: Nîmes, Ville
- 6M 6535: Répertoire des associations déclarées
- 10M 260: Recensement, Ville de Nîmes, 1906
- 10M 261: Recensement, Ville de Nîmes, 1906
- 10M 262: Recensement, Ville de Nîmes, 1906
- 10M 274: Dénombrement général de 1906: état numérique de fonctionnaires départementaux et communaux
- 12M 24: Statistique agricole, 1811
- 12M 222: Statistique agricole, arrondissements d'Uzès et du Vigan, 1900
- 12M 263: Situation industrielle, 1870-1879
- 14M 337: Foires et marchés
- 14M 340: Foires et marchés
- 14M 370: Foires et marchés
- 14M 371: Situation industrielle
- 14M 445: Grèves, 1899-1901
- 14M 446: Grèves, 1892-1900
- 14M 469: Industrie, affaires diverses, 1880-1898
- 14M 534: Grèves, 1904-1907
- 14M 584: Procès-verbaux, infractions
- 14M 587: Situation industrielle, 1891-1903

(3) Series S: Travaux Publics
- 5S 6: Chemin de Fer: personnel, assermentations, mouvement, 1850-1887
- 5S 7: Chemin de Fer: personnel, assermentations, mouvement, 1888-1896
- 5S 8: Chemin de Fer: personnel, assermentations, mouvement, 1897-1904

(4) Series R: Affairs Militaires
- 1847-1895 Classes des conscrits

Archives départementales de la Lozère

(1) Series E: Etat Civil
E80 f1: Recensements, Langogne, 1861
4E 80: Etat civil, Langogne, 1845-1872
4E 198: Etat civil, Villefort, 1845-1872

(2) Series M: Personnel, Police et Administration Générale
M3030: Statistique agricole, arrondissement de Mende, 1897-1906
M4113: Enquête sericiculture, 1879-1903
M4127: Foires et marchés, Langogne
M4131: Foires et marchés, Villefort
M4173: Situation industrielle et commerciale, 1880-1882, 1886-1888
M4198: Statistique agricole, pesage de grains, 1871-1886
M4199: Statistique agricole, pesage de grains, 1887-1901

(3) Series O: Administration et Comptibilité Communale
3O 893: Villefort, vicinalité

(4) Series R: Affaires Militaires
1870-1898 Classes des conscrits

(5) Series T: Instruction Publique
T3148: Monographies communales faites par les instituteurs, II Empire

Archives municipales de Nîmes

Series F: Recensements, Commerce et Industrie, Agriculture
F7 54: Syndicats
F7 55: Syndicats
F7 55-2: Bureaux de placement

Greffe du Tribunal d'Instance à Mende

Etat civil, Langogne, 1873-1914
Etat civil, Villefort, 1873-1914

Greffe du Tribunal d'Instance au Vigan

Etat civil, Le Vigan, 1873-1914

Greffe du Tribunal d'Instance à Nîmes

Etat civil, Le Vigan, 1873-1914
Etat civil, Nîmes, 1873-1914

Archives du Consistoire de Nîmes

C53: Registres électoraux de l'Eglise de Nîmes, 1900-1901

Ia. Local Newspapers and Government Publications

Annuaire du Gard, 1861, 1880, 1881, 1892, 1889

Bulletin Municipal de la ville de Nîmes, 1900-1910

Guide du Gard, 1904-1907

Le Petit Midi, Nîmes, daily, 1906

Le Petit Républican du Midi, Nîmes, daily, 1901, 1904, 1906

II. SECONDARY SOURCES

Abrams, Philip [ed.] *Towns in Societies.* Cambridge: Cambridge University Press, 1978.

Ackerman, Evelyn B. *Village on the Seine.* Ithaca, NY: Cornell University Press, 1979.

Agulhon, Maurice *Une ville ouvrière au temps du socialisme utopique: Toulon de 1815 à 1851.* Paris: Mouton, 1970.

——— "Les chambrées en Basse-Provence: histoire et ethnologie," *Revue historique* 498 (1971), 337-368.

——— with Gabriel Désert and Robert Specklin *Histoire de la France rural,* Vol. 3: *Apogée et crise de la civilisation paysanne, 1789-1914.* Paris: Editions Seuil, 1976.

Åckerman, Sune "Swedish migration and social mobility: the tale of three cities." *Social Science History* 1 (Winter 1977), 178-209.

——— "Towards an understanding of emigrational processes." *Scandinavian Journal of History* 3 (1978), 131-154.

Anderson, Grace *Networks of Contact: The Portuguese and Toronto.* Waterloo, Canada: Wilfrid Laurier University, 1974.

Anderson, Michael *Family Structure in Nineteenth-Century Lancashire.* Cambridge: Cambridge University Press, 1971.

——— "Urban migration into nineteenth century Lancashire: some insights into two competing hypotheses." *Annales de démographie historique* (1971), 13-26.

——— "Household structure and the Industrial Revolution: mid-nineteenth century Preston in comparative perspective," in P. Laslett, ed., *Household and Family in Past Time.* Cambridge: Cambridge University Press, 1972.

——— "Marriage patterns in Victorian Britain: an analysis based on registration district data for England and Wales." *Journal of Family History* 1 (1976), 55-78.

André, Lucien "L'épopée du chemin de fer: La Levade-Villefort." *Almanach Cévenol* 6 (1974), 161-168.

Anglade, Jean *La vie quotidienne dans le Massif Central au XIXe siècle.* Paris: Hachette, 1971.

Armengaud, André, "Un siècle délaissé: le XIXe." *Annales de démographie historique* (1971), 299-309.

——— "Industrialisation et démographie dans la France du XIXe siècle," in P. Léon et al., eds., *L'industrialisation en Europe au XIXe siècle: cartographie et typologie.* Paris: Editions du C.N.R.S., 1972.

Association Française pour l'Avancement des Sciences. *Nîmes et le Gard,* 2 vols. Nîmes: Imprimerie Cooperative, 1912.

Audiganne, Armand *Les populations ouvrières et les industries de la France,* 2 vols. New York: Burt Franklin [1860], 1970.

Azais, l'Abbé P. "La charité à Nîmes." *Mémoires de l'Académie de Nîmes,* ser. 6 (1874), 27-139.

Barton, Josef *Peasants and Strangers: Italians, Rumanians, and Slovaks in An American City, 1890-1950.* Cambridge, MA: Harvard University Press, 1975.

Barbot, Jules *Le Paysan Lozérian.* Mende: Privat, 1899.

Baumès, Jean Babtiste Timothée and J. C. Vincens *Topographie de la ville de Nismes et de sa banlieu.* Nîmes: n.p., 1802.

Beltramone, André *La mobilité graphique d'une population.* Paris: Gauthier-Villars, 1966.

Benoit, Eugène *Association des Employées de Commerce et de l'Industrie de la ville de Nîmes.* Nîmes: La Laboreuse, 1907.

Benoît-Germain, Fernand "Commerce et Industrie," in Association Française pour l'Avancement des Sciences, ed., *Nîmes et le Gard,* 2 vols. Nîmes: Imprimerie Cooperative, 1912.

Berkner, Lutz K. "The stem family and the developmental cycle of the peasant household: an eighteenth-century Austrian example." *American Historical Review* 77 (April 1972), 398-418.

Bernard, Marc. *Pareils à des enfants.* Paris: Gallimard, 1941.

——— *Salut, Camarades.* Paris: Gallimard, 1955.

Bertaux, Isabelle "The life history approach to the study of internal migration." *Oral History* 7 (1979), 26-32.

Beteille, Roger *Les aveyronnais.* Poitiers: Imprimerie l'Union, 1974.

——— "L'originalité de l'emigration rouergate: filières, migrations et comportement socioprofesional." *Actes de XLIII Congrès d'Etudes de la Fédération Historique du Languedoc Méditerranéen et du Roussillon.* Rodez: 1974.

Biraben, Jean Noël "Inventaire des listes nominatives de recensement en France." *Population* 18 (1962), 305-328.

Bigot, Antoine *Li bourgadieiro: poesies patoises.* Nîmes: n.p., 1881.

Blanchard, Raoul *Le comté de Nice.* Paris: Arthème Fayard, 1960.

Blanquet, D. M. "De la mendicité dans le département de la Lozère." *Mémoires de la Société des Lettres, Sciences et Arts de la Ville de Mende* 15 (1845-1846), 58-69.

Boegner, Marc, André Siegfried, and Pierre Lestringant [eds.] *Protestantisme français.* Paris: Plon, 1945.

Boutin, Emile "La propriété batie." *Journal de la Société de Statistique de Paris* 32 (July 1891), 221-248.

Bouvier, Jean *Le Crédit Lyonnaise de 1863 à 1882.* Paris: SEVPEN, 1961.

Boyer, Armand "Les migrations saisonnières dans la Cévenne vivaroise." *Revue de Géographie Alpine* 22 (1934), 571-609.

Bozon, Pierre *La vie rurale en Vivarais.* Valence-sur-Rhône: Réunies, 1963.

Brandes, Stanley *Migration, Kinship and Community Tradition in a Spanish Village.* New York: Academic Press, 1975.

Braudel, Fernand *Le Méditerranée et le monde Méditerranéen à l'époque de Philippe II.* Paris: Armand Colin, 1949.

Bravard, Yves "Sondages à propos de l'emigration dans les Alpes du Nord." *Revue de Géographie Alpine* 45 (1957), 91-112.

——— *Le dépeuplement des hautes-vallées des Alpes-Maritimes.* Grenoble: Allier, 1961.

Brettell, Caroline "Hope and nostalgia: Portuguese women immigrants in Paris." Ph. D. dissertation, Brown University, 1979.

Brossard, René "Les chemins de fer dans le Gard, leurs origines, leur développement," in Association Française pour l'Avancement des Sciences, ed., *Nîmes et le Gard,* 2 vols. Nîmes: Imprimerie Cooperative, 1912.

Brown, J. S., H. K. Schwartzweller, and J. Mangalam "Kentucky migration and the stem family: an American variation of a theme by Le Play." *Rural Sociology* 28 (1963), 48-69.

Brugier, Victorien *La Bourse du Travail à Nîmes*. Nîmes: Imprimerie L'Idéale, 1925.

Caralp-Landon, Raymonde *Les Chemins de Fer dans le Massif Central*. Paris: Imprimerie Nationale, 1959.

Cayez, Pierre "Une proto-industrialisation décalée: la ruralisation de la soierie lyonnaise dans la première moitié du XIXe siècle." *Revue du Nord* 63 (1981), 95-103.

Chaballier, Claude "La population du Gard: étude démographique." *Bulletin de la Société languedocienne de Géographie*, ser. 2 (1934), 160-190.

Chabanon, Jules *Villefort-du-Gévaudan*. Mende: Ignon-Renouard, 1920.

Chamson, André *The Road*. New York: Scribner's, 1929.

Chamson, Lucie Mazauric *"Belle Rose, Ô Tour Magne"*. Paris: Plon, 1969.

Chastel, Rémy *La Haute Lozère, jadis et nagère*. Paris: Roudil, 1976.

Chatelain, Abel "La main-d'oeuvre et la construction des chemins de fer au XIXe siècle." *Annales: Economies, Sociétés, Civilisations* 8 (1953), 502-506.

——— "Migrations et domesticité féminine urbaine en France, XVIIIe siècle-XXe siècle." *Revue d'histoire économique et sociale* 47 (1969), 506-528.

——— *Les migrants temporaires en France de 1900 à 1914*, 2 vols. Lille: Publications de l'Université de Lille, 1976.

Chevalier, Louis *La formation de la population parisienne au XIXe siècle*. Paris: Presses Universitaires Françaises, 1950.

——— *Les parisiens*. Paris: Hachette, 1967.

——— *Laboring Classes and Dangerous Classes in Paris during the First Half of the Nineteenth Century*. New York: Fertig, 1973.

Chojnaka, Helen "Nuptiality patterns in agrarian society." *Population Studies* 30 (July 1976), 203-241.

Choldin, Harvey M. "Kinship networks in the migration process." *International Migration Review* 7 (1973), 163-175.

Cholvy, Gérard "Une chrétienté au XIXe siècle: la Lozère." *Revue du Gévaudan* 18-19 (1972-1973), 365-382.

"Collecte annuelle pour les pauvres par les membres du Consistoire et du Diaçonat (1904)." *Bulletin de l'Eglise Reformée de Nîmes* 18 (January 1905), 1-11.

Conseil Municipal de Langogne "Délibération de la ville de Langogne pour être le chef-lieu d'un département (1789)." *La Lozère Pittoresque* 4 (1900), 42-45.

Corbin, Alain *Archaïsme et modernité en Limousin au XIXe siècle, 1845-1880*, 2 vols. Paris: Marcel Rivière, 1975.

——— *Les filles de noce: misère sexuelle et prostitution (19e et 20e siècles)*. Paris: Aubier Montaigne, 1978.

Cosson, Armand "Industrie de soie et population ouvrière à Nîmes de 1815 à 1848," in G. Cholvy, ed., *Economie et société en Languedoc-Roussillon de 1789 à nos jours*. Montpellier: Université Paul Valéry, 1978.

Crew, David F. *Town in the Ruhr: A Social History of Bochum, 1860-1914*. New York: Columbia University Press, 1979.

Demos, John and Virginia Demos "Adolescence in historical perspective." *Journal of Marriage and the Family* 32 (November 1969), 632-639.

Desgraves, Louis, with Georges Dupeux. *Bordeaux au XIXe siècle*. Bordeaux: Fédération Historique du Sud-Ouest, 1969.

Dugrand, Raymond *Villes et campagnes en Bas-Languedoc*. Paris: Presses Universitaires Françaises, 1963.

Dupeux, Georges. "Immigration urbaine et secteurs économiques: l'exemple de Bordeaux au début du XXe siècle." *Annales du Midi* 85 (1973), 209-220.

——— "La croissance urbaine en France au XIXe siecle." *Revue d'histoire économique et sociale* 52 (1974), 173-189.

Dutil, Léon *L'état économique du Languedoc à la fin de l'ancien régime (1750-89)*. Paris: Hachette, 1911.

Duveau, Georges *La vie ouvrière en France sous le second Empire*. Paris: Gallimard, 1946.

——— *Les instituteurs*. Paris: Deuil, 1966.

Elder, Glen "Family history and the life course." *Journal of Family History* 2 (Winter 1977), 279-304.

Estienne, P. "Un demi-siècle de dépeuplement dans le Massif Central." *Revue de Géographie Alpine* 44 (1956), 463-472.

Fabre, Daniel and Jacques La Croix *La vie quotidienne des paysans du Languedoc au XIXe siècle*. Paris: Hachette, 1973.

Fairchilds, Cissie *Poverty and Charity in Aix-en-Provence, 1640-1789*. Baltimore: Johns Hopkins University Press, 1976.

Fermaud, Alice "La lycée de jeunes filles de Nîmes." *Revue économique de la Chambre de Commerce de Nîmes-Uzès-Le Vigan* 4, no. 35 (1953), 16-18.

Foulquier, l'Abbé Achille *Notes Historiques sur les Paroisses des Cévennes*. Mende: n.p., 1907.

Foner, Nancy "Women, work and migration: Jamaicans in London." *Urban Anthropology* 4 (1975), 229-249.

France: Statistique generale *Industrie. Résultats généraux de l'enquête effectuée pendant l'année 1848*. Paris: Imprimerie Nationale, 1848.

——— *Annuaire statistique de la France, 1905*. Paris: Imprimerie nationale, 1905.

——— *Résultats statistiques du recensement général de la population effectué le 4 mars 1901*, 5 vols. Paris: Imprimerie nationale, 1904-1907.

——— *Statistique des families en 1906*. Paris: Imprimerie nationale, 1912.

Frey, Michel "Du mariage et du concubinage dans les classes populaires à Paris (1846-1847)." *Annales: ESC* 33 (1978), 803-829.

Fruit, Elie *Les Syndicats dans les Chemins de Fer (1890-1910)*. Paris: Editions ouvrières, 1976.

Furet, François and Jacques Ouzouf *Lire et Ecrire*. Paris: Editions du Minuit, 1977.

Gaillard, Jean-Michel "Le mouvement ouvrier dans le Gard (1875-1914)." Mémoire de Maîtrise, Université de Nanterre, 1969.

Gallon, G. "Le mouvement de la population dans le département du Gard, 1821-1920." *Mémoires de l'Académie de Nîmes* 48 (1928-1930), 81-117.

——— "Le mouvement de la population dans le département de la Lozère au cours de la période 1821-1920." *Bulletin de la Société des Lettres de la Lozère, Chroniques et Mélanges* (1933), 1-40.

Garden, Maurice "L'attraction de Lyon à la fin de l'ancien régime." *Annales de démographie historique* (1970), 205-222.

——— *Lyon et les Lyonnais au XVIIIe siècle*. Paris: Société d'editions "Les Belles Lettres," 1970.

Gérard, Guillaume *Notes sur cent ans d'histoire en Lozère*. Mende: Chaptal, 1969.

Gillis, John R. *Youth and History: Tradition and Change in European Age Relations, 1770 to the Present*. New York: Academic Press, 1974.

Glasco, Laurence A. "The life course and household structure of American ethnic groups: Irish, Germans, and native-born whites in Buffalo, New York, 1855." *Journal of Urban History* 1 (May 1975), 339-364.

Glenn, Norval, Andreain Ross, and Judy Corder-Tully "Patterns of intergenerational mobility of females through marriage." *American Sociological Review* 39 (1969), 638-699.

Goiffron, l'Abbé Etienne *Les hôpitaux et les oeuvres charitables à Nîmes*. Nîmes: Jouve, 1896.

Goldstein, Sidney "Circulation in the context of total mobility in Southeast Asia." East-West Population Institute, 1978.

Gorlier, Pierre *Le Vigan à travers les siècles: histoire d'une cité languedocienne*. Montpellier: Editions de la Licorne, 1955.

Granovetter, Mark *Getting a Job*. Cambridge, MA: Harvard University Press, 1974.

Gross, Edward "Plus ça change . . . ? The sexual structure of occupations over time." *Social Problems* 16 (1968), 198-207.

Geurin, Pierre " Des types de famille et des causes de désorganisation de la famille dans une commune rurale du Midi." *Mémoires de l'Académie de Nîmes* ser 7 (1913), 63-75.

Guillaume, Pierre *Démographie historique*. Paris: Armand Colin, 1970.

——— *La population de Bordeaux au XIXe siècle: essai d'histoire sociale*. Paris: Armand Colin, 1972.

Haines, Michael *Fertility and Occupation: Population Patterns in Industrialization*. New York: Academic Press, 1979.

Hajnal, John "Age at marriage and proportions marrying." *Population Studies* 7 (1953), 111-136.

Hareven, Tamara "Family time and historical time." *Daedalus* 106 (Spring 1977), 57-70.

Hartwell, R. M. "The tertiary sector in the English economy during the Industrial Revolution," in P. Léon et al., eds., *L'industrialisation en Europe au XIX siècle: cartographie et typologie*. Paris: Editions du CNRS, 1972.

Higonnet, Patrice *Pont-de-Montvert: Social Structure and Politics in a French Village, 1700-1914*. Cambridge, MA: Harvard University Press, 1971.

Higounet, Charles *Bordeaux au XVIIIe siècle*. Bordeaux: Fédération historique du Sud-Ouest, 1968.

Hochstadt, Steve "Migration and industrialization in Germany, 1815-1977." *Social Science History* 5 (1980), 445-468.

Hohenberg, Paul "Migrations et fluctuations démographiques dans la France rurale, 1836-1901." *Annales ESC* 29 (1974), 461-497.

Hood, James "Patterns of popular protest in the French Revolution: the conceptual contribution of the Gard." *Journal of Modern History* 48 (June 1976), 259-293.

Hufton, Olwen *The Poor of Eighteenth-Century France*. Oxford: Clarendon Press, 1974.

Igolen, L. C. "La garrigue et les masets nimois." *Mémoires de l'Académie de Nîmes* ser. 7 (1931-1932), 32-93.

Jacquemes-Dolle, Jocelyne "Les industries de la chaussure, de la bonneterie et de la confection dans l'agglomeration nimoise." Mémoire de Maîtrise, Université Paul Valéry, Montpellier III, 1971.

Jacquet, Joseph *Les cheminots dans l'histoire sociale de la France*. Paris: Editions sociales, 1967.

Journal d'Agriculture Pratique "Une école de fermières à New York." *Bulletin de la Société d'Agriculture de la Lozère* 50 (1878), 131-136.

Jouverte, Gilberte and Janine Dumas "La vie religieuse dans le diocèse de Nîmes sous l'épiscopat de Mgr. Besson (1875-1888)." Mémoire de Maîtrise, Université Paul Valéry, Montpellier III, 1972.

Katz, Michael *The People of Hamilton, Canada West: Family and Class in a Mid-Nineteenth-Century City*. Cambridge, MA: Harvard University Press, 1975.

Kett, Joseph "Adolescents and youth in nineteenth-century America," in Theodore Rabb and Robert Rotberg, eds., *The Family in History*. New York: Harper & Row, 1971.

——— *Rites of Passage: Adolescence in America, 1790 to the Present*. New York: Basic Books, 1977.

Knodel, John "Town and country in 19th-century Germany: a review of urban-rural differentials in demographic behavior." *Social Science History* 1 (Spring 1977), 356-382.

Köllmann, Wolfgang "The process of urbanization in Germany at the height of the industrialization period." *Journal of Contemporary History* 4 (1969), 59-76.

Kronborg, Bo and Thomas Nilsson "Social mobility, migration and family building in urban environments," in D. Ganut et al., eds., *Chance and Change: Social and Economic Studies in Historical Demography in the Baltic Area*. Odense, Denmark: Odense University Press, 1978.

Kucsynski, Jurgen *The Rise of the Working Class*. New York: McGraw-Hill, 1967.

Lamorisse, René *La population de la Cévenne languedocienne*. Montpellier: Paysan du Midi, 1975.

Landes, David *The Unbound Prometheus*. Cambridge: Cambridge University Press, 1972.

Laslett, Barbara and Margaret Little "Adolescence in historical perspective." Unpublished manuscript, University of California at Los Angeles, 1977.

Laslett, Peter *The World We Have Lost*. London: Metheun, 1965.

——— [ed.] *Household and Family in Past Time*. Cambridge: Cambridge University Press, 1972.

Laurans, Alain "Villefort dans le Diocèse d'Uzès, 1700-1789." Mémoire de Maîtrise, Université Paul Valéry, Montpellier III, 1974.

Lautier, G. "La sericiculture et les industries de la soie dans le pays cévenol." *Bulletin de la Société Languedocienne de Géographie* ser. 2 (1930), 79-86.

Lee, J.J. "Aspects of urbanization and economic development in Germany, 1815-1914," in Philip Abrams, ed., *Towns in Societies*. Cambridge: Cambridge University Press, 1978.

Lees, Lynn "Irish slum communities in nineteenth century London," in Stephen Thernstrom and Richard Sennett, eds., *Nineteenth Century Cities*. New Haven, CT: Yale University Press, 1970.

Léon, Pierre "La région lyonnaise dans l'histoire économique et sociale de la France: une esquisse (XVI-XXe siècles)." *Revue historique* 237 (1967), 31-62.

——— with François Crouzet and Richard Gascon [eds.] *L'industrialisation en Europe au XIXe siècle: cartographie et typologie*. Paris: Editions du CNRS, 1972.

Léonard, Emile *Le Protestant français*. Paris: Presses Universitaires de France, 1955.

Lequin, Yves "Les bases d'une cartographie industrielle de l'Europe au XIXe siècle," in P. Léon et al., eds., *L'industrialisation en Europe au XIXe siècle: cartographie et typologie*. Paris: Editions du CNRS, 1972.

——— *Les ouvriers de la région lyonnaise (1848-1914)*, 2 vols. Lyon: Presses Universitaires de Lyon, 1977.

Le Roy Ladurie, Emmanuel *Les paysans de Languedoc*. Paris: SEVPEN, 1966.

Lewis, Gwynne *Life in Revolutionary France*. London: Batsford, 1972.

——— *The Second Vendée*. New York: Oxford University Press, 1978.

Loubère, Leo *Radicalism in Mediterranean France: Its Rise and Decline, 1848-1914*. Albany, NY: State University of New York Press, 1974.

Lowenstein, Steven "The rural community and the urbanization of German Jewry." *Central European History* 8 (1980), 218-237.

MacDonald, John S. and Leatrice MacDonald "Chain migration, ethnic neighborhood formation and social networks." *Milbank Memorial Fund Quarterly* 42 (1964), 82-97.

McQuillan, Kevin "Economic factors and internal migration: the case of nineteenth-century England." *Social Science History* 4 (1980), 479-499.

Marcelin, Paul *Les compagnons du tour de France à Nîmes du XVIIe siècle à nos jours*. Nîmes: Pradier, 1963.

——— *Souvenirs d'un passé artisanal*. Nîmes: Chastanier, 1967.

Marrès, Paul "L'évolution de la viticulture dans le Bas-Languedoc." *Bulletin de la Société languedocienne de Géographie* (1935), 26-60.

——— *Les Grands Causses*, 2 vols. Tours: Arrault, 1935.

——— "Modernisation de la vie rurale cévenole," in M.J. Blache, ed., *Mélanges offerts au Doyen Bénévent*. Gap: Ophrys, 1954.

Martin, Georges *Nîmes à la Belle Epoque*. Brussels: Editions Libro-Sciences, 1974.

Martinez, Catherine "Commerce et le marché de détail dans une ville moyenne et ses environs: Nîmes." Thèse de 3e cycle, Université Paul Valéry, Montpellier, III, 1974.

Mazel, Elie "Statistique démographique de la ville de Nîmes comparée (1876-1888)." *Mémoires de l'Académie de Nîmes* ser. 7 (1887), 213-266.

Mazel, Henri "Nîmes en 1880." *Mémoires de l'Académie de Nîmes* ser. 7 (1939-1941), 149-173.

McBride, Theresa *The Domestic Revolution: The Modernisation of Household Service in England and France, 1820-1920*. New York: Holmes and Meier, 1976.

——— "A woman's world: department stores and the evolution of women's employment, 1870-1920." *French Historical Studies* 10 (1978), 664-683.

Merlin, Pierre *La Dépopulation des plateaux de Haute Provence*. Paris: La Documentation française, 1969.

——— *Exode rural*. Paris: Presses Universitaires françaises, 1971.

Moch, Leslie Page "Migrants in the city: newcomers to Nîmes, France at the Turn of the century." Ph.D. dissertation, University of Michigan, 1979.

——— "Adolescence and migration to Nîmes, 1906." *Social Science History* 5 (1981), 25-51.

——— "Marriage, migration and urban demographic structure: a case from France in the Belle Epoque." *Journal of Family History* 6 (1981), 70-88.

Modell, John and Tamara Hareven "Urbanization and the malleable household: an examination of boarding and lodging in American families." *Journal of Marriage and the Family* 35 (August 1973), 467-479.

Modell, John, Frank Furstenberg, Jr. and Theodore Hershberg "Social change and transitions to adulthood in historical perspective." *Journal of Family History* 1 (1976), 7-32.

Néaber et al. [eds.] *Dictionnaire biographique du Gard.* Paris: Flammarion, 1905.

Neuman, Allen "The influence of family and friends on German internal migration, 1880-1885." *Journal of Social History* 13 (1979), 277-288.

Nouschi, A. [ed.] *Les migrations dans les pays méditerranéens au XVIIIème et au début du XIXe.* Nice: Centre de la Méditerranée Moderne et Contemporaine, 1973.

Obermann, Karl "De quelques problèmes et aspects socioéconomiques des migrations allemandes du XVIe au XIXe siècle." *Annales de démographie historique* (1971), 120-132.

Parent-Duchâtelet, A.-J.-B. *De la prostitution dans la ville de Paris,* 2 vols. Paris: Baillière, 1836.

Parnes, Herbert *Research on Labor Mobility.* New York: Social Science Research Council, 1954.

Pech, Rémy *Entreprise viticole et capitalisme en Languedoc-Roussillon (du phylloxera aux crises de mévent).* Toulouse: Université de Toulouse-Le Mirail, 1975.

Perlman, Janice *The Myth of Marginality: Urban Poverty and Politics in Rio de Janeiro.* Berkeley: University of California Press, 1976.

Perrot, Michelle *Les ouvriers en grève, France, 1871-1890,* 2 vols. Paris: Mouton, 1974.

——— "De la nourrice à l'employée . . . Travaux de femmes dans la France du XIXe siècle." *Le mouvement social* 105 (1978), 3-10.

Picard, Thomas *Nîmes autrefois, Nîmes aujourd'hui.* Nîmes: Gervais-Bedot, 1901.

Pinkney, David "Migrations to Paris during the Second Empire." *Journal of Modern History* 25 (1953), 1-12.

Pitié, Jean *Exode rural et migrations intérieures en France: l'exemple de la Vienne et du Poitou-Charentes.* Poitiers: Norois, 1971.

Pleck, Elizabeth "Two worlds in one." *Journal of Social History* 10 (Winter 1976), 178-195.

Pontier, l'Abbé "Il y a deux cent ans: on discutait de grands travaux routiers dans la région Villefort-Langogne." *Revue du Gévaudan* 6 (1960), 178-180.

Poujol, Olivier "Réflexions sur les limites des Cévennes." *Revue du Gévaudan* 16 (1970), 118-131.

Poussou, Jean-Pierre "Introduction à l'étude des mouvements migratoires en Espagne, Italie et France méditerranéens au XVIIIe siècle," in A. Nouschi, ed., *Les migrations dans les pays méditerranéens au XVIIIème et au début du XIXe.* Nice: Centre de la Méditerranée Moderne et Contemporaine, 1973.

——— "Note sur la mobilité urbaine dans la deuxième moitié du XVIIIe siècle vue à travers les registres de sépultures de l'hôpital Saint-André de Bordeaux," in *Sur la population française au XVIIIe et au XIXe siècles, Hommage à Marcel Reinhard.* Paris: Société de Démographie Historique, 1973.

——— "Les rélations villes-campagnes en Aquitaine dans la deuxième moitié du XVIIIe siècle: quelques reflexions méthodologiques sur les attractions urbaines et les échanges migratoires," in Centre d'histoire économique et sociale de la région lyonnaise, ed., *Démographie urbaine.* Lyon: Université de Lyon II, 1977.

Pred, Allen "Behavior and location: foundations for a geographic and dynamic location theory." *Lund Studies in Geography* 27, series B (1967).

Reboul, Henri *L'industrie nîmoise du tissage au XIXe siècle.* Montpellier: Fermin et Montane, 1914.

Reboul, J. and E. Auguier *Hôtel-Dieu actuel et nouvel hôpital à Nîmes.* Nîmes: Gustave Gory, 1901.

Reddy, William "Family and factory: French linen weavers in the Belle Epoque." *Journal of Social History* 9 (Winter 1975), 201-212.

Reymond, Pierre [ed.] *Atlas historique de la France Contemporaine, 1880-1965.* Paris: Armand Colin, 1966.

Riegelhaupt, Joyce "Saloio women: an analysis of informal and formal political and economic roles of Portuguese peasant women." *Anthropological Quarterly* 40 (July 1967), 109-126.

Rieutort, André *Langogne.* Mende: Ecole Normale de Mende, 1960.

Riou, Michel "L'immigration dans les villes du Vivarais au XIXe siècle," in *Vivaris et Languedoc: Actes du XLIVe Congrès de la Fédération Historique du Languedoc Méditerranéen et du Roussillon.* Montpellier: Université Paul Valéry, 1972.

Ritchey, P. Neal "Explanations of migration." *Annual Review of Sociology* 2 (1976), 363-404.

Rivoire, Hector *Statistique du département du Gard,* 2 vols. Nîmes: Ballivet & Fabre, 1842.

——— "Notice sur l'industrie de la ville de Nîmes." *Mémoires de l'Académie de Nîmes* (1853), 268-297.

Roque, Jean-Daniel "L'église nationale protestante de Nîmes de 1870 à la veille de la séparation des Eglises et de l'Etat," 2 vols. Mémoire de Maîtrise, Université Paul Valéry, Montpellier III, 1969.

——— "Nouveaux aperçus sur l'église protestante de Nîmes dans la seconde moitié du XIXe siècle." *Bulletin de la Société de l'Histoire du Protestantisme* 120 (1974), 48-96.

——— "Positions et tendancies politiques des protestants nimois au XIXe siècle." *Droite et gauche en Languedoc-Roussillon: Actes du colloque de Montpellier, 9-10 Juin 1973.* Montpellier, 1975.

Roubin, Lucienne *Chambrettes des Provençaux.* Paris: Plon, 1970.

Rouger, Hubert "Nîmes en 1870: la ville, sa population, sa vie économique." *Revue économique de la Chambre de Commerce de Nîmes-Uzès-Le Vigan* 4, no. 31 (1953), 14-16.

——— "La vie à Nîmes à la fin du siècle dernier." *La revue économique de la Chambre de Commerce de Nîmes-Uzès-Le Vigan* 7, no. 61 (1956), 14-17.

Rouquette, Alain "Une colonie gévaudanaise dans les basses Cévennes: les lozériens à Anduze." *Cévennes et Gévaudan: Actes du XLVIe Congrès de la Fédération historique du Languedoc Méditerranéen.* Mende, 1974.

Roussel, Théophile "Rapport au préfet au sujet de l'enquête sur l'utilité publique du chemin de fer de Brioude à Alès." *Bulletin de la Société d'Agriculture de la Lozère* 12 (1861), 172-183, 192-211.

Roussy, Michael "Evolution démographique et économique des populations du Gard." Thèse de droit, Université de Montpellier, 1949.

Sarran, l'Abbé Achille *Les masets nimois*. Nîmes: Imprimerie Générale, 1898.

Schofield, R. S. "Age-specific mobility in an eighteenth-century rural English parish." *Annales de démographie historique* (1970), 261-274.

Schram, Stuart *Protestantism and Politics in France*. Alençon, France: Corbière et Jugain, 1954.

Scott, Joan Wallach *The Glassworkers of Carmaux*. Cambridge, MA: Harvard University Press, 1974.

——— and Louise A. Tilly "Women's work and the family in nineteenth-century Europe." *Comparative Studies in Society and History* 17 (January 1975), 36-64.

Secondy, Louis "L'établissement secondaire libre de Langogne au XIXe siècle." *Revue du Gévaudan* 18-19 (1972-1973), 383-396.

Sharlin, Allan "Historical demography as history and demography." *American Behavioral Scientist* 21 (1977), 245-262.

——— "Natural decrease in early modern cities: A reconsideration." *Past and Present* 79 (1978), 126-138.

Sewell, William "The structure of the working class of Marseille in the middle of the nineteenth century." Ph. D. dissertation, University of California at Berkeley, 1971.

——— "Social change and the rise of working-class politics in nineteenth-century Marseille." *Past and Present* 65 (1974), 75-109.

——— "Social mobility in a nineteenth-century European city." *Journal of Interdisciplinary History* 7 (1976), 217-233.

Siegfried, André "Le groupe Protestant Cévenol sous la III République," in Marc Boegner et al., eds., *Protestantisme français*. Paris: Plon, 1945.

Snyder, David and Paula Hudis "Occupational income and the effects of minority competition and segregation: a reanalysis and some new evidence." *American Sociological Review* 41 (1976), 209-234.

Société Internationale des Etudes Pratiques d'Economie Sociale. *Les ouvriers des deux mondes,* Vol. 2. Paris: Société Internationale des Etudes Pratiques d'Economie Sociale, 1858.

Sorre, Max "La répartition des populations dans le Bas-Languedoc." *Bulletin de la Société languedocienne de Géographie* ser 1 (1906), 105-136, 237-278, 364-387.

Stevenson, Robert Louis *Travels with a Donkey in the Cevennes*. New York: Scribner's, 1905.

Stouffer, Samuel "Intervening opportunities: A theory relating mobility and distance." *American Sociological Review* 5 (1940), 845-867.

Sullerot, Evelyne *Histoire et sociologie du travail feminin*. Paris: Gonthier, 1968.

Syndicat de la Bonneterie "Origine de la bonneterie gardoise." *Revue économique de la Chambre de Commerce de Nîmes-Uzès-Le Vigan* 3-4, nos. 23-32 (1952), 2.

Thadani, Veena N., with Michael Todaro "Female migration in developing countries: a framework for analysis." Center for Population Studies, Population Council, 1980.

Thernstrom, Stephen *The Other Bostonians: Poverty and Progress in the American Metropolis, 1880-1970*. Cambridge, MA: Harvard University Press, 1973.

Thérond, Etienne "L'industrie nimoise de la chaussure, ses fabrications, ses specialités, ses possibilités." *Revue économique de la Chambre de Commerce de Nîmes-Uzès-Le Vigan* 3, no. 25 (1952), 7-9.

Thintoin, Robert "Structure sociale et démographique du Gévaudan aux XVIIIe et XIXe siècles." *Revue du Gévaudan* 4 (1958), 116-145.

——— "Le commerce en Gévaudan au XVIIIe siècle." *Revue du Gévaudan* 16 (1970), 76-89.

Thomas, Louis-J. "L'emigration temporaire dans le Bas-Languedoc et le Roussillon au commencement du XIXe siècle." *Bulletin de la Société languedocienne de Géographie* ser. 1 (1910), 301-308.

Thompson, Edward P. *The Making of the English Working Class*. London: Gollanscz, 1963.

Tilly, Charles. *The Vendée*. New York: John Wiley, 1967.

——— "Migration in modern European history," in William McNeill and Ruth Adams, eds., *Human Migration: Patterns and Policies*. Bloomington: Indiana University Press, 1978.

——— [ed.] *Historical Studies of Changing Fertility*. Princeton, NJ: Princeton University Press, 1978.

——— "Flows of capital and forms of industry in Europe, 1500-1900." University of Michigan, 1982.

——— with C. Harold Brown, "On uprooting, kinship and the auspices of migration." *International Journal of Comparative Sociology* 8 (1968), 139-164.

Tilly, Louise "Occupational structure, women's work and demographic change in two French industrial cities, Anzin and Roubaix, 1872-1906," in J. Sundin and E. Soderlund, eds., *Time, Space and Man: Essays on Microdemography*. Atlantic Highlands, NJ: Humanities Press, 1979.

——— "Industrial production and the redistribution of capital and labor in nineteenth-century Lombardy," in Michael Hanagan and Charles Stephenson, eds., *Workers and Industrialization: Comparative Studies of Class Formation and Worker Militancy*. New York: Greenwood Press, forthcoming.

——— with Joan Scott *Women, Work, and Family*. New York: Holt, Rinehart & Winston, 1978.

Tipton, Frank *Regional Variations in the Economic Development of Germany During the Nineteenth Century*. Middletown, CT: Wesleyan University Press, 1976.

Trial, Louis "Un ennemi de la famille: le logement insalubre." *Revue du Midi* 28 (1900), 944-963.

Tugault, Yves *La mesure de la mobilité: cinq études sur les migrations internes*. Paris: PUF, 1973.

Un vieux Nimois "La rue de Nîmes en 1900." *La revue économique de la Chambre de Commerce de Nîmes-Uzès-Le Vigan* 6, no. 50 (1955), 27-28.

Van de Walle, Etienne *The Female Population of France in the Nineteenth Century*. Princeton, NJ: Princeton University Press, 1974.

Varillon, P. "Conférence de St. Vincent de Paul dans le département du Gard au XIXe siècle." Mémoire de Maîtrise, Université Paul Valéry, Montpellier III, 1972.

Vauriot, Dr. "Assistance publique et privé," in Association française pour l'Avancement des Sciences, ed., *Nîmes et le Gard,* 2 vols. Nîmes: Imprimerie cooperative, 1912.

Vidal, Jean-Claude "La croissance de la ville de Nîmes." Mémoire de Maîtrise, Université de Montpellier, 1970.

Vincienne, Monique *Du village à la ville: le systeme de mobilité des agriculteurs.* Paris: Mouton, 1972.

Volle, Jean-Paul "La croissance urbaine de Nîmes." *Bulletin de la Société languedocienne de Géographie* ser. 3 (1968), 345-364.

Weber, Adna *The Growth of Cities in the Nineteenth Century.* Ithaca, NY: Cornell University Press, 1899.

Weber, Eugen *Peasants into Frenchmen: The Modernization of Rural France, 1870-1914.* Stanford, CA: Stanford University Press, 1976.

Zeldin, Theodore *France 1848-1945,* Vol. I: *Ambition, Love and Politics.* Oxford: Clarendon Press, 1973.

Index

ABOUT THE AUTHOR

Leslie Page Moch earned a bachelor's degree at the University of Washington in Seattle and a Ph. D. in history at the University of Michigan. She is currently Assistant Professor of History at the University of Texas at Arlington. She is coeditor, with Gary Stark, of *Essays on the Family and Historical Change* and the author of scholarly articles on migration, France, women and the family for social science and history journals.